MODERN HUMANITIES RESEARCH ASSOCIATION
TEXTS AND DISSERTATIONS
VOLUME 86

THE PROSE OF SASHA SOKOLOV
REFLECTIONS ON/OF THE REAL

MODERN HUMANITIES RESEARCH ASSOCIATION
TEXTS AND DISSERTATIONS

Established in 1970, the series promotes important work by younger scholars by making the most accomplished doctoral research available to a wider readership. Titles are selected and edited by a Board of distinguished experts from across the modern Humanities.

Editorial Board
English: Professor Catherine Maxwell, Queen Mary, University of London
French: Professor William Brooks, University of Bath
Germanic: Professor Ritchie Robertson, University of Oxford
Hispanic: Professor Derek Flitter, University of Exeter
Italian: Professor Brian Richardson, University of Leeds
Portuguese: Professor Thomas Earle, University of Oxford
Slavonic: Professor David Gillespie, University of Bath

Managing Editor: Dr Graham Nelson

The Prose of Sasha Sokolov

Reflections on/of the Real

by
Elena Kravchenko

Modern Humanities Research Association
2013

Published by

*The Modern Humanities Research Association
1 Carlton House Terrace
London SW1Y 5AF
United Kingdom*

© *Modern Humanities Research Association, 2013*

Elena Kravchenko has asserted her right under the Copyright, Designs and Patents Act 1988 to be identified as the author of this work. Parts of this work may be reproduced as permitted under legal provisions for fair dealing (or fair use) for the purposes of research, private study, criticism, or review, or when a relevant collective licensing agreement is in place. All other reproduction requires the written permission of the copyright holder who may be contacted at rights@mhra.org.uk.

Copy-Editor: Nigel Hope

First published 2013

*ISBN 978-1-907322-52-5 (hardback)
ISBN 978-1-907322-95-2 (paperback)
ISSN (MHRA Texts and Dissertations) 0957–0322*

CONTENTS

	Preface	vii
	Introduction	1
1	Metaphor of Origin: Narcissism as a Constructive Principle in *School for Fools*	19
2	A Realized Metaphor: The Eucharist Miracles in *Between Dog and Wolf*	51
3	A Lie That Tells the Truth: Mediation of Reality in *Palisandriia*	99
	Conclusion	129
	Bibliography	135
	Index	152

PREFACE

My interest in Sokolov originates from 2003, when I met an actor who played Nymphea, the protagonist of Sokolov's first novel, *Shkola dlia durakov* (*School for Fools*). He presented me with the book. Then I read the rest of Sokolov and saw Andrei Moguchii's adaptation of *Mezhdu sobakoi i volkom* (*Between Dog and Wolf*) in Nice in 2004. This story is on the cover of the book: a still from Moguchii's play featuring Axel Schrick as Iakov Palamakhterov.

I began my research on Sokolov for my MA dissertation at King's College London: a comparative study of the representation of madness in *School for Fools* and Faulkner's *The Sound and the Fury*. I continued my academic engagement with Sokolov's texts in my doctoral thesis, which I defended at UCL in 2010 and which became the foundation for this monograph.

Before I proceed I would like to thank a few people who played an important role in the making of this book. I would like to thank Axel Schrick for the gift of his friendship and the book.

I would like to acknowledge gratefully my advisers at the School of Slavonic and East European Studies, Dr Maria Rubins and Dr Seth Graham, who supervised my thesis, for their patience, support, and advice. I would also like to express my gratitude to my viva voce examiners, Professor Julian Graffy and Professor Andrei Zorin, for their expertise, encouragement, and kindness. My research was also shaped by the knowledgeable advice of many other specialists and I would like to thank Professor Barbara Heldt, Professor Don Johnson, Jean Murray, and Professor Gerry Smith.

A very special person I would like to thank for his unfailing support, trust and generosity with his time is Professor Arnold McMillin. He made this book happen. Special thanks to the Student So-and-So for his many insights and for being an inspiration to me. And finally, I am very grateful to Irina Savitskaia, a poet and a friend of mine, who walked my daughter in a pram for hours, rain or shine, while I worked on this book, and my husband, Martin Cullen, for his understanding and love.

E. K., June 2012

INTRODUCTION

~

> 'Everything passes through language' means = language creates everything: metaphor creates tact; in humanist discourse, one would have said: metaphor creates civilization [...]. — I would go as far as saying: language creates reality; in choosing one's language, one chooses one's real [...].[1]
>
> Without language there is no life. Language, like music, can exist without life and after life. All texts will survive after your personal death and the death of society. Real art is pure energy, and it prevails, and it is dissolved into space. It is forever, it's eternal, a part of eternity, whereas life is just a very short thing. It's temporary.[2]
>
> Так, но с чего же начать, какими словами? Все равно, начни словами.[3]

The year 2009 saw the first edition of Sasha Sokolov's collected works.[4] The oeuvre amounts to one volume of 600 pages *in toto* and comprises three novels and eleven essays. The edition features no preface, which is just as well, since the critical self-reflexivity of Sokolov's texts threatens to reduce any prelude to a cento. The eleven essays that are included in the volume and which, in essence, constitute a meta-commentary on Sokolov's larger texts and the author's relationship with them, fulfil the function of an afterword. Written for conferences and public lectures in the period from 1983 to 2006, they are part manifestos of the writer's 'art-for-art's-sake' aesthetics, part imaginative and poetic discussions of the relationship between art and the artist and the essence of language.

The edition does not include three of Sokolov's most recent works: *Rassuzhdenie (Meditation)* (2007),[5] *Gazibo (Gazebo)* (2009),[6] and *Filornit (Philornite)* (2010).[7] These texts were gathered in a separate newly published volume, *Triptikh (Triptych)*.[8] Here Sokolov's proverbial disdain for the plot-line, chronology, and causal structures reaches its zenith,[9] resulting in a complex verbal construct oscillating between poetry and prose. These rarefied texts are pure expression of what Sokolov calls 'proetry' ('proeziia').[10] Structured as a polyphonic dialogue, they represent an allegorical meditation on art and all that pertains to it: its context, reception, and aesthetics. Reflecting on his aesthetics, Sokolov describes himself as a practitioner of the art-for-art's-sake philosophy:

> I am a poet of pure art [...]. This direction in literature [...] sets as its goal, or more precisely, it sets no extra-literary goals, and simply develops language, aesthetics, taste, imagination. Of course, it is not up to me to proclaim that language has all the prerequisites of a self-sufficient, infinite phenomenon.[11]

Strangely, this type of linguistic sensibility has been traditionally regarded as abstracted from reality. And yet what could be more tactile and physical than language for a poet?

In a recent film documentary,[12] Sokolov compared language to music and its workings to a form of dance:

> Для меня важно, как работает язык, этот своего рода лингвистический танец. Если бы я родился в другое время, в другом месте, в другой семье, я бы стал композитором, потому что язык одна из форм музыки. И, наконец, все зависит от состояния, ноты.[13]

This comparison is illuminating not only because dance is a form of communication that is used to tell stories and a mnemonic device: before the arrival of writing, ritual dance and formulaic poetry were methods of passing myths from generation to generation. Dance is also a fitting metaphor for a text because it is physical. It embodies sound just as the text gives visual form to language.

The physical impact of Sokolov's art was strangely prefigured by his first publications. In 1968, the Soviet national magazine for the blind, *Nasha zhizn'*, formerly known as *Zhizn' slepykh*, published Sokolov's sketch about a blind accordion player, *Vse tsveta radugi* (*All the Colours of the Rainbow*).[14] In 1971 another of his short stories, *Staryi shturman* (*The Old Helmsman*), appeared in *Nasha zhizn'*, which won Sokolov his first prize as 'the best story about the blind'.[15] They were published in Braille, the language by which meaning is retrieved through touch. In his later works, this linguistic corporality took the centre stage, outlasting the evanescence of life. Language became the only artefact of reality: not its expression but its embodiment. In the following study I will explore the way reflection and language, as one of its forms, signifies or creates reality in/through Sokolov's three novels. Fading away into its reflection, reality, paradoxically, finds its essence and substance: it becomes real.

Reflection as a source of integrity has been an object of contemplation for some time. Perhaps one of the earliest, and still one of the most influential, meditations on this is the myth of Narcissus. Narcissus, a child of reflecting bodies, was born to the blue-water nymph, Liriope, after she had been ravished by the river-god Cephisus. One day, Liriope consulted the blind seer Tiresias as to whether her son would live to old age. The answer was: 'if he ne'er knows himself'.[16] The prophecy was fulfilled when Narcissus turned sixteen years of age. One day, while on a stag hunt, he was followed by the nymph Echo, who was longing to call him, but unable to speak. Echo was dispossessed of her voice except for the senseless repetition of another's words: a punishment inflicted by Juno. When Narcissus called out 'Is anyone here', she echoed 'Here'. Surprised, Narcissus invited her to come out. So she did, and flew to embrace him. Appalled by her reaction, Narcissus proudly pushed her away. The nymph spent the rest of her days pining away until only her voice remained and her bones took on the appearance of stones. Shortly afterwards, on another stag hunt, Narcissus leaned over a pool to quench his thirst. As he drank he saw an image which captivated him. Narcissus was finally in love and overcome by desire. However, soon he realized that the other was his own self, in despair transformed into a flower.[17]

The extraordinary reflexivity of the myth has given rise to a variety of theoretical and artistic speculations.[18] This study will engage with a number of thinkers whose preoccupation with mirrors will provide scaffolding for the ensuing analysis of Sokolov's reflections. One of the most crucial theoretical models in terms of this inquiry has been advanced by Mikhail Bakhtin. In the next few pages I will proceed to outline the key concepts developed by Bakhtin, placing this preview within a wider theoretical framework.

One of the important framing elements is Jacques Lacan's theory of 'mirror stage', which postulates narcissistic illusion as a part of an identification process.[19] Lacan's idea rests upon an assumption that infants go through a stage of psychic development — the 'mirror stage' — in which they define their identity in accordance with the image reflected in the mirror. This mirror image is the foundation upon which the 'I' will be constructed. This stage represents Lacan's 'imaginary' order, which is based on identification (imitation), and which allows for the idea of the completion through the other. Thus, if we assume this image, which the child sees as unified, to be an accurate representation of the self, it enters into a dialectical process between the self and the other. For Lacan this figure in the mirror is a fiction that introduces a break with the real. Subjectivity then depends upon the recognition of an irreducible distance separating the self from the other, thus turning psychic life into a series of irremediable losses and misrecognitions (Lacanian méconnaissance).[20]

For Bakhtin, a mirror reflection of the self is far from perfect: it is vacuous and ghostly. The effect of its 'eerie loneliness'[21] is produced by its being locked in the loop of a single consciousness. To break it is to include the 'evaluating' other, and thus to apprehend oneself through the eyes of this other and oversee the reflection of one's life in the plane of his consciousness.[22] Thus the discovery of the irreducible distance between the self and the other is a gift: it guarantees the need of one for another and hence foregrounds the human capacity for empathy and love.[23] If genuine, this love is not based on identification (internalization) but on aestheticization (externalization). Bakhtin defines this fundamental ontological condition as 'outsidedness' ('vnenakhodimost''), a position that presupposes a 'surplus of vision' ('izbytok videniia') which allows one to give meaning, form, and context to the object of perception.[24] This relationship between the self and the other is defined as an 'aesthetic need':

> В этом смысле можно говорить об абсолютной эстетической нужде человека в другом, в видящей, помнящей, собирающей и объединяющей активности другого, которая одна может создать его внешне законченную личность, этой личности не будет, если другой ее не создаст: эстетическая память продуктивна, она впервые рождает внешнего человека в новом плане бытия.[25]

The key Bakhtinian idea of the relationship between the self and the other — or the origin and its representation — re-emerges in Jacques Derrida's affirmation that '[n]o thing is complete in itself; it can only be completed by what it lacks'.[26] The 'originary lack', contained in the original purity of a thing, requires a supplement: a sign that 'replaces the center in its absence — this sign is added, occurs as a surplus, as a *supplement*'.[27] In socio-economical terms, the Bakhtinian 'need' — demand — is met by the Derridian 'supply': literally, supplemented.

As has been noted, Bakhtin's scheme of 'objectification' of the self through and of the other has come under much unsympathetic scrutiny, lamenting the loss of the individual self in the overwhelming otherness.[28] However, for Bakhtin, it is not a question of the prevalence of one side over the other or their mutual neutralization. Neither is it for Derrida, as attested by his notion of *différance*, a blend of difference and deferral, which makes a singularity of meaning impossible. In fact, it is the inadequacy of the subject to himself — the non-correspondence of the referent and the signifier — that constitutes a precondition for any ethico-aesthetic act, that is reflection. It is precisely at the point of reflexion (*prelomlenie*) that meaning — that is the real — emerges:

> Точка зрения извне, ее избыточность и ее границы. Точка зрения изнутри на себя самого. В чем они принципиально не могут покрыть друг друга, не могут слиться. Именно в этой точке несовпадения, а не в едином духе (равнодушном к точке зрения изнутри или извне) совершаются события. Вечная тяжба в процессе самосознания 'я' и 'другого'.[29]

In his desire to be a signified and a signifier that perfectly, without loss or distortion, mirror each other, Narcissus disdains the gap between the self and the other. By excluding the other, Narcissus excludes the possibility of a metaphor. Since he fails to symbolize, he is unable to exist as a subject.[30] As Echo is losing her body, Narcissus is losing his link with reality. To reach for the real, metaphor proves to be a necessity. By rejecting Echo, he precludes sound from becoming word, vision from becoming embodied, and reality from becoming meaningful. Thus, Sokolov turns to metaphors, reducing — or elevating — reality to language. Reflected through the echo, it acquires substance — and ideality — for the echo does not distinguish between the physical and the metaphysical.

The fusion of physics and metaphysics has been pointed out in Iosif Brodskii's discussion of the formal — metrical — organization of poetry:

> The seemingly most artificial forms for organizing poetic language — terza rima, sestinas, decimas, and so forth — are in fact nothing more than a natural, reiterative, fully detailed elaboration of the echo that followed the original Word.[31]

Sokolov does precisely that. He reminds us of the beginning by taking language as his end. Metaphysics for him is inscribed in language, manifest in its phonetics, syntax, and grammar that capture the subject and the object in time and space.

Before I proceed, I will briefly trace the history of the three novels and attempt to determine Sokolov's situation in the present cultural context.

Sokolov began as a poet. He presented his poetry, heavily influenced by Aleksandr Blok, Boris Pasternak, and the French symbolists as he admitted, at the readings on the Mayakovskii Square in Moscow. This was followed by his association with SMOG,[32] an unofficial literary group, which gathered young underground poets and writers.[33] Sokolov described the group as some elemental force, an anarchic energy that took over the lives of its members. Unable to bear the 'excess energy', he escaped this context in order to get a formal education.[34] Graduating from the Faculty of Journalism at Moscow State University — the most liberal department in Soviet Russia, according to Sokolov — he practised his trade at a number of remote outposts where he wrote for local newspapers,[35] and at *Literaturnaia Rossiia*, a weekly paper of the Union of Writers. In May 1972, as he realized that he was ready to write 'seriously', Sokolov gave up his position in *Literaturnaia Rossiia* and took a job as a gamekeeper in a hunting reserve on the upper Volga. He settled on the periphery, where distractions were few — the hunters would arrive once a week — lived alone, and wrote.[36] This period of nearly two years on the Volga (from May 1972 to November 1973) resulted in a manuscript of *Shkola dlia durakov* (*School for Fools*).

Realizing the sheer impossibility of its publication in the Soviet Union, he sent the manuscript abroad. It re-emerged in Alexandria, Egypt, and eventually found its way to the hands of Ellendea and Carl Proffer of Ardis. As the only publishing house outside Russia dedicated to Russian literature, Ardis played a seminal role in the Russian letters of the twentieth century, and in Sokolov's life. It was founded in 1971 in Ann Arbor, Michigan, with a mission to publish the 'lost library' of twentieth-century Russia — the works of Mandel'shtam, Tsvetaeva, and Nabokov, amongst others — and to bring translations of contemporary authors writing in the Soviet Union to the West.

As Ellendea Proffer recollects, at the beginning of the 1970s they received a photocopy of a manuscript (most likely this was towards the end of 1973 and the beginning of 1974 as Sokolov completed *School for Fools* in Russia in May 1973), which arrived from Egypt (as someone said, with an 'Egyptian stamp'). Famously, one of the first readers of the manuscript was Brodskii, then a chief consultant on Russian literature at Ardis. The text was anonymous — its title page followed a few weeks later — which led Brodskii to conclude that it was an outstanding new work by Vladimir Maramzin.[37] However, upon learning that it was written by Sokolov rather than Maramzin, he considered it unsafe to publish an unknown author.[38] Although slightly put off by its dubious origin, the Proffers believed that they 'had a masterpiece on our hands' and proceeded with the novel's publication.[39]

The pre-publication promotion of the novel, written by an emerging author, proved extremely difficult. In fact, Sokolov and his text were met with outright hostility by the established Russian and émigré writers, which was exacerbated by Sokolov's peculiar sense of humour, which, as attested by Ellendea Proffer, drove many people away.[40] It was Nabokov, however, who sealed the writer's future. Upon reading the manuscript, he responded to Carl Proffer that the novel was 'by far the best thing you have published in the way of modern Soviet prose', defining it as 'an enchanting, tragic, and touching work',[41] a description that appeared on the first edition of the novel.

Thus, blessed by Nabokov, *School for Fools* appeared in the United States in early 1976. It was received enthusiastically by critics and the literary circles of the first-wave émigré community, among whom were such literati as Vladimir Weidle and Nina Berberova. However, in Soviet critical circles, the novel's publication hardly received any notice and it was met with general incomprehension. According to Ellendea Proffer, who came to Moscow to introduce *School for Fools*, the Soviet audience was not 'prepared' for this type of prose: 'To understand *Shkola dlia durakov*, it was necessary to know other modernist writers, to sense the structure of the narrative, and appreciate its intoxicating language'.[42]

Indeed, many critics view Sokolov's first novel as a successor to the Modernist tradition, the link back to the Silver Age and the Russian Symbolists. His narrative technique has also been associated with the surrealist movement, particularly with the writing of André Breton (*Surrealist Manifestos*) and Salvador Dali (*Secret Life of Salvador Dali*).[43] It has also invited comparisons with the works of James Joyce, Virginia Woolf, and William Faulkner.[44] However, one of the main 'influences' on Sokolov's experimental rhythmic prose has been identified with his benefactor, Nabokov. Aleksandr Genis nominated Sokolov as the first Russian writer who 'returned the Nabokovian concept of literature to our homeland'.[45] Don Barton Johnson, the principal and most devoted scholar of Sokolov's works, reports that after having read Nabokov's *Lolita* and *The Gift*, Sokolov was dismayed by the similarities between the style of his *School for Fools* and Nabokov's prose technique. However, as argued by Johnson, the parallels drawn between the two writers are not so much a question of influence (Sokolov claims he had not read any Nabokov prior to emigration) as of a shared concern with style and language play.[46] The writer himself singles out Nikolai Gogol', Aleksandr Kuprin, Edgar Allan Poe, and James Joyce as his precursors.[47]

Although the publication of *School for Fools* in Russia had to wait until 1989, when it appeared in the journal *Oktiabr'*,[48] by the early 1980s Sokolov's work acquired a cult-like 'underground' status, thanks to its circulation in *samizdat*.[49] The name of Sokolov was first introduced to the official Soviet press by Tatiana Tolstaia, who, invited by Oleg Khlebnikov, the co-editor of the journal *Ogonek*, 'pled the Sasha Sokolov case' before the chief censor, Vladimir Solodin.[50] As a result of her appeal, an excerpt from *School for Fools*, with a brief introduction by Tolstaia, appeared in *Ogonek* in August 1988.[51] In 1990, the same journal was to publish *School for Fools* and *Between Dog and Wolf*, Sokolov's second novel, in one volume, which became Sokolov's first book edition in Russia.[52]

The first public response to *School for Fools*, or more precisely its excerpt in *Ogonek*, was an interview with the critic Natalia Ivanova, who described Sokolov as a 'true writer, endowed with an idiosyncratic vision, who has no analogues in contemporary Russian literature'.[53] The same year saw the first public academic discussion of *School for Fools*. At a Moscow Symposium in October 1988, the young scholar Sergei Golubitskii presented a paper 'Neistovaia radost' i vostorg Nimfei Al'by ili udovletvorenie pochul'', in which he hailed the entrance of a gifted contemporary émigré writer with an 'unprecedentedly insignificant delay of a decade'.[54] By the mid-1990s, academic interest in Sokolov's work had been confirmed by many conference presentations, scholarly articles, and doctoral theses both in Russia and abroad.[55] The novel has been translated into eighteen languages — its English translation, by Carl Proffer, appearing in 1977 — and is probably the best known of Sokolov's works to this day. In 2006, the thirtieth anniversary of the publication of *School for Fools* was commemorated by a special issue of *Canadian–American Slavic Studies*, which featured papers by a new generation of Russian scholars.[56]

Sokolov's second novel, *Mezhdu sobakoi i volkom* (*Between Dog and Wolf*), considered his best by the author,[57] follows a rather different trajectory. Falling into a 'grey' area of Sokolov scholarship, it exacts enormous demands on the reader and is the most hermetic of his works. The reason for this is the nearly impenetrable linguistic jungle, a combination of dialecticisms, archaisms, esoteric rustic phraseology, extended word play, and general 'disregard' for the (traditional) reader's comfort, that constitutes the text. The novel has been compared to Joyce's *Finnegans Wake* by virtue of its linguistic, semantic, and cultural density, which leaves an almost physical impression of viscosity. Despite many attempts, its translation has yet to see the light of day.[58]

Although Sokolov started working on *Between Dog and Wolf* before his emigration in 1975, much of it was written in the West, where his cultural and literary context was considerably broadened. As reported by Johnson, upon reading Nabokov, Sokolov was alternatively dismayed and flattered by the parallels between *School for Fools* and Nabokov's work. This resulted in his determination to produce a text as far removed from Nabokov's style as possible.[59] If Nabokov's presence has indeed drastically faded in *Between Dog and Wolf*, much of the history of Russian and European art made an enthusiastic appearance, intentionally this time. The linguistic registers constituting *Between Dog and Wolf*, sweep from the 'word-weaving' ('pletenie sloves') of the ancient Rus' epic of *Zadonshchina* to Velemir Khlebnikov's trans-sense ('zaum'') and Andrei Platonov's prose,[60] incorporating almost the entire nineteenth-century Russian literary legacy.[61]

The first version of the text, one and a half times the book's final length, was completed in 1978. Carl Proffer's response was almost complete incomprehension:

> I cannot get through a page [...] without tremendous difficulties. The problem is mostly lexical — I have to look up so many words; this, combined with the narrative's elliptical style and with your indirectness of plot and characterization [leave me] totally lost. I've tried three times [starting at] different points in the novel, but it's hopeless. Even after discussing it with Alesha [poet Aleksei Tsvetkov] (and he is very enthusiastic) and trying to get certain general things straight, I could not get through. And I don't think it could be translated.[62]

According to Johnson, Sokolov had not realized the complexity of his work — in his mind it was written on the level of Vladimir Vysotskii's song lyrics — and decided to rewrite and shorten the novel.[63] Although Proffer still found the text impossible, the final version of the manuscript was published in February 1980. As Proffer envisioned, several attempts to translate the novel came to naught, and unlike the triumphant entrance of *School for Fools*, *Between Dog and Wolf* was received with a puzzled silence, broken by four reviews scattered around the Russian émigré press.[64] Generally, the novel found a very limited readership in the West and scholarly response was slow in coming.

The first critical assessment of *Between Dog and Wolf* in the Soviet Union appeared in 1981. Although not published in Russia until 1989, when it appeared in a serialized version in the journal *Volga*,[65] just as Sokolov's first novel, *Between Dog and Wolf* was circulating in *samizdat*. It gained almost immediate recognition and in 1981 it won Sokolov the Andrei Belyi Prize for the best Russian prose, awarded by the Leningrad *samizdat* journal *Chasy*.[66] The first 'official' review, Vladimir Potapov's 'Ocharovannyi tochilshchik: Opyt prochteniia' ('An Enchanted Grinder: An Experiment at Reading'), appeared as an afterword to the novel's publication in *Volga* in 1989. In December of the same year Andrei Zorin's review of Sokolov's first and second novels came out in *Novyi mir*.[67] Viewing Sokolov as the force that transformed Russian prose,[68] the scholar reads these texts as attempts to overcome time and its consequences through the dissolution of human existence in the substance of language. Zorin's article was followed by almost a decade of silence, when in the late 1990s *Between Dog and Wolf* entered wider scholarly research.

Between Dog and Wolf, which remains the least read and studied of Sokolov's texts thank to its linguistic inaccessibility, won Sokolov the honours of being one of the most hermetic writers in contemporary Russian literature. Sokolov counters that by comparing himself to Khlebnikov:

> It seems to me that I write and think in intelligible categories, but my texts simply demand greater effort from the reader. Faulkner used to say about his works: 'My books need to be read two of three times to be understood', and in response to reader complaints: 'I've already read your book twice or three times, but I still don't understand', Faulkner countered, 'Read it one more time. No one declared reading entertainment; it is hard work'. [...] It takes several years of preparation to understand Khlebnikov, but it is well worth it. After Khlebnikov, Sokolov will be easy.[69]

Indeed, especially with regard to *Between Dog and Wolf*, Sokolov's texts require perseverance. And it pays. The impact of this text on the development of the Russian cultural make-up is undeniable. The director of *Formal'nyi Teatr*, Andrei Moguchii, whose adaptation of *Between Dog and Wolf* received the First Prize at the Nice Theatre Festival in 2004 and Zolotaia Maska in Moscow in 2006,[70] defined the novel as an 'epochal' text:

> Я испытал эстетическое удивление и этическое потрясение, когда его прочел. Вообще в профессиональном отношении Саша Соколов оказал на меня очень большое влияние, я очищаюсь его языком. На первый взгляд он крайне специфичен и сложен, однако при многократном прочтении, он оказывается ясным и даже прозрачным.[71]

Sokolov's third and still most recent novel, *Palisandriia* (*Astrophobia*), differs strikingly from the first and the second texts not only in terms of style and language but because of its conspicuous and unprecedented turn to content and context. Discouraged by the ambivalent reception of *Between Dog and Wolf*, Sokolov allegedly decided to produce a work more accessible and commercially successful. Thus, in the summer of 1980, in California, he embarked on *Palisandriia*, completing the first draft in 1983. After showing it to Proffer, Sokolov had to revise it substantially. Proffer, hoping for a wide readership thanks to the novel's sensationalism about Soviet political figures and its perverse eroticism,[72] dissuaded the author from his more radical stylistic innovations such as the absence of capital letters and full stops and their replacement by a 'strophic' graphic layout.[73] *Palisandriia* finally emerged in the United States in April 1985, followed by its English translation, *Astrophobia*, in 1989.

As a counterbalance to his ambition to produce a work that would read and sell, Sokolov endeavoured 'to write a novel that would end the novel as a genre'.[74] Indeed, *Palisandriia*'s subversive streak has probably been the most celebrated topic of scholarly interest. It has been labelled as 'anti-novel',[75] dystopia,[76] 'a story of the anti-epoch',[77] 'inverted' *Lolita*,[78] and 'perverted' narcissism.[79] Its subversion is generally interpreted in the parodic key. Thus, Aleksandr Zholkovskii argues that in its general style and design, the novel belongs to the Sternian tradition of parodic narrative with its idiosyncratic characters preoccupied with time, masculinity, military prowess, and physical deformity.[80] Johnson views *Palisandriia* as a parody of multiple genres, including the epic, the folkloric, the confessional memoir, the pornographic novel, and the political thriller. He establishes two major subtexts in the novel: Eduard Limonov's *Eto ia — Edichka* (*It's Me Eddy*) and Nabokov's *Lolita*.[81] Olga Matich believes that the key target of the novel's parodic *tour de force* is the dissident culture, with its claims to 'first-hand' information about Soviet history and its literary and historical self-indulgence.[82]

By virtue of its engagement with history and politics — unprecedented for Sokolov — *Palisandriia* has been identified with what Linda Hutcheon called 'historiographic metafiction'.[83] This type of fiction is marked by a return to history, combined with a questioning of the seeming neutrality and objectivity of historical accounts.[84] Owing to this focus on Soviet history, *Palisandriia* has also been associated with sots-art, an artistic trend that appeared in the Soviet Union in the 1970s.[85]

While Sokolov's two first texts seem to elude periodization — *School for Fools* oscillates between the titles of 'the last modernist work' and 'the first postmodernist work'; *Between Dog and Wolf* falls 'between dog and wolf' — *Palisandriia* is viewed as quintessentially postmodern. This is due, above all, to its exploration of the 'last things and apocalyptic ugliness'.[86] The apocalyptic intonation of *Palisandriia* is conveyed through the effect of blurriness and monotony. This, in turn, is achieved through the imprinting of all the possible authorial positions, registers and styles, and then reducing the difference between them, and thus the individual value of each, to zero.[87] Mikhail Epshtein defines this type of literature, developed in Russia in the 1980s, as 'arrière-garde'.[88] According to Epshtein, if the avant-garde vigorously advanced new forms — rejecting the past and present for the sake of the future — and strove to explode the norm, the arrière-garde makes no difference between old or new, authentic or fake and abolishes the norm by elevating everything to a rule. It is compared to verbalized silence — the white noise — in which 'literature is no more than language, facing its own failure to express'.[89]

As contrasted with *Palisandriia*, Sokolov's first two novels belong to what is designated 'phenomenalism': 'a poetics of pure presence [that] occupies a middle zone between myth and parody, between metaphysical seriousness and linguistic playfulness, lying between the depth of the object and the comic inversion of this depth'.[90] When combined, these two categories give a good idea of Sokolov's writing (and much of contemporary literature): it is not more and not less than language and precisely because of that, it leaves the impression of immediacy — 'presence'. However, this 'pure presence' conceals pure absence and the effect of immediacy turns out to be an attempt to transcend it.

Mark Lipovetskii, among others, identifies this transcendence urge with neo-Baroque, a trend in Russian (and Latin American) postmodernism, and considers Sokolov its practitioner.[91] The other category of Russian postmodern art, according to Lipovetskii, is conceptualism.[92] If conceptualism is associated with the ritual and derives from the avant-garde aesthetics (OBERIU, in particular), neo-Baroque relates to high Modernism, represented in Russian literature by Andrei Belyi and Nabokov, and has a structure of a labyrinth, or fractal. Conceptualism demythologizes cultural discourse, while neo-Baroque remythologizes whatever is left of it. Thus conceptualism substitutes the author's voice for a system of impersonal discursive rituals (linguistic formulae, clichés, and so on), when neo-Baroque works with the individual authorial myth (albeit in the parodic key as in *Palisandriia*).[93]

Sokolov is not an easily categorized author. His texts can be compared to the polystylistic technique developed in music by Alfred Schnittke.[94] On the one hand, the self-reflexive (fractal) structure of Sokolov's texts, his tendency to equate the subject and the object of the narrative, and other means of engagement with the authorial myth place him firmly in the neo-Baroque category. On the other hand, his linguistic sensibility does not allow him to forego play with linguistic and cultural clichés, practised by conceptualists. However, both praxes are ultimately attempts to represent the unrepresentable, for, to quote Fredric Jameson, 'the world is not unknowable, but it is merely unrepresentable'.[95] And, perhaps, one of the ways to know it is to represent it. This conception of the relationship between art and reality will be an important focus of my analysis.

In my first chapter, 'Metaphor of Origin: Narcissism as a Constructive Principle in *School for Fools*', which constitutes a discussion of Sokolov's first novel, I will examine an aesthetic (trans)formation of reality and reconstruction of the self through a series of metaphors. The project is framed by a number of readings — from classical to postmodern — of the myth of Narcissus as a metaphor for the dynamics between the 'real' and the 'constructed', presented as a series of juxtapositions, which informs Sokolov's novel: the self and the other; the context and the text; the present and the past; presence and absence; an event and its remembrance/representation.

The myth of Narcissus constitutes for *School for Fools* what Lucien Dällenbach called the 'metaphor of origin', or a 'transcendental *mise en abyme*' — a pre-text which motivates and underlies a narrative.[96] In my adoption of 'narcissism' as a model, I will examine the aesthetic and psychological implications of self-reflexivity and its role in the construction of the text, the context and the self in *School for Fools*. In this I will engage with Julia Kristeva's and Mikhail Bakhtin's reading of reflection as a constitutive element of identity, Linda Hutcheon's concept of 'narrative narcissism', and the theoretical models advanced by Lucien Dällenbach (*mise en abyme*). I will also apply Louis Sass's reading of schizophrenia as a form of hyper-reflexivity rather than a regression into the primitive state. This hyper-awareness of the real will be demonstrated through the schizophrenic understanding of language, which lies at the basis of Sokolov's narrative. By these means, I hope to illuminate how memory, instead of retrieving the past, signifies it, and how language, instead of expressing reality, engenders it.

My second chapter, 'A Realized Metaphor: The Eucharist Miracles in *Between Dog and Wolf*', constitutes a reading of *Between Dog and Wolf* as a re-enactment of the Eucharist. In this re-enactment representation of reality becomes represented reality, in which language does not so much communicate as embody what is absent. In my endeavour I will trace Sokolov's engagement with a series of reflections of reality, which is used to demonstrate how perception thereof is often preconditioned by its representation. I will then proceed to explore Sokolov's mediation of the real through the constructed, conceptualized as a dialogue between one's own and the other's, the old and the new, the content and the form, space and time, speech (spirit) and writing (letter), culminating in the fusion of the context and the text. Employing the technique of deconstruction in my analysis, I will attempt to demonstrate how reality is grounded by its representation as the latter is grounded in its medium: language.

My third chapter, 'A Lie that Tells the Truth: Mediation of Reality in *Palisandriia*', is a reading of Sokolov's third novel as an expression of 'abject'. Julia Kristeva's term, 'abject', is described as 'something that disturbs identity, system, order. What does not respect borders, positions, rules'.[97] *Palisandriia*, a text that pretends to be a memoir, a chronicle written by an eye-witness, a novel of an aesthete, deconstructs all these presumptions with grotesque preciousness. This approach is identified with an aesthetic sensibility called Camp: a postmodern version of dandyism. Camp is argued to be an answer to the problem of authenticity and taste in the age of mass culture and total simulacrum. By taking this aesthetic stance Sokolov's chronicler becomes a perfect referent, a supplement to the lost historical and cultural signified. Transcending the loss through incarnation/verbalization, he mediates between the context and the text.

In this fusion of history and his story, Sokolov's hero also reminds us that, in fact, there is very little outside this verbalization, to distort the famous dictum. In one way or another, the real has to be mediated in order to be appreciated or even experienced. It is not a negation of the real or the past, but recognition that historical reality is discursive reality: we receive and know it already as a text — the only artefact remaining. By treating history — individual and national — as a vehicle for aesthetics, Sokolov's text allows a glimpse — an intuition — of the real among its total discrediting.

Notes to the Introduction

1. Roland Barthes, *The Neutral*, trans. by Rosalind E. Krauss and Denis Hollier (New York: Columbia University Press, 2007), p. 34.
2. David Remnick, 'Wellspring of the Russian Writer: Thirsting for his Native Language, Sasha Sokolov Returns', *Washington Post*, 28 September 1989, interview with Sasha Sokolov.
3. Sasha Sokolov, *Shkola dlia durakov* (hereafter 'Shkola') (St Petersburg: Symposium, 2001), p. 11.
4. Sasha Sokolov, *Shkola dlia durakov. Mezhdu sobakoi i volkom. Palisandriia. Esse* (St Petersburg: Azbuka-klassika, 2009).
5. Sasha Sokolov, 'Rassuzhdenie', *Zerkalo*, 29 (2007) <http://magazines.russ.ru/zerkalo/2007/29/ss2.html> [accessed November 2007].
6. Sasha Sokolov, 'Gazibo', *Zerkalo*, 33 (2009) <http://magazines.russ.ru/zerkalo/2009/33/s01.html> [accessed December 2009].
7. Sasha Sokolov, 'Florinit', *Zerkalo*, 35 (2010) <http://magazines.russ.ru/zerkalo/2010/35/2s0.html> [accessed December 2010].
8. Sasha Sokolov, *Triptikh* (Moscow: OGI, 2011).
9. See Sokolov's interview with Maksim Gureev: 'Сюжет — меня эта сторона литературы никогда не увлекала. Сюжет — это надуманная вещь, сюжет — это на продажу'. In Maksim Gureev, 'Snimaetsia dokumental'noe kino' (hereafter 'Maksim Gureev'), *Voprosy Literatury*, 2 (2011) <http://magazines.russ.ru/voplit/2011/2/gu5.html> [accessed November 2011].
10. See Ivan Podshivalov, 'A Conversation with Sasha Sokolov: Moscow, 1989', *Canadian-American Slavic Studies*, 40 (2006) (hereafter 'Slavic Studies 40'), trans. by Ludmilla Litus, 352–66 (p. 352). Interview with Sasha Sokolov. Originally published in *Moskovskii Komsomolets* (20 August 1989).
11. Slavic Studies 40, p. 354.
12. In September 2008, Maksim Gureev presented at the Kinoshok Film Festival in Anapa a short documentary on Sasha Sokolov: *A peizazh bezuprechen* (*But the Landscape is Impeccable*). The title is a line from Sokolov's 2007 *Rassuzhdenie*, an authorial reading

of which constitutes the second part of the film. The first part, shot at the train station in Feodosiia, Ukraine, is an evocation of the imagery of Sokolov's first novel: a train station, a bicycle shop, a drunk, a queue. The film shows Sokolov — walking around, resting on a bench and intimately musing about language as a form of music or dance — against the background of this 'impeccable landscape'.

13. Maksim Gureev.
14. Sasha Sokolov, 'Vse tsveta radugi', *Nasha zhizn'*, 9 (1968), 9–11, in D. Barton Johnson, 'Literary Biography' (hereafter 'Johnson Literary Biography'), *Canadian-American Slavic Studies*, 21 (1987), 203–30 (p. 205).
15. Johnson Literary Biography, pp. 206–07 (A letter of 6 May 1988 from Sokolov to Johnson).
16. Ovid, *Metamorphoses*, trans. by Frank Justus Miller, 2 vols (London and Cambridge, MA: Loeb Classical Library, 1960), I.
17. Ibid.
18. An exhaustive study of the myth's retellings has been undertaken by Louis Vinge in Louis Vinge, *The Narcissus Theme in Western European Literature up to the Early 19th Century*, trans. by Robert Dewsnap and Nigel Reeves (Lund: Skånska Centraltryckeriet, 1967).
19. Needless to say, all the psychological studies on narcissism — whether in opposition to or in agreement with — derive from Sigmund Freud's interpretation of the myth, articulated in his 1914 article 'On Narcissism: An Introduction'. Sigmund Freud, 'On Narcissism: An Introduction', in *The Standard Edition of the Compete Psychological Works of Sigmund Freud: On the History of the Psycho-Analytic Movement, Papers on Metapsychology and Other Works*, 24 vols, trans. by James Strachey (London: The Hogarth Press and the Institute of Psycho-Analysis, 1957), XIV, 73–102.
20. Jacques Lacan, 'The Mirror Stage as the Formative of the Function of the I' (hereafter 'Lacan'), in *Écrits: A Selection*, trans. by Alan Sheridan (London: Routledge, 1993), pp. 1–7.
21. Mikhail Bakhtin, 'Avtor i geroi v esteticheskoi deiatel'nosti' (hereafter 'Avtor i geroi'), in *Sobranie sochinenii*, 7 vols (Moscow: Russkie slovari, 1997–2003), I (2003), pp. 69–263 (p. 110)
22. Ibid., p. 110.
23. Ibid., pp. 126–30; see Caryl Emerson, 'The Next Hundred Years of Mikhail Bakhtin (The View from the Classroom)' (hereafter 'Emerson'), *Rhetoric Review*, 19 (2000), 12–27 (p. 14).
24. 'Avtor i geroi', pp. 95–96.
25. Ibid., p. 115.
26. Jacque Derrida, *Dissemination* (hereafter 'Derrida Dissemination'), trans. by Barbara Johnson (London: The Athlone Press, 1981), p. 304.
27. Jacques Derrida, 'Structure, Sign and Play in the Discourse of the Human Sciences', in *Writing and Difference* (hereafter 'Derrida Difference'), trans. by Alan Bass (London and New York: Routledge Classics, 2004), pp. 351–70 (p. 365). Italics in the original. Derrida borrows the term 'supplement' from Jean-Jacques Rousseau's *Essay On the Origin of Languages*, analysed in Derrida's *Of Grammatology*.
28. Emerson, p. 19.
29. Mikhail Bakhtin, 'Ritorika v meru svoei lzhivosti', in *Sobranie sochinenii*, 7 vols (Moscow: Russkie slovari, 1997–2003), V (1997), pp. 63–70 (p. 64).
30. For Lacan subjectivity is marked by the entrance into the symbolic order, represented by language. See Jacques Lacan, 'The Psychoses, 1955–1956', in *The Seminar of Jacques Lacan*, Book III, ed. by Jacques-Alain Miller, trans. by Russell Grigg (New York: Norton, 1993).

31. Joseph Brodsky, 'A Poet and Prose', in *Less Than One: Selected Essays* (New York: Farrar, Straus, Giroux, 1986), pp. 176–94 (p. 186).
32. Among the interpretations of the acronym are *'smelost', mysl', obraz i glubina'* (courage, thought, image and depth); *Samoe Molodoe Obshchestvo Geniev* (Society of Youngest Geniuses), and *'szhatyi mig otrazhennoi giperboly'* (Condensed Moment of Reflected Hyperbole). 'Smog' is also a past perfect of the verb 'to be able to': 'smoch'', thus yielding 'I was able to', or 'I did it'.
33. Among its founding members were a poet Leonid Gubanov; Vladimir Aleinikov, a poet who received the Andrei Belyi Prize; Iurii Kublanovskii, a poet and a publicist; Nikolai Bokov, an editor of the samizdat journal *Sheia* (Moscow) and later an emigrant journal *Kovcheg* (Paris); Vladimir Batshev, a writer and an editor of the journal *Literaturnyi evropeets* (Germany).
34. Slavic Studies 40, pp. 370–71.
35. Feeling at odds with institutional life, Sokolov resolved to complete his studies by correspondence. For much of 1968 he worked for *Kolkhoznaia Pravda* (*The Collective Farm Truth*) in the village of Morki in Mariiskii Republic on the middle Volga. See Johnson Literary Biography, pp. 205–06.
36. Slavic Studies 40, p. 372.
37. Maramzin was a well-known figure in the Leningrad literary circles in the 1960s. The style of his prose was considered absolutely original but many critics associated it with the works of Nikolai Leskov, Iurii Olesha, and Andrei Platonov.
38. Irina Vrubel'-Golubkina, 'Ia vsiu zhizn' vybiraiu luchshee. Chashche vsego bessoznatel'no ...' (hereafter 'Vrubel'-Golubkina'), *Zerkalo*, 37 (2011). Interview with Sasha Sokolov. <http://magazines.russ.ru/zerkalo/2011/37/6so.html> [accessed December 2011].
39. Ellendea Proffer quoted in Aleksandr Genis, 'Lessons of *Shkola dlia durakov* (Over the Barrier: A Special Broadcast in Honor of Sasha Sokolov's 60th Birthday)', Slavic Studies 40, 341–49 (p. 344).
40. Ibid., pp. 343–44.
41. Ibid., pp. 344–45; Johnson Literary Biography, p. 213.
42. Ellendea Proffer in Slavic Studies 40, p. 344.
43. D. Barton Johnson, 'A Structural Analysis of Sasha Sokolov's *School for Fools*: A Paradigmatic Novel' (hereafter 'Johnson Structural Analysis'), *Fiction and Drama in Eastern and Southeastern Europe; Evolution and Experiment in the Postwar Period*, ed. by Henrik Birnbaum and Thomas Eekman (Bloomington, IN: Slavica Publishers, Inc., 1980), pp. 207–237 (p. 215); Fred Moody, 'Madness and the Pattern of Freedom in Sasha Sokolov's *A School for Fools*', *Russian Literature Triquarterly*, 16–17 (1979), 7–32 (p. 32).
44. Arnold McMillin, 'Aberration or the Future: The Avant-Garde Novels of Sasha Sokolov', in *From Pushkin to Palisandriia: Essays on the Russian Novel in Honour of Richard Freeborn*, ed. by A. McMillin (London: Macmillan, 1990), pp. 229–43 (pp. 231–35); Erzsebet Vari, '"Literatura [...] — iskusstvo obrashcheniia so slovom": Zametki o povesti "Shkola dlia durakov" Sashi Sokolova', *Studia Slavica Academiae Scientiarum Hungaricae*, 47 (2002), 427–50 (p. 430); Vladimir Tumanov, 'A Tale Told by Two Idiots: Krik idiota v "Shkole dlia durakov" S. Sokolova i v "Shume i iarosti" U. Folknera', *Russian Language Journal*, 48 (1994), 137–55.
45. Slavic Studies 40, p. 345.
46. D. Barton Johnson, 'Saša Sokolov and Vladimir Nabokov', *Russian Language Journal*, 41 (1987), 153–62 (pp. 154).
47. Vrubel'-Golubkina.
48. Sasha Sokolov, 'School for Fools', *Oktiabr'*, 3 (1989).

49. Andrei Bitov, in his afterword to *School for Fools* in *Oktiabr'*, recollects that as a teacher in the Gor'kii Institute of World Literature he assigned readings from *School for Fools*: Andrei Bitov, 'Grust' vsego cheloveka', *Oktiabr'*, 3 (1989), 157-58.
50. Oleg Khlebnikov, 'The Orderly on Duty by the Time Switch', Slavic Studies 40, 389-90 (p. 390). An excerpt from Oleg Khlebnikov, 'Leshii tam brodit, no chudes net. Chem zakonchilas' moia sluchainaia sviaz' s tsenzuroi. Ispoved'', *Novaia gazeta*, 40 (6 June 2000), trans. by Ludmilla Litus.
51. Tat'iana Tolstaia, 'O Sashe Sokolve', *Ogonek*, 33 (1988), 20-23.
52. Sasha Sokolov, *Shkola dlia durakov. Mezhdu sobakoi i volkom* (Moscow: Ogonek-variant: Sovetsko-britanskaia tvorcheskaia assotsiatsiia, 1990).
53. Natal'ia Ivanova, 'Neestestvennyi otbor', interview by Ivan Podshivalov, *Moskovskii Komsomolets*, 215 (18 September 1988); in Slavic Studies 40, p. 408.
54. *Al'manakh prisutstvie* (22 March, 2000), in Slavic Studies 40, p. 408.
55. The first scholarly response to *School for Fools* appeared in the West in 1979. See full bibliography in Ludmilla L. Litus and D. Barton Johnson, 'Sasha Sokolov: A Selected Annotated Bibliography (1967-2006)', Slavic Studies 40, 425-94 (pp. 442-44 and 450-70).
56. Slavic Studies 40.
57. Ibid., p. 409.
58. The only translation available today is Polish, by Aleksandr Boguslawski: *Miedzy psem a wilkiem* (Warsaw, 2000).
59. D. Barton Johnson, 'Background Notes on Sokolov's *School for Fools* and *Between Dog and Wolf*: Conversations with the Author', Slavic Studies 40, 331-39 (p. 337).
60. Sokolov denies any 'ties' with Platonov: 'Platonov did not influence me at all; I felt absolutely nothing for Platonov. [...] Of course, I read him, but I never felt influenced by him. His first book, a collection of stories, appeared at the time we were completing school, around 1960, perhaps a little earlier, and that started a Platonov craze. His works were read aloud and discussed at evening literary gatherings in Moscow.' (quoted in Slavic Studies 40, p. 368). Despite these assertions, there are a number of correspondences, mostly manifest in their 'subordination' to language. Both writers illuminate absurdity built into language yet insist that language is the only way out of this dead end. Hence the shared sense of the futility and emptiness of the human condition, which is evoked in their works. Sokolov describes his second novel as 'a testament to the resilience of the human spirit, to the permanence and isolation of human existence' (quoted in Slavic Studies 40, p. 401). There are also lexical 'lapses' into 'Platonovshchina' in Sokolov — such as the word 'bobyl'' (an unmarried /celibate man). See Platonov's *Chevengur*.
61. A detailed analysis of the novel's intertextual links is provided in, among others, D. Barton Johnson, 'Sasha Sokolov: The New Russian Avant-garde', *Critique: Studies in Contemporary Fiction*, 30 (1989), 163-78; Gerald S Smith, 'The Verse in Sasha Sokolov's *Between Dog and Wolf*', *Canadian-American Slavic Studies*, 21 (1987), 321-45.
62. A letter from Carl Proffer to Sokolov (28 June 1978), quoted in Slavic Studies 40, pp 338-39.
63. A conversation with Johnson (20 June 1983), in Slavic Studies 40, p. 339.
64. Boris Vel'berg, 'Mezhdu sobakoi i volkom', *Novyi amerikanets*, 206 (2 February 1984), 14-15; Igor' Burikhin, 'S. Sokolov. Mezhdu sobakoi i volkom. Ardis, Ann Arbor, 1980', *Grani*, 118 (1980), 273-74; I. Maler, 'Imeiushchii v rukakh tsvety', *Dvadtsat' Dva*, 16 (1980), 219-20.
65. Sasha Sokolov, 'Mezhdu sobakoi i volkom', *Volga*, 8 (1989), 62-92; and 9 (1989), 70-107.
66. Johnson Literary Biography, pp. 216-19.

67. Andrei Zorin, 'Nasylaiushchii Veter', *Novyi Mir*, 12 (1989), 250–53.
68. Zorin calls Sokolov 'the sender of the wind' ('nasylaiushchii veter') — borrowing Sokolov's own image of the semi-mythical character from *School for Fools*.
69. Slavic Studies 40, p. 358.
70. Moguchii's production of *School for Fools*, which opened in St Petersburg in 1998, also won a number of prizes: Zolotoi Sofit (2000), Zolotaia Maska (2001), Edinburgh Fringe First Award (2001), and the Grand Prix Award at the Belgrade International Theatre Festival (2001). See Slavic Studies 40, pp. 417–18.
71. Interview with Zhanna Zaretskaia in BIA, 20 February 2000 <http://bia-news.ru/news/36757.> [accessed January 2010].
72. Johnson Literary Biography, pp. 221–22 (A letter from Carl Proffer to Sasha Sokolov, 2 May 1983).
73. These 'intricacies' appeared in the first selection from the novel, published in *Dvadtsat' Dva*, 30 (1983).
74. Johnson Literary Biography, p. 217. A letter from Lilia Sokolov, Sokolov's partner at the time, to Johnson (29 March 1988).
75. Laura Beraha, 'The Last Rogue of History: Picaresque Elements in Sasha Sokolov's *Palisandriia*' (hereafter 'Beraha'), *Canadian Slavonic Papers*, 35 (1993), 201–20.
76. Larissa Rudova, 'The Dystopian Vision in Sasha Sokolov's *Palisandriia*', Slavic Studies 40, 163–77 (hereafter 'Rudova Slavic Studies 40').
77. Kira Sapgir, 'V Russkoi Mysli — pisatel' Sasha Sokolov', *Russkaia mysl'*, 3386 (12 November 1981), p. 11.
78. Johnson Literary Biography, p. 217.
79. Alexander Zholkovsky, 'Vliublenno-blednyie nartsissy o vremeni i o sebe' (hereafter 'Zholkovsky Beseda'), *Beseda*, 6 (1987), 144–77 (p. 148).
80. Alexander Zholkovsky, 'The Stylistic Roots of Palisandriia' (hereafter 'Zholkovsky Roots'), *Canadian-American Slavic Studies*, 21 (1987), 369–400 (pp. 378–79).
81. Johnson, D. Barton, 'Saša Sokolov's Palisandrija', *Slavic and East European Journal*, 30 (1986), 389–403.
82. Olga Matich, 'Sasha Sokolov and his Literary Context', *Canadian-American Slavic Studies*, 21 (1987), 301–19 (p. 315). Among other parodic subtexts Matich names Aesopian language, literary graphomania, the émigré novel and émigré nostalgia, the spy novel, sensationalism, literary taboo-lifting, the Freudian craze and Jungian psychoanalytic mythology, Western liberalism, civil rights, Western popular culture.
83. Mark Lipovetsky, *Russian Postmodernist Fiction: Dialogue with Chaos* (hereafter 'Lipovetsky') (Armonk, NY: M. E. Sharpe, 1998), p. 174; Rudova Slavic Studies 40, p. 176.
84. Linda Hutcheon, *A Poetics of Postmodernism: History, Theory, Fiction* (New York and London: Routledge, 2005), pp. 24–25.
85. Boris Grois, 'Zhizn' kak utopiia i utopiia kak zhizn': iskusstvo sots-arta' (hereafter 'Grois Utopia'), *Sintaksis*, 18 (1987), 171–81 (pp. 171–72); Lipovetsky, p. 180.
86. Beraha, p. 220.
87. Grois Utopia, p. 179; Lipovetsky, p. 180.
88. Mikhail Epstein, *After the Future: The Paradoxes of Postmodernism and Contemporary Russian Culture* (hereafter 'After Future'), trans. by Anesa Miller-Pogacar (Amherst, MA: University of Massachusetts Press, 1995), pp. 93–94; Mikhail Epstein, *Postmodern v russkoi literature* (hereafter 'Epshtein Postmodernism') (Moscow: Vysshaia shkola, 2005), p. 226.
89. After Future, pp. 88–94; Epshtein Postmodernism, pp. 226–27.
90. After Future, pp. 84–85; Epshtein Postmodernism, pp. 215–16.

91. Mark Lipovetskii, *Paralogii: Transformatsiia (post)modernistskogo diskursa v kul'ture 1920–2000-h godov* (hereafter 'Paralogii') (Moscow: Novoe literaturnoe obozrenie, 2008), p. 267. Other neo-Baroque authors are Andrei Bitov, Tatiana Tolstaia and Viktor Erofeev.
92. Paralogii, p. 265. In the conceptual category Lipovetskii lists Vladimir Sorokin, Lev Rubinstein, Dmitrii Prigov, among others.
93. Paralogii, pp. 241–73.
94. A comparison was suggested by Arnold McMillin at a conference where I presented a paper on *Between Dog and Wolf*.
95. Fredric Jameson, 'Postmodernism, or The Cultural Logic of Late Capitalism', *New Left Review* (1984) 146, 53–92 (p. 91).
96. Lucien Dällenbach, *The Mirror in the Text* (hereafter 'Dallenbach'), trans. by Jeremy Whiteley and Emma Hughes (Cambridge: Polity Press, 1989), pp. 105–06.
97. Julia Kristeva, *Powers of Horror: An Essay on Abjection*, trans. by Leon S. Roudiez (New York: Columbia University Press, 1982), p. 4.

CHAPTER 1

~

Metaphor of Origin: Narcissism as a Constructive Principle in *School for Fools*

Our perceptions are undoubtedly interlaced with memories, and, inversely, a memory [...] only becomes actual by borrowing the body of some perception into which it slips. These two acts, perception and recollection, always interpenetrate each other, are always exchanging something of their substance as by a process of endosmosis.[1]

Narcissus, then, goes to the secret fountain in the depths of the woods. Only there does he feel that he is naturally doubled. He stretches out his arms, thrusts his hands down toward his own image, speaks to his own voice. Echo is not a distant nymph. She lives in the basin of the fountain. Echo is always with Narcissus. She is he. She has his voice. She has his face. He does not hear her in a loud shout. He hears her in a murmur, like the murmur of his seductive seducer's voice. In the presence of water, Narcissus receives the revelation of his identity and of his duality; of his double powers, virile and feminine; and, above all, the revelation of his reality and his ideality.[2]

In the instance of a disease arising wholly out of the imagination of the sufferer, it is reasonable enough to suppose that a similar experience of the imagination would effect the cure.[3]

In her recollection of the publication of *School for Fools*, Ellendea Proffer says that no one whom they approached with a request to write a review agreed to do so. As an unknown émigré author-debutant, Sokolov needed exposure and a solid recommendation. As the last resort, Carl Proffer came to Nabokov, whom he knew personally, imploring him to read the book and write a short review. Strikingly and unprecedentedly, Nabokov, infamous for his extreme haughtiness and strong opinions in the matters of his craft, consented and wrote an endorsement that determined Sokolov's future.[4]

As Andrei Zorin noted, Nabokov's epithets, 'enchanting, tragic, and touching', which adorned the first edition of *School for Fools*,[5] speak not so much of Sokolov's gift as a writer as of the emotional impact of the book on the reader. Sokolov's 'poetry of childhood', in Zorin's words, is a motif of many of Nabokov's novels, and especially in *Drugie berega* (*Speak, Memory*), a lyrical recollection of the writer's childhood in pre-Revolutionary Russia.[6] *School for Fools* is also a recollection of someone's life, but a life that goes loose and splits into the remembered and the remembering, thus forever confusing as to who or what originated whom: the remembered or the remembering. As in *Drugie berega*, there is a play with reflections and symmetries, and there is an irreplaceable loss at the core of it all, which the author-narrator-hero tries to substitute. That is why reflection and metamorphosis are the main tropes. Highly self-conscious, *School for Fools* composes itself by contemplating its own reflection and reproducing itself *en abyme*.

Shkola dlia durakov (*School for Fools*)[7] is a short novel presented as a retrospective account of a young nameless man afflicted with either multiple personality disorder or schizophrenia, or perhaps both. The recollection is constructed as a dialogue between the narrator and his alter ego, intercepted with long rambling monologues (recollections proper) which incorporate mini-dialogues with other characters of the novel.

The story (*fabula*) of *School for Fools* — a figure of speech as far as Sokolov is concerned,[8] is 'scandalously traditional', in Aleksandr Genis's view. It is the initiation of the hero into the adult world, and his discovery of the existential fundamentals: love and death.[9] The narrator (who lives with his parents — the state prosecutor father, a cruel, loveless, and generally unpleasant man, and a detached yet smothering and submissive mother) is a student in a special school for the mentally deficient. He undergoes a series of losses, constituting his formative experiences, which he recollects in his attempt to remember his shattered self. One of the main traumatic experiences is his unrequited love for a young woman, Veta Acatova,[10] whose protean image oscillates between a neighbour, a classmate, and a teacher. The other event is the loss of his mentor, Pavel Norvegov, a geography teacher in the special school, and the narrator's father figure. And, finally, there is the loss of his parents' dacha, a symbol of the narrator's innocence and serenity. As a result of these traumas the narrator develops something like a multiple personality disorder, characterized by amnesia — 'selective memory' ('izbiratel'naia pamiat'') as it is referred to in the novel[11] — which allows him to construct an alternative version of the experience. The dialogue, or interplay between the two versions — the real (within the coordinates of the story) and the constructed — constitutes the *sujet* of the novel.

* * * * *

Narcissus, it was foretold, would live long 'if he knows himself — not'.[12] True to the prophecy, soon after he becomes aware of himself through his reflection, he dies. By mistaking his reflection for another, Narcissus reveals 'otherness' within himself. Unable to bear it, he withers away, leaving in his stead a flower — a symbol of the inward (Narcissistic) gaze.

The narrator of *School for Fools* also undergoes a metamorphosis into a flower: Nymphea — a Latin name for a white water lily (*Nymphaea alba*). In his free re-enactment of the myth of Narcissus, Sokolov duly invokes images of Tiresias — the blind seer who promised Narcissus a long life as long as he did not know himself — in the guise of a cuckoo, and the nymph Echo, 'disembodied' into the sound of music:

> Была (есть, будет) очень хорошая погода, а река — тихая и широкая, а на берегу, на одном из берегов, куковала кукушка (кукует, будет куковать), и она, когда я бросил (брошу) весла, чтобы отдохнуть, напела (напоет) мне много лет жизни. Но это было (есть, будет) глупо с ее стороны, потому что я был совершенно уверен (уверен, буду уверен), что умру очень скоро, если уже не умер. [...] я находился в одной из стадий исчезновения. Видите ли, человек не может исчезнуть моментально и полностью, прежде он превращается в нечто отличное от себя по форме и по сути — например, в вальс, в отдаленный, звучащий чуть слышно вечерний вальс, то есть исчезает частично, а уж потом исчезает полностью. [...] что касается моего случая с лодкой, рекой, веслами и кукушкой, то я, очевидно, тоже исчез. Я превратился тогда в нимфею, в белую речную лилию с длинным золотисто-коричневым стеблем, а точнее сказать так: я ч а с-т и ч н о исчез в белую речную лилию.[13]

According to the myth, Narcissus confers his name on a flower. Sokolov's nameless narrator, often referred to as 'student so-and-so' ('uchenik takoi-to'), acquires a name (identity) — Nymphea — through his transformation. Unlike Narcissus, who loses himself discovering the 'true' identity of the other, the narrator in *School for Fools* regains his self through the other, slipping into the introspective space, presented as 'a desire for the former self' ('zhelanie sebia prezhnego'):

> Это было хуже, чем если бы я стал призраком, потому что призрак, по крайне мере, может пройти сквозь стену, а я не прошел бы, мне было бы нечем пройти, от меня ведь ничего не осталось. И опять неверно: что-то осталось. Осталось желание себя прежнего, и пусть я не сумел вспомнить, кем я жил до исчезновения, я чувствовал, что тогда, то есть д о, жизнь моя текла интересней, полнее, и хотелось стать снова тем самым неизвестным, забытым таким-то.[14]

The book becomes a quest for a 'former self': an attempt at remembering the self, 'stringing the beads of memory':[15]

> Песня лет, мелодия жизни. Все остальное — не ты, все другие — чужие. Кто же ты сам? Не знаешь. Только узнаешь потом, нанизывая бусинки памяти. Состоя из них. Ты весь — память будешь.[16]

It has been argued that this passage represents a surfacing of an 'I', coming into existence through a 'you' — the former self discovered under the layers of memories and associations.[17] Such self-objectification, achieved through a split of the self into the reflecting and the reflected, is an essential part of the narrative structure. If for Narcissus this cleft is a deadly obstacle, for Sokolov's narrator, it provides a position of the Bakhtinian outsideness (*vnenakhodimost'*) — the 'otherness' that constitutes a precondition of an aesthetic act:

> Отсюда вытекает и общая формула основного эстетически продуктивного отношения автора к герою. Отношения напряженной вненаходимости автора всем моментам героя, пространственной, временной, ценностной и смысловой вненаходимости, позволяющей собрать *всего* героя, который изнутри себя самого рассеян и разбросан в заданном мире познания и открытом событии этического поступка, собрать его и его жизнь и восполнить *до целого* теми моментами, которые ему самому в нем самом недоступны [...].[18]

In Sokolov's narrative, the split is motivated by a psychological condition: a fusion of schizophrenia and multiple personality disorder. Although technically different — split mind versus split personality — both conditions are characterized by dissociation and self-objectification, albeit experienced slightly differently.[19]

A textbook case of split personality, Nymphea has a double, or an 'alter ego', with whom he engages in conversations, arguments, and activities — a condition called 'co-consciousness'. The practice of the 'multiples' to refer to themselves as *we*, and to use their 'alters' to 'share' duties, is also explored in the narrative.[20] Schizophrenia is more about dissociation from one's own emotions and body rather than one's experience as in multiple personality disorder. Louis Sass describes the schizophrenic experience as filled with doubting and detachment: 'a division or doubling in which the ego disengages from normal forms of involvement with emotions, instincts and the body, often taking itself [...] as its own object'.[21] Along with the myth of Narcissus, these discourses constitute the mode and the subject of the novel.

The novel is dedicated to a 'retarded boy Vaitis Danstin': 'Слабоумному мальчику Вите Пляскину, моему приятелю и соседу'.[22] 'Vitia Pliaskin' is a reference to St Vitus's dance (*pliaska sviatogo Vitta*), also known as chorea. It is a disorder of nervous system, usually affecting children, and is characterized by quick, patterned muscular contractions of the face and limbs. The name of the condition derives from a Christian saint, St Vitus, who suffered martyrdom by dismemberment in AD 303 during the persecution of the Christians.

The St Vitus cult spread in the Middle Ages, especially among Germans and Slavs, owing to his alleged miraculous powers against seizures: the sufferers were brought before his image when they were stricken with convulsions.[23] St Vitus is listed as one of the 'auxiliary saints' — the Fourteen Holy Helpers — a group of saints venerated together in Roman Catholicism because their intercession was thought to be particularly effective against a range of diseases. This group originated in the fourteenth century in the Rhineland, largely as a result of the epidemic that became known as the Black Death.[24] In the *Litany of the Fourteen Holy Helpers* St Vitus is referred to as a 'special protector of chastity' and is invoked to 'teach us the value of our soul'.[25]

According to the legend Vitus was the son of a Sicilian senator in Syracuse, who between the ages of seven and twelve was converted to Christianity under the influence of his tutor Modestus and his nurse Crescentia, without the knowledge of his father. He resisted his father's attempts, which included various forms of torture, to make him renounce his Christian faith. He fled with his tutor and nurse to Lucania, from where he was taken to Rome to exorcise a demon which had taken possession of a son of the emperor Diocletian. This he did, and yet, because he refused to abandon the Christian faith, he was tortured together with his tutors. Vitus was cast into a cauldron filled with molten lead, from which he miraculously emerged unscathed. A lion to which he was fed crouched before him and licked his feet (hence his frequent portrayal with a dog or another animal). Finally he was racked on the iron horse until his limbs were dislocated. At this point a storm arose which destroyed many temples, killing a multitude of pagans.[26]

Sokolov's story takes place in the twentieth-century Soviet Empire, presented in the miniature form of a school for fools. The protagonist and the narrator is a martyr of the school's 'slipper system': every student is forced to change into slippers, which are carried in a bag with the student's 'credentials'. There is also a despotic father and a mentor — a geography teacher with apostolic proclivities, manifest in his name: Pavel (Paul), also known as Savl (Saul). Other biblical allusions include the elusive figure of the Sender of Wind — a version of the Holy Spirit — and the narrator's name, Nymphea, a white lily, a traditional symbol of purity and virginity associated with the Virgin Mary. All of this, along with the evocations of the storm, Nymphea's struggle with his father, and references to a burning cauldron (tended by a witch-neighbour in the corridor of his flat), resonates with St Vitus' legend. Perhaps one of the striking evocations of St Vitus' image, with the usual dog or another animal,[27] occurs in the description of the school yard:

> Перед фасадом ты мог видеть некоторые скульптуры: в центре — два небольших меловых старика, один в кепке, а другой в военной фуражке. Старики стояли спиной к школе, а лицом к тебе, бегущему

> по аллее во вторую смену, и у того и другого одна из рук была вытянута вперед, словно они указывали на что-то важное, происходившее там, на каменистом пустыре перед школой, где нас заставляли раз в месяц бегать укрепляющие кроссы. По левую сторону от стариков коротала время скульптура девочки с небольшой ланью. И девочка, и лань тоже светились бело, как чистый мел, и тоже глядели на пустырь. А по правую сторону от стариков стоял мальчик-горнист, и он хотел бы играть на горне, он умел играть, он мог бы играть все, даже внешкольный чардаш, но беда в том, что горна у него не было, горн выбили у него из рук, вернее, белый гипсовый горн разбился при перевозке, и у мальчика из губ торчал лишь стержень горна, кусок ржавой проволоки. Разреши мне поправить тебя, насколько я помню, белая девочка действительно стояла во дворе школы, но то была девочка не с ланью, а с собакой, меловая девочка с простой собакой; когда мы ехали на велосипеде из пункта А в пункт Б, эта девочка в коротком платье и с одуванчиком в волосах шла купаться; ты говоришь, что меловая девочка у нас перед школой стоит (стояла) и смотрит (смотрела) на пустырь, где мы бегаем (бегали) укрепляющие кроссы, а я говорю тебе: она смотрит на пруд, где скоро станет купаться. Ты говоришь: она гладит лань, а я говорю тебе: эта девочка гладит свою простую собаку. И про белого мальчика ты рассказал неправду: он не стоит и не играет на горне, и хотя у него изо рта торчит какая-то железка, он не умеет играть на горне, я не знаю, что это за железка, возможно, это игла, которой он зашивает себе рот, дабы не есть бутербродов матери своей, завернутых в газеты отца своего.[28]

In a series of metamorphoses the statue of a little girl with a small deer becomes a little girl with an 'ordinary dog': one of Veta's — whose name is a feminized version of Vitus — guises by virtue of the 'ordinary dog' that lives in the Acatovs' garden.[29] The reference to 'vneshkol'nyi chardash' (extra-curricular czardas) goes back to Nymphea's proposed accordion performance for Veta.[30] Nymphea is also identified with the boy's figure through the comparison of the iron rod protruding from the figure's mouth to a needle for sewing one's mouth in rejection of the mother's sandwiches wrapped in the father's papers.[31] The epithet 'melovoi' (chalk) is a symbol/symptom of death. The 'etymology' of the symbolism leads back to a town called Mel (Chalk). In this town, where everything is made of chalk, people are dying from a disease which they call 'melovaia' (the chalky).[32] The impersonation of Savl's death is described by the narrator as 'melovaia zhenshchina' (a chalky woman).[33] Contextualized within two other chalk statues, unambiguously representing Lenin (an old man in a civilian cap) and Stalin (an old man in a military cap), the scene is a representation of the narrator's torturous, 'mortified' conditions. A student in the school for fools (a metaphor for Soviet Russia, as has been stated a number of times),[34] Nymphea escapes this madness by raising it to the second degree: going mad.

Incidentally, in his (successful) attempt to drop out of the Military Institute of Foreign Languages in Moscow, Sokolov feigned madness. As reported by Johnson, among his favourite rehearsed delusions were that his chest was a taut drumhead with internal Aeolian harp strings waiting to be plucked and that he was an unexploded bomb.[35] The three months he spent in a military mental hospital must have been informative for an aspirant writer — a kind of field research for *School for Fools*, a text 'modelled' on the schizophrenic discourse.[36]

According to Eugen Bleuler, the man who coined the term 'schizophrenia', one of the most seminal traits of schizophrenic speech, responsible for its deviant quality, is the loosening of associations.[37] It is also referred to as a 'thought disorder', described as 'a logic failure, resulting from the erroneous equation of phenomena on the basis of identical predicates rather than identical subjects'.[38] Sass argues that a more precise name for this condition is 'formal thought disorder', as it concerns not so much the content of thought or the understanding of language *per se* as the person's entire mode of thinking. It is reflexive of the schizoid tendency to order the world in accordance with highly idiosyncratic and impractical, or unconventional, perspectives, based on criteria different from those accepted in a given culture.[39]

One of the major features of schizophrenic thought processes, according to Sass, is a condition called glossomania. It involves the ordering of speech by acoustic qualities, or by irrelevant connotations of words, rather than by communicative function. Thus, neglecting the overall meaning of something read or heard, schizophrenics focus on the sound of words or their graphic appearance. Also, unlike persons with organic brain syndromes, often resisting the notion that one word can have several meanings, schizophrenics are hypersensitive to the polysemantic nature of language and are often aware of a large number of the potential, but irrelevant, meanings of words. Hence, their tendency to make puns and to feel overwhelmed with multiple meanings.[40]

Glossomania is a major mechanism of the narrative construction in *School for Fools*. Thus some of the book's characters 'materialize' from a homonymic play, activated through associative phonetic patterns:

> Это пятая зона, стоимость билета тридцать пять копеек, поезд идет час двадцать, северная ветка, ветка акации или, скажем, сирени, цветет белыми цветами, пахнет креозотом, пылью тамбура, куревом, маячит вдоль полосы отчуждения, вечером на цыпочках возвращается в сад и вслушивается в движение электрических поездов, вздрагивает от шорохов, потом цветы закрываются и спят, уступая настояниям заботливой птицы по имени Найтингейл; ветка спит, но поезда, симметрично расположенные на ней, воспаленно бегут в темноте цепочками, окликая по имени каждый цветок [...]; но ветка спит, сомкнув лепестки цветов, и поезда, спотыкаясь на стыках, ни за что

не разбудят ее и не стряхнут ни капли росы — спи спи пропахшая креозотом ветка утром проснись и цвети потом отцветай сыпь лепестками в глаза семафорам и пританцовывая в такт своему деревянному сердцу смейся на станциях продавайся проезжим и отъезжающим плачь и кричи обнажаясь в зеркальных купе как твое имя меня называют Веткой я Ветка акации я Ветка железной дороги я Вета [...].[41]

Starting off as a railway branch line ('*vetka* zheleznoi dorogi'), the figure dissolves into its homonym, a bough of acacia ('*vetka* akatsii'), and, by aural association, evolving into a name — Veta Acatova.

In shifting its focus from expression to impression, language becomes the source of control over the narrative. An illuminating instance of this is a 'dissection' of the verb 'issiaknut'' (to dry up). Yielding a word 'siaku' — a Japanese measure unit, the metamorphosis engenders a scene which is utterly disruptive of the flow of the narrator's story — if one is still following — but is seminal as a manifestation of linguistic 'transubstantiation' of reality. The scene, initially taking place at a railway postal depot, evolves into a stylization of Yasunari Kawabata, a Japanese writer. It features some railway post office workers, drinking tea, and unexpected visitors, enigmatically referred to 'te, kto prishli' (those who came), with a request to hear something from the Japanese classics. Incidentally, one of the workers, Semen Nikolaev, has a Kawabata on him. The reading of random passages from Kawabata, followed by some stylization of Dogen's poetry, metamorphoses into their enactment, with Nikolaev and his colleague, Fedor Muromtsev, gradually assuming the roles of Tsuneo Nakamura and F. Muromatsu — the alleged protagonists of the story — discussing cold spells and arguing about how many 'siaku' of snow winter brings. The artifice of the scene, emphasized by its highly stylized opening, presented as a description of a stage setting of a theatre play, results in the ambiguity as to what reality is real: that of the railway workers or the Japanese winter. The answer to the absurd question is either, since the only tangible thing in *School for Fools* is language from which scenes and characters derive as if independently of the author's or narrator's will. By flaunting its aural, graphic and semantic resourcefulness, and, sorcerer-like, invoking scenes and images from its morphemes, language celebrates its materiality.

Apart from morphological dissection and homonymy, this schizoid tendency is manifest in the use of paronomasia, presented as misspellings. Thus 'Barkarola–barrakuda', a pair meant to designate a musical instrument, is a reference to the narrator's music lessons that were a pretext, a sad euphemism, for his mother's adultery. Another paronomastic pair is 'konstruktor–konstriktor', in which a set of construction toys becomes a constrictor, revealing the ominous side of engineering, a profession into which all fools of the special school are being forged.[42] A similar pair is 'konduktor–konstriktor'. A metamorphosis of a train conductor into 'constrictor' intimates the nature of the train/railway motif in Sokolov's work. Trains and railway tracks are recurrent symbols and hubs of violence, promiscuity, mutilation, and death in all three Sokolov's novels. In his second novel, *Between Dog and Wolf*, the theme of sexual violence and death on the tracks takes the centre stage. In *Palisandriia*, the railway motif is curiously avoided for the entire length of the novel, just to emerge at its denouement, in the hero's final and phallic return — a triumphant entrance on the train — to the mother/land. Standing for masculinity, violence, and death, the theme of the railway is also associated with memory in *School for Fools*. All the instances of the emergence of traumatic memories are connected with or take place at the railway station, the tracks, or the train. Thus if the river brings oblivion and solace — a theme further developed in Sokolov's second novel — the railway is identified with memories.

Examining a paronomastic pair 'politika–kalitika', Ludmilla Litus traces the stem of 'kalitika' to 'kalit', meaning 'to harden' (as in Ostrovskii's *Kak zakalialas' stal'*), or to 'kalita', translated as 'a purse', suggesting the toughening effect of the politics and the link between politics and money.[43] In my reading, Sokolov's neologism refers to the crippling effect of politics, jumbling 'politika' (politics) with 'kaleka' (a cripple) or its verbal form 'kalechit' — 'to cripple', as is attested by the inner-textual (and extra-textual) context. The narrator is given an absurd task of rewriting newspaper lead articles, 'чтобы мы лучше разбирались в вопросах внешней и внутренней к а л и т и к и' ('so that we would have a better understanding of internal and external *polyticks*').[44] When the prosecutor comes to check on the son's progress, the image of the narrator (in fact, Nymphea has managed to escape, leaving behind his alter ego) leaves little doubt as to the meaning of 'kalitika':

> Он видит, как ты сидишь за письменным столом и старательно — старание выражено в том, что ты склонил свою наголо стриженую голову набок и нелепо изогнул спину, будто тебя всего изломали, да, сбросили на камни с высокого обрыва, а затем подошли и еще больше изломали с помощью кузнечных щипцов, которыми держат раскаленные болванки — пишешь.[45]

The extra-textual context of many a Soviet unofficial artist/writer is well known. Although *School for Fools* cannot be reduced to a veiled commentary on the absurdities and horrors of Soviet reality,[46] this instance is evocative indeed of artists' dire fate during the Soviet regime, forced to compromise their professional integrity. After all, Sokolov's emigration was caused by the impossibility of writing or being published.[47]

The pair 'obrazovanie — oborzovanie' is also discussed by Litus, who tracks down the root 'borz' to 'borzopisets' — a graphomaniac. 'Borzyi' is an archaism for 'fast', and thus 'oborzovanie', by analogy, can mean 'quick education', or 'poor education'.⁴⁸ A colloquial derivative of the stem 'borz' — a verb 'oborzet" (to become impudent and offensive) — may need to be taken into consideration. The narrator is resisting his 'oborzovanie' by refusing to comply with the obtuse rules of the system, epitomized by the 'slipper system' ('tapochnaia sistema'). The 'slipper system' implies that each student changes his street footwear into slippers, carried in a specially labelled bag. Thus by forcing its mad students into home footwear, the school 'domesticates' chaos. Generally, the shod and shoeless dilemma occupies an important place in Sokolov's juxtaposition of the institutionalized and creative worlds.⁴⁹ Thus, the state prosecutor — the embodiment of the state power — despises (and envies) the geography teacher, Pavel/Savl Norvegov, for wearing no shoes.⁵⁰ The symbolism of shoes as a sign of conformity emerges strongly in the episode of Savl's pending suspension:

> [...] да, я хорошо помню, что Перилло хотел уволить меня по-щучьему. Но, подумав, он дал мне испытательный срок — две недели, и чтобы не вылететь с работы, я решил проявить себя в лучшем виде. Я решил стараться и стараться. Я решил не опаздывать в школу, решил купить и носить сандалии, я поклялся вести уроки строго по плану. Я отдал бы кому-нибудь половину дачного лета, лишь бы остаться с вами, друзья мои.⁵¹

If the geography teacher resists the system by refusing to wear shoes, Nymphea, forced into shoes, boots, galoshes, and slippers, neutralizes his 'shod' condition on the level of language. On his way to the post office (in a desperate attempt to be initiated into the mysteries of sex so as not to appear before Veta as a good-for-nothing), Nymphea reads a store sign 'Obuv" ('Footwear') as 'liubov" (love).⁵² Framed in the context of the chapter 'Skeerly'– an onomatopoeic representation of sex — such reading not only conveys the narrator's resistance to his immediate reality, but equally reflects the boy's enamoured state and prepares for the episode to come: Nymphea's 'amorous' advances at the post office. In fact, the trip to the post office, represented as a list of store signs, is a remarkable portrayal of Nymphea's semioticization and control of reality. The cityscape turns into a mindscape, presented as a sort of a library catalogue, wherein each label indicates or conceals a micro-story, which charts out not so much the outer environment as the narrator's inner state.

Umberto Eco, in *The Infinity of Lists*, writes that the ancient use of the 'catalogue' technique, a prime example of which is Homer's list of ships from the *Iliad*, is a way to convey the ineffability and the immensity of the object of description.⁵³ The technique thus is a way to give form — an underlying order — to the potentially 'unknowable' phenomenon. Indeed, *School for Fools* is literally overrun with lists, one of its main means of organization. In fact, one of the first catalogues is a reference to Homer's celebrated list, which, befittingly, conveys the narrator's difficulty in representing reality:

вечер добрый билеты би леты чего нет Леты реки Леты ее нету вам аи цвета ц Вета ц Альфа Вета Гамма и так далее чего никто не знает потому что никто не хотел учить нас греческому было непростительной ошибкой с их стороны это из-за них мы не можем перечислить толком ни одного корабля [...].[54]

The importance of this technique is announced in one of the novel's epigraphs. It is a list of irregular verbs, which constitute an exception to the rule of verbal conjugation:

> Гнать, держать, бежать, обидеть,
> слышать, видеть, и вертеть,
> и дышать, и ненавидеть,
> и зависеть, и терпеть.

Группа глаголов русского языка, составляющих известное исключение из правил; ритмически организована для удобства запоминания.[55]

According to Johnson, its meaning lies solely in the form, pointing to one of the devices of Sokolov's narrative — the use of rhythmically organized lists.[56] Although some catalogues are indeed constructed on the basis of sound similarity, which is hardly surprising, considering Sokolov's linguistic sensitivity, I do not think that they are semantically insignificant.

One of the traits of the schizophrenic discourse is an extreme terseness and the use of cryptic words, resulting in a 'telegraphic' form of speech, reminiscent of the 'catalogue' technique. It is identified with a failure to monitor one's speech in accordance with the social requirements of conversation: as if the words and phrases were packed with meaning, which remains inaccessible as no contextual cues are supplied to the listener. Sass maintains that it is a manifestation of a need to avoid a direct confrontation with the reality of disturbing themes, or to convey experiences that are inherently ineffable.[57]

Bearing this in mind along with the primary function of an epigraph, the list of verbs may be read as a summary prefiguring the events unfolding in the novel. Apart from the ominous ring to the combination of the verbs, the epigraph prefigures the uniqueness and nonconformity of the narrator's perception, suggested by the rules of exception. His eccentricity is reflected in his peculiar approach to manipulating concepts and categories, which parallels the schizophrenic modes of classification and identification. The ways in which perceived identities, differences, and similarities are used to form categories point to the narrator's unusual manner of allocating attention. It supplies him with a critical distance from things that are normally taken for granted by an ordinary person. One such instance occurs at the very beginning of the novel, presented as the setting of the story to come:

> Обычная станция — сама станция, но вот то, что за станцией — то представлялось очень хорошим, необыкновенным: пруд,

> высокая трава, танцплощадка, роща, дом отдыха и другое. На
> околостанционном пруду купались обычно вечером, после работы,
> приезжали на электричках и купались. Нет, но сначала расходились,
> шли по дачам. Устало, отдуваясь, вытирая лица платками, таща
> портфели, авоськи, екая селезенкой. Ты не помнишь, что лежало в
> авоськах? Чай, сахар, масло, колбаса; свежая, бьющая хвостом рыба;
> макароны, крупа, лук, полуфабрикаты; реже — соль. Шли по дачам,
> пили чай на верандах, надевали пижамы, гуляли — руки-за-спину
> — по садам, заглядывали в пожарные бочки с зацветающей водой,
> удивлялись множеству лягушек — они прыгали всюду в траве, —
> играли с детьми и собаками, играли в бадминтон, пили квас из
> холодильников, смотрели телевизор, говорили с соседями. И если
> еще не успевало стемнеть, направлялись компаниями на пруд —
> купаться. А почему они не ходили к реке? Они боялись водоворотов
> и стрежений, ветра и волн, омутов и глубинных трав. А может быть
> реки просто не было? Может быть. Но как же она называлась? Река
> называлась.[58]

At first glance, this enumeration of everyday activities strikes us as superfluous and empty. Especially random is the catalogue of the contents of the shopping bag — '*avos'ka*', a name of great significance. An '*avos'ka*', a purely Soviet phenomenon, is a foldable knitted bag, whose name derives from '*avos*' ('what if?'), suggesting the anxiety about the constant food and consumer goods shortages in the Soviet Union. The apparent absurdity and incongruity of the contents of Sokolov's '*avos'ka*' have an underlying logic: they are sorted into 'breakfast', 'lunch', and 'dinner' categories (Russian/Soviet breakfast traditionally consisting of tea and a sandwich). Inserted in the overall context of the list, they not only strengthen the sense of rigidity and conventionality of the narrator's environment, but also reflect on the absurdity of its order. In retrospect it becomes obvious that the list is an oblique portrayal of the narrator's father, identified through the images of pyjamas, briefcase, and walks 'with arms behind their backs', which spring up throughout the narrative connected with the father.[59] The static nature of this character is conveyed through a striking image of his white face upon which two black flies (common attributes of the corpse) trickle down like tears.[60]

Sokolov's lists present non-obvious or idiosyncratic logical patterns, which reorganize perception of the world by bringing out unexpected, and seemingly absurd, links between distant things and challenging the ones commonly accepted. These qualities relate to Eco's definition of the modern lists (from Rabelais to Joyce to Borges), which, contrary to the Homeric impulse to order, are made in contempt of this order, made out of 'love of excess, hubris and a greed for words, for the joyous […] science of the plural and the unlimited'.[61] One of the prime examples of such a list is Borges's catalogue of animals from his 1942 essay *John Wilkins' Analytical Language*:

These ambiguities, redundancies, and deficiencies recall those attributed by Dr. Franz Kuhn to a certain Chinese encyclopedia called the *Heavenly Emporium of Benevolent Knowledge*. In its distant pages it is written that animals are divided into (a) those that belong to the emperor; (b) embalmed ones; (c) those that are trained; (d) suckling pigs; (e) mermaids; (f) fabulous ones; (g) stray dogs; (h) those that are included in this classification; (i) those that tremble as if they were mad; (j) innumerable ones; (k) those drawn with a very fine camel's-hair brush; (l) etcetera; (m) those that have just broken the flower vase; (n) those that at a distance resemble flies.[62]

The disconcerting effect of Borges's list stems from its defiance of its own criteria of categorization, since one of the categories can include all the others. Thus category (a) consisting of animals that belong to the emperor can enclose (b), (c), etc. Moreover, Borges's list exhausts its limits by including itself within its own classification, '(h) those that are included in this classification', thus breaking any commonsensical order. Sokolov's taxonomy and purpose are not dissimilar to Borges's. For instance, there are lists that defy the purpose of a list: to represent the world of abundance and consumption, which is employed often in mass media and advertisements, as the only model of an ordered universe.[63] Sokolov's answer to that is a catalogue of the objects and phenomena that are not:

[З]десь я должен в скобках заметить, что станция, где происходит действие, никогда, даже во времена мировых войн, не могла пожаловаться на нехватку мела. Ей, случалось, недоставало шпал, дрезин, спичек, молибденовой руды, стрелочников, гаечных ключей, шлангов, шлагбаумов, цветов для украшения откосов, красных транспарантов с необходимыми лозунгами в честь того или совершенно иного события, запасных тормозов, сифонов и поддувал, стали и шлаков, бухгалтерских отчетов, амбарных книг, пепла и алмаза, паровозных труб, скорости, патронов и марихуаны, рычагов и будильников, развлечений и дров, граммофонов и грузчиков, опытных письмоводителей, окрестных лесов, ритмичных расписаний, сонных мух, щей, каши, хлеба, воды.[64]

There are lists that cancel themselves out through the disintegration of the syntax:

И если случится, что вы разберетесь во всем этом первый, немедленно сообщите, адрес вы знаете: стоя над рекой на закате дня, когда умирают укушенные змеей, звонить велосипедным звонком, а лучше — звенеть деревенской косой, приговаривая: коси, коса, пока роса, или: коси-коси, ножка, где твоя дорожка, и так далее, пока загорелый учитель Павел не услышит и, приплясывая, не выйдет из дома, не отвяжет лодку, не прыгнет в нее, не возьмет в руки самодельные греби, не перегребет Лету, не сойдет на твоем берегу, не обнимет, не поцелует, не скажет добрых загадочных слов, не получит, нет, не прочитает отправленного письма, ибо его, вашего учителя, нету в

> живых, вот беда, вот незадача, нету в живых, а вы — живите, пока не умрете [...].⁶⁵

The Russian construction 'poka ne' (until) dissolves into a pure negation ('ne poluchit'), thus annulling the preceding and the ensuing actions in the list.

The chaos of the surrounding reality, resisting the logic of grammar, accumulates in a collage-like picture compiled of its disjointed fragments that, paradoxically, captures its very essence. This palimpsest of traces turns into a Stendhal's mirror of sorts, which moves across the country bearing its image:

> Наконец поезд выходит из тупика и движется по перегонам России. Он составлен из проверенных комиссиями вагонов, из чистых и бранных слов, кусочков чьих-то сердечных болей, памятных замет, деловых записок, бездельных графических упражнений, из смеха и клятв, из воплей и слез, из крови и мела, из белым по черному и коричневому, из страха смерти, из жалости к дальним и ближним, из нервотрепки, из добрых побуждений и розовых мечтаний, из хамства, нежности, тупости и холуйства. Поезд идет, [...] и вся Россия, выходя на проветренные перроны, смотрит ему в глаза и читает начертанное — мимолетную книгу собственной жизни, книгу бестолковую, бездарную, скучную, созданную руками некомпетентных комиссий и жалких, оглупленных людей.⁶⁶

The image of the train crossing the country is a metaphor for Sokolov's text. Its brown or black walls evoke a school blackboard, written upon with a chalk — a deathly entity in the novel — which illuminates the allegorical layer of the school for fools: a metaphor for the country of suffering idiots. It also actualizes one of the narrative techniques of Sokolov's novel: text within the text (Iurii Lotman's 'tekst v tekste').⁶⁷ These auto-reflexive miniature models, or *mise en abyme*, function as a kind of 'self-regulation' of the narrative, reacting to its context and reversing it. Dällenbach, in his *Mirror in the Text*, distinguishes two types of *mise en abyme*: repeated and single.⁶⁸ Chapter 2, entitled 'Now', is a good example of this technique that combines both types.

As a single *mise en abyme* it divides the text into two, challenging its unity and splitting it into two jarring tones: 'realistic' and 'imaginary'. It functions like the 'Yershalaim' chapters do in Bulgakov's *The Master and Margarita*: providing a 'verisimilar' context to the phantasmagoria of 'Moscow' chapters. Appearing as totally extraneous to the body of the text, it clashes with the lyricism and incantation-like sensitivity of other chapters. It is a collection of sketches written in a stark minimalistic key in a tone of 'objective' detachment. Sokolov wrote these stories first, in Moscow, later developing and integrating them in the text of *School for Fools*.⁶⁹ Embedded into the main narrative, they paradoxically contain it within them and serve as its context.

As suggested by its title — 'Now' — the chapter functions as a present-tense framework of the novel, constituting the 'realistic' backbone of *School for Fools*.

The narrative voice of the vignettes is identified with a young man, an aspiring writer, who has been discharged from military service, and who is living in a dacha settlement and writing sketches about his experiences and encounters. The uncannily 'objectivized' manner of presentation results in a defamiliarized version of the events, taking place in other parts of the narrative. The objectivization is achieved through the use of the third-person singular — he, or in the stylized form of *skaz*, as in 'As Always on Sunday' and 'The Tutor'. The sketches written in the first-person singular are still deliberately emptied of any form of subjectivity. For instance in 'Amid the Wastelands', Sokolov reverses the function of the 'constituting consciousness' by presenting the narrator, the I/eye of the story, not as a subject but as an object of perception: 'Я закурил и пошел обратно, к тому дому, в котором что-то делали с моей невестой и который издали пристально смотрел мне в глаза.'[70]

The chapter also features an overview of the personages and incidents that affect the narrator's existence most significantly as well as providing thematic ties with the rest of the novel.[71] Thus the first vignette, 'The Last Day', 'picks up' exactly at the point Nymphea left it: underneath Veta's window. The sketch depicts a young man in the throes of unrequited love for a woman whose windows he spends nights watching.[72] The woman re-emerges in the closing sketch, suggestively called 'Now': the protagonist, who has returned from the army, sees her dancing with a strange man — an image that 'spills' into the next chapter, 'Savl', which opens with Veta dancing in a restaurant.[73] In another sketch, the narrator shares a train compartment with a young woman making sexual advances:

> Красивая молодая женщина, которая ехала с ним в купе, совсем не стеснялась его и перед сном раздевалась, стоя перед дверным зеркалом, и он видел ее отражение, и она знала, что он видит, и улыбалась ему. В последнюю ночь пути она позвала его к себе, вниз, но он притворился, что спит, и она догадалась об этом и тихо смеялась над ним в темноте узкого и душного купе, а тем временем поезд кричал и летел сквозь черную пургу, и пригородные уже полустанки растерянно кивали ему вослед тусклыми фонарями.[74]

This bleak detachment of presentation is a 'realistic' take on the associative incantation of Veta's introduction in chapter one:

> спи спи пропахшая креозотом ветка утром проснись и цвети потом отцветай сыпь лепестками в глаза семафорам и *пританцовывая в такт своему деревянному сердцу смейся на станциях продавайся проезжим и отъезжающим плачь и кричи обнажаясь в зеркальных купе как твое имя меня называют Веткой* я Ветка акации я Ветка железной дороги я Вета беременная от ласковой птицы по имени Найтингейл я беременна будущим летом и крушением товарняка вот берите меня берите я все равно отцветаю это совсем недорого я на станции стою не

> больше рубля я продаюсь по билетам а хотите езжайте так бесплатно ревизора не будет он болен погодите я сама расстегну видите я вся белоснежна ну осыпьте меня совсем осыпьте же поцелуями никто не заметит лепестки на белом не видны.[75]

The chapter could be compared to a mirror placed in the middle of the text, which, collapsing, scatters a myriad of its pieces into the most hidden corners of the surrounding space. Its working into the fabric of the novel is accomplished through the recurrence of identical elements — in the form of an epithet, a phrase, or an image, which signals a connection between things, suggesting their proximity, or sameness.

Generally, the superimposition of recurrent images or epithets is the basic mechanism of narrative construction in *School for Fools*. They constitute a leitmotif, serving as an indicator of plot, producing links between the characters and events, sometimes of the most surprising nature. A good example of this technique is the neologism 'skeerly', mentioned earlier. Presented as a text within the text — a tale recollected by the narrator — *Skeerly* is a hybrid of two popular Russian folk tales: *Masha and the Bear* (*Masha i medved'*) and *Wooden Leg* (*Lipovaia noga*). The first tale features a bear and a clever little girl, Masha, who outsmarts the bear by making it carry her home, disguised as gifts (pies) for her parents. The second is a story of a one-legged bear, haunting a village at night, accompanied by the screeching noise of his wooden leg. In Nymphea's tale, the bear, whose prosthesis makes the same screeching noise — onomatopoeically presented as 'skeerly' — abducts the little girl, carrying her off in a wicker basket into his lair where he does the unthinkable with her. The *Skeerly* tale is impressed upon the narrator's psyche through a record, played by his neighbour Sheina Solomonovna, who, once in a while, borrows his broken record player (and magically makes it work). It is a recording of the screechy — skeerlying — voice of her late husband, reading the tale.[76]

Most importantly, 'skeerly' is associated with the noise suggesting the sound of bedsprings, heard from a room where Veta is — as prompted by the alter ego — with a man. The association is so strong that in his account of the tale the narrator communicates a terrifying suspicion that the abducted little girl 'might not be a girl, but a certain woman acquaintance of mine, with whom I have close relations'.[77]

> Когда я вспоминаю С к и р л ы — хотя я стараюсь не вспоминать, лучше не вспоминать — мне мерещится, будто девочка та — не девочка, а одна моя знакомая женщина, с которой у меня близкие отношения, вы понимаете, конечно, мы с вами — не дети, и мне мерещится, что медведь — тоже не медведь, а какой-то неизвестный мне человек, мужчина, и я прямо вижу, как он что-то делает там, в номере гостиницы, с моей знакомой, и проклятое с к и р л ы слышится многократно, и меня тошнит от ненависти к этому звуку, и я полагаю,

что убил бы того человека, если бы знал, кто он. Мне тяжело думать про сказку С к и р л ы, сударь, но, поскольку я редко делаю домашнее задание, меня часто оставляют после уроков делать уроки на завтра и на вчера, и оставшись один в классе, я обычно выхожу пройтись в коридор, а выйдя, встречаюсь там с Тинберген, а когда я вижу ее, грядущую искалеченной, но вместе и какой-то почти веселой, танцующей походкой, и слышу тоскливый — как крик одинокого козодоя — скрип ее протеза, то — увольте, сударь, — не могу не думать о сказке С к и р л ы, потому что звук именно тот самый, как в гостинице [...].[78]

Further sexual references re-emerge in the narrator's dreadful recollections of his music lessons, during which he memorizes 'sextets', while his mother and the 'maestro' seek privacy in the tower up the 'skeerlying' stairs.[79] As a symbol of the mysterious sex act, 'skeerly' ties in one knot the ominous figure of the rapist bear and the nymphomaniac witchlike Sheina, intimating the mother's and Veta's promiscuity.

Apart from serving as a 'plot-marker', such a-chronological superimposition of recurrent elements is a way to collapse time, a category that is constantly suppressed in the narrative. This technique is exposed in Nymphea's presentation of his life as a chaotic agglomeration of dots on a piece of paper, each indicating this or that day, rather than an ordered calendar-like sequence, which he terms 'poetic nonsense'.[80] The notion of time is also undermined through his doing away with the tense system: all three tenses are often used simultaneously. Such an approach to time in the narrative is captured in the image of two trains, circuiting the city and thus eliminating movement and time:

> Поезда, которые минуют наш дом, движутся по замкнутой, а следовательно — бесконечной кривой вокруг нашего города, вот почему из нашего города выехать почти невозможно. Всего на кольцевой дороге работает два поезда: один идет по часовой стрелке, другой — против. В связи с этим они как бы взаимоуничтожаются, а вместе — уничтожают движение и время.[81]

This sketch, a part of a *mise en abyme*, presented as Nymphea's course essay, entitled 'My Morning', illuminates the role of duplication as the motivator of the narrative.

School for Fools belongs to a trend in metafiction that Linda Hutcheon called a 'narcissistic narrative'. It is defined as 'a self-reflective and/or self-conscious text, which forms itself by refracting its own process — producing itself by a series of duplications'.[82] Hutcheon distinguishes two types of 'narrative narcissism': overt and covert, which operate on two levels: linguistic and narrative (diegetic). In overtly narcissistic texts the self-consciousness and self-reflexivity are manifested through an explicit 'thematization' within the fiction. In covert forms of narcissism, this process is internalized — or 'actualized'.[83]

In Sokolov's text, it is achieved by means of the trope of madness, manifested as schizophrenic discourse on the linguistic level and the theme of the double on the diegetic plane.

The theme of the double, which permeates all levels of the text, is introduced in the third epigraph to the novel: a quotation from Edgar Allan Poe's *William Wilson*. Poe's Doppelganger is one of many portrayals of duality, which saturated the romantic fiction of the nineteenth century: Dostoevskii, Gogol', Wilde, and Stevenson, to name a few. However, as Alexandra Karriker notes, the alter ego of Sokolov's narrator does not function as the conscience of Poe's tale.[84] Nor does it fulfil the role of the personality's dark side, the emerging id, as depicted in *The Picture of Dorian Gray* or *Dr Jekyll and Mr Hyde*. In fact, Sokolov's use of the trope of the double is closest to Dostoevskii's *The Double* (*Dvoinik*). Goliadkin-like, Nymphea creates an alter ego who is able to achieve things that the narrator could only dream about. Or rather, he projects his inefficiencies and complexes onto the other, thus remaining free to act as his imagination commands. On the narrative level this process is presented as a dialogue between the two versions of reality — 'objective' and personal, conceptualized as the interplay between the emergence and repression of traumatic memories. The narrator's alter ego seems to function as an agent of 'objective' reality. His is the voice of a critic, who constantly undermines the veracity of the narrator's story by pestering him for details, 'refreshing' his memory, and pressing Nymphea to admit to his escapism. The nature of this relationship transpires from the very opening of the novel, when one of the voices tries to undo the other's elusiveness by insisting that it knows the (non-existent) river's name in the dacha settlement.[85] The river is, of course, Lethe: the river of oblivion, on whose banks Nymphea seeks refuge.

Sokolov's use of the double is not only a mode of destabilizing perspective consistency. His adaptation of the Doppelganger is resonant with Nabokov's parodic treatment of the genre in *Lolita*, based on constant undermining of the reader's expectations. Inviting the reader to draw parallels, through the allusions to Poe and his representation of the double, Sokolov infests the text with doubling and multiplicity, turning it into a pure projection of the narrator's divided self. Imitating the protagonist, each character sports a double, who provides a 'surplus' meaning. This supplementary function of the double focuses on the superior faculties possessed by most of the characters in the novel. (Ab)using Bakhtin's 'surplus of seeing' ('izbytok videniia'), which allows one to construct a unified image of an event or a being ('so-bytie'),[86] Sokolov's narrator solipsizes his environment.

Another — perhaps the most seminal within the text — function of the double is illuminated in a parable, 'The Carpenter in the Desert', told by Savl at his last class, which uncannily anticipates his death. It features a carpenter in the desert, who after a period of unbearable idleness due to the absence of tools and materials, turned into a bird in his joy as he finally found two planks of wood and a nail and built a cross. Later, tempted with grain by some strangers, he crucified a man, who turned out to be his own self.[87] The imagery of the tale unmistakably evokes the Passion scene, aligning the parable's hero with the figure of Christ as carpenter and martyr. It also recalls the biblical legend of Christ's temptation in the desert, according to which the devil promised him the world if he would agree to compromise his faith. This led Karen McDowell to read the tale as an account of the writer's fate in Soviet Russia, forced to compromise his or her integrity as a true artist.[88] This insight, although valuable, cannot be taken completely in earnest. In Sokolov's adaptation the biblical motif is desecrated by the secular echoes of Poe's Doppelganger,[89] where the killing of one's double or, as in Oscar Wilde's *The Picture of Dorian Gray*, of one's representation, leads to death. The identification of the image of the double with death in literature and popular beliefs (a superstition of breaking a mirror) can be traced back to the myth of Narcissus.[90] Thus, in its incorporation of a number of references to the role of the double, Savl's parable seems to suggest that reality is a form of representation: it exists as and as long as reflection does.

Counteracting Nymphea's dissociation with the self, his narrative reveals a strong urge to be reflected. There are multiple instances in which the narrator perceives himself in reflection, literally through the eyes of the other:

> Оглянувшись, ты увидел ее большие глаза цвета пожухлой травы, в них медленно оживали слезы и отражались какие-то высокие деревья с удивительной белой корой, тропинка, по которой ты ехал, и ты сам со своими длинными худыми руками и тонкой шеей, и ты — в своем неостановимом движении о т.[91]

A manifestation of this 'reflexive' compulsion is Nymphea's fascination with the echo:

> Пожарная бочка манит тебя пустотой своей, и пустота эта, и тишина, живущая и в саду, и в доме, и в бочке, скоро становятся невыносимыми для тебя, человека энергического, решительного и делового. Вот почему ты не желаешь больше размышлять о том, что кричать в бочку — ты кричишь первое, что является в голову: я — Нимфея, Нимфея! — кричишь ты. И бочка, переполнившись несравненным гласом твоим, выплевывает излишки его в красивое дачное небо, к вершинам сосен — и по дачным душным мансардам и чердакам, набитым всяческим барахлом, по волейбольным площадкам, где никто никогда не играет, по вольерам с тысячами ожиревших кроликов, по гаражам, провонявшим бензином, по верандам, где на полу разбросаны детские игрушки и чадят керосинки, по огородам и вересковым пустошам вкруг дачных поселков — несется эхо — излишки твоего крика: ея-ея-ея-ея-яяяяя-а-а![92]

The lasting reverberation of 'Nymphea-ia-ia' turns into 'ia' — a Russian for 'I', filling the void of the barrel as water would do. By evoking the self in the shout and equating it with the medium of reflection — water — the narrator reaches for the 'I'.

Reflected in the surrounding objects and voices, he attains his essence — 'immortality of the non-existent':

> Когда мы покидаем поезд и спускаемся с платформы, я оглядываюсь: я вижу, как весь вагон смотрит нам вслед. Мы, идущие своей дорогой, отражаемся в глазах и стеклах набирающего скорость состава: моя среднего роста мама в демисезонном коричневом жакете с воротником из болезненной степной лисы, мама в чешуйчатой, твердой на вид, шляпке, сделанной неизвестно из чего, в ботах; и я — худой и высокий, в темном пыльнике на шести пуговицах, перешитом из прокурорской шинели отца, в ужасной бордовой кепке, в ботинках с полузаклепками и с галошами. Мы отлетаем от станции все дальше, растворяясь в мире пригородных вещей, звуков и красок, с каждым движением все более проникаем в песок, в кору деревьев, становимся оптической ложью, вымыслом, детской забавой, игрой света и тени. Мы *преломляемся* в голосах птиц и людей, мы обретаем бессмертие несуществующего.[93]

This coming into existence through a reflection[94] is illuminated in the creation of the novel's characters, the majority of whom materialize from some form of representation. Thus the postman Mikheev/Medvedev emerges from a picture of Ivan Pavlov, a Russian physiologist.[95] Sheina Trakhtenberg/Tinbergen comes to 'life' from a reference to Niko Tinbergen's study of mimicry in the insect.[96] Savl's image as a reflection of a publishing logo recurs in the text.[97] At one point the teacher's portrayal on the window sill of the school toilet, in a position perfectly imitating the publisher's logo, eventually metamorphoses into the image of the narrator:

> И вот мы посмотрели на него, сидящего таким образом, сбоку, в профиль: издательский знак, экслибрис, серия книга за книгой, силуэт юноши, сидящего на траве или на голой земле с книгой в руках, темный юноша на фоне белой зари, мечтательно, юноша, мечтающий стать инженером, юноша-инженер, если угодно, кудрявый, довольно кудрявый, книга за книгой, читает книгу за книгой на фоне, бесплатно, экслибрис, за счет издательства, один и тот же, все книги подряд, очень начитан, он очень начитан, ваш мальчик — нашей доброй любимой матери — Водокачка, учительница по предметам литература и русский язык письменно и устно, маме сказала, даже слишком, мы бы не рекомендовали все подряд, особенно западных классиков, отвлекает, перегрузка воображения, дерзит, заприте на ключ, не больше пятидесяти страниц в день, для среднего школьного возраста […].[98]

The narrator walks off the page of the book — right onto the page we are reading. Later in the narrative, in his conversation with Acatov, Nymphea, tongue-in-cheek, finds himself speaking 'like in a novel', which, of course, he is:

> Уважаемый Аркадий Аркадьевич, я чрезвычайно ценю ваше изобретение, однако сейчас я сам нуждаюсь в вашем совете — и даже в большей степени, чем вы — в моем, у вас вопрос честолюбия, а у меня — извините, я говорю, как в романе и оттого мне как-то неловко и смешно, — у меня к вам вопрос целой жизни.[99]

This meta-ironic affirmation of the interdependence of life and its representation is often conveyed through the application of literary tropes in the rendering of reality. Thus Savl demands a clarification of his status — dead or living — with the aid of a metaphor. Strictly speaking, what he demands is the metaphor of a metaphor, since his death appeared in the form of a strange 'chalky' ('melovaia') woman,[100] informing Nymphea of Savl's departure to his dacha, across the river Lethe. As a response to Savl's enquiry, Nymphea comes up with a series of poetic and idiosyncratic representations of death:

> Но мне снова тревожно, я хочу опять возвратиться к разговору о той женщине, я жду очередных подробностей. Скажите, с кем или с чем вы могли бы сравнить ее, дайте метафору, дайте сравнение, а то я не слишком четко представляю ее себе. Дорогой отставник, мы могли бы сравнить ее с криком ночной птицы, воплощенным в образе человеческом, а также с цветком отцветающей хризантемы, а также с пеплом отгоревшей любви, да, с пеплом, с дыханием бездыханного, с призраком, и еще: женщина, отворившая нам, была тот бабушкин меловой ангел с одним надломленным крылом, тот — ну, вы, наверное, знаете.[101]

By cramming metaphor upon metaphor Nymphea seems to 'secure' the existence of the object described, as if attempting to breathe life back into its deathliness. An illuminating instance of this process is the figure of Veta Acatova.

Denied any tangibility, Veta exists only as a metaphor, in her myriad of guises, mediated through the narrator's impressions, free associations, memories, and fantasies. In the two instances of her bodily description in the novel she appears in the form of representation: photographic, pictorial and plastic.[102] When Nymphea is asked to describe Veta by giving her 'portretnaia kharakteristika' (a character's summary, literally translated as 'portrait-like characterization), he does precisely that: actualizing a figure of speech — a literary term — he presents Veta through a reference to a portrait by Leonardo da Vinci, *La Gioconda*:

> А почему бы тебе не рассказать, как именно она выглядела, когда входила, почему бы не дать, как говорит Водокачка, портретную

> характеристику? Нет-нет, невозможно, бесполезно, это лишь загромоздит нашу беседу, мы запутаемся в определениях и тонкостях. Но ты только что вспоминал о просьбе Леонардо. Тогда, у него в мастерской, мы, кажется, сумели описать Вету. Сумели, но описание наше было лаконичным, ибо и тогда мы не могли сказать больше того, что сказали: дорогой Леонардо, представьте себе женщину, она столь прекрасна, что когда вы вглядываетесь в черты ее, то не можете сказать н е т радостным слезам своим. И, — спасибо, юноша, спасибо, — отвечал художник, — этого достаточно, я уже вижу этого человека.[103]

This fusion of Mona Lisa and Veta, as her prototype, gives another dimension to Sokolov's narrative.

According to his biographer, Giorgio Vasari,[104] Leonardo da Vinci was never painting anything but the object of his desire, a fixation of which *La Gioconda* and her famous smile is the perfect embodiment.[105] In his essay 'Leonardo da Vinci', Sigmund Freud traces this obsession back to Leonardo's relation to his mother. Examining the artist's biography and work, Freud speaks about the importance of the artist's childhood experience, which haunted him throughout his life. It became most visible in Leonardo's art, which Freud interprets as sublimation. This essay, written four years prior to his 'On Narcissism: An Introduction', establishes a link between narcissism and homosexuality through the schema of identification with the mother.

An illegitimate child of a Florentine notary, Piero Antonio of Vinci, Leonardo spent the first years of his life with his mother, who, in Freud's reading, took her son in place of her husband, and 'by the too early maturing of his erotism robbed him of a part of his masculinity'.[106] By identifying with his mother, Leonardo established his own person as a model for his love objects and incorporated into himself her desire (for him), which resulted in auto-eroticism instead of true love of the other:

> What he has in fact done is to slip back to auto-eroticism: for the boys whom he now loves as he grows up are after all only substitutive figures and revivals of himself in childhood — boys whom he loves in the way in which his mother loved *him* as a child. He finds the objects of his love along the path of *narcissism*, as we say; for Narcissus, according to the Greek legend, was a youth who preferred his own reflection to everything else and who was changed into the lovely flower of that name.[107]

As Steven Bruhm notes in his study of narcissism, Freud's Narcissus bypasses his own reflection in the waters and seeks his mother, a water nymph Liriope, who returns his idealized image by loving him, affirming his worth, and holding him together: preventing him from splitting into two.[108] The embodiment of this reflecting idealized/ing other — imago in psychology — in *School for Fools* is Veta, Nymphea's biology teacher (and a common mother figure). Since the imago that becomes an object of love is identified with a lost and an idealized part of the self,[109] the restoration of the protagonist's identity depends on the reconstruction of Veta's image. As with Leonardo's idealized imago (his mother), rather than his reflection, Veta is a medium — the spring over which Nymphea leans in search of the self. If Leonardo's desire took a turn through sublimated homosexuality to get back to the mother (as the eternal feminine, *La Gioconda*), Sokolov's narrator detours through heterosexuality only to get back to a narcissistic reflection, that is a reflection of his 'former self'.

Like Leonardo's works, Nymphea's narrative speaks of nothing but his desire (for his former self), displaced into his desire for Veta. The displacement is acknowledged in the verbal equation of Veta's photo and Nymphea's desire for the former self as the only 'things' that remained: 'Это было хуже, чем если бы я стал призраком, [...] от меня ведь ничего не осталось. И опять неверно: что-то осталось. Осталось желание себя прежнего'.[110] Veta's photo — another thing that remains — re-emerges in the passage that concentrates the novel's key points, quoted earlier, in an almost identical verbal context: 'Улыбнись, постарайся не шевелиться, это будет фотография. Единственная, которая останется после всего, что будет'.[111] Echoing Leonardo's Mona Lisa, whose 'unfathomable smile, always with a touch of something sinister in it, [...] plays over all Leonardo's work',[112] Veta's illusive image is distilled in the novel's texture, culminating in her photo:

> А над всем этим, щурясь от белого зимнего солнца — в енотовой шубке — на фоне сугроба и дачного заснеженного леса — сияла, летела, царила — твоя несравненная Вета — учительница по анатомии, ботанике, биологии [...] Господи сударь какая изумительная фотография она здесь как живая то есть нет я ошибся стилистическая ошибка я хотел сказать как настоящая как на уроке красивая и недоступная кто это снимал когда почему я ничего не знаю какой-нибудь подлец с фотоаппаратом кто он в каких они отношениях здесь или в другом месте легион вопросов.[113]

Veta is a metaphor. For Julia Kristeva the term metaphor signifies not so much a classical juxtaposition of figurative versus plain, but 'a meaning being acted out'.[114] As metaphor, Veta gives, or 'acts out' Nymphea's meaning.

Victoria Hamilton, in her psychoanalytical study of the figure of Narcissus, argues that Narcissus's life turns into a tragedy when 'he ceases to be a hero and comes to exist as a representation, as an object completed and fixed'.[115] Although Hamilton's reading of representation as completion (the end) of the subject echoes Bakhtin's notion of outsideness as completion, for Bakhtin, the self can attain value and meaning only through this act of completion/formation (literally, 'oformlenie') through the other:

> Наружность бытия, фактическая наличность, определенность

(именно так, а не иначе), плоть бытия в человеке, его обращенность вовне себя может быть ценностно осмыслена, просветлена только через другого и для другого, т.е. в ценностной категории другого. Наружность выражает не меня, а отношение ко мне другого, Бога, здесь я не создаю себя, но или я просто и тупо оказался таким, каким я есмь (данность моя) или: меня создали таким, т.е. я осмыслен в создавшей меня активности другого.[116]

Similarly, for Kristeva, the subject comes into being by seeing himself as an object for the other, existing only inasmuch as it identifies with this (idealized) other. After all, ego has nothing to close in on except a void. And along with identifications and projections, representations, supplied by the other, constitute a means of exorcizing this emptiness.[117] The other comes first: Narcissus's tenuous identity is shaped by his representation. In Sokolov too, the double reigns supreme.

Constructed as a dialogue between Nymphea and his alter ego, the novel eventually discloses another narrative voice. A character, introduced as an author, on several occasions intrudes into the narrative: 'Dear student so-and-so, I, the author of this book'.[118] Interestingly, the voices of the 'author' and the alter ego seem to coincide, often interrupting the narrator's monologue, questioning, offering some corrections, and demanding more information. One of the instances of coincidence between the narrator's double and the surrogate author is their participation in 'how do you begin?' dialogues, which opens the novel, and re-emerges on several occasions later in the text.[119] At the end of the novel, in a scene reminiscent of the second part of *Don Quixote*, the narrator and the authorial persona engage in a friendly chat about the book they are in.[120] These authorial intrusions into the narrative establish what Dällenbach referred to as a 'reciprocal relationship' between reality and fiction, precluding any distinction being drawn between cause and effect, the original and the copy.[121]

Imitating Nymphea imitating Narcissus, the author exists in two forms. By splitting his self off into a fictional alter ego, he becomes at once the creator and the character of his own fiction. The authorial doubling, in the manner of Cervantes and his Cid Hamete, the Moorish chronicler who is presumably the true author of *Don Quixote*, is seminal for Sokolov's project. Creating an antithesis, a parodic mirroring of his own work, the artist interposes a necessary distance between himself and his project that enables him to perform his aesthetic act. If Veta Acatova is the mirror for the narrator, for the author figure this reflecting medium is the book.

School for Fools — a book about writing a book — is permeated with references to the role of books in the construction of the narrative and the self. One of the lengthiest invocations of the theme occurs during Nymphea's trip to the post office, presented as a sequence of the store signs. One of the signs reading 'Knigi' ('Books') opens into a list of random slogans and proverbs concerning books, disjointed excerpts from Russian and Soviet classics, folklore, and nursery rhymes:

> КНИГИ. Книга — лучший подарок, всем лучшим во мне я обязан книгам, книга — за книгой, любите книгу, она облагораживает и воспитывает вкус, смотришь в книгу, а видишь фигу, книга — друг человека, она украшает интерьер, экстерьер, фокстерьер, загадка: сто одежек и все без застежек — что такое? отгадка — книга. Из энциклопедии: статья к н и ж н о е д е л о н а Р у с и: книгопечатание на Руси появилось при Иоанне Федорове, прозванном в народе первопечатником, он носил длинный библиотечный пыльник и круглую шапочку, вязаную из чистой шерсти. И тогда некий речной кок дал ему книгу: на, читай. И сквозь хвою тощих игол, орошая бледный мох, град запрядал и запрыгал, как серебряный горох. Потом еще: я приближался к месту моего назначения — все было мрак и вихорь. Когда дым рассеялся, на площадке никого не было, но по берегу реки шел Бураго, инженер, носки его трепетал ветер. Я говорю только одно, генерал, я говорю только одно, генерал: что, Маша, грибы собирала? Я часто гибель возвращал одною пушкой вестовою. В начале июля, в чрезвычайно жаркое время, под вечер, один молодой человек. А вы — говорите, эх, вы-и-и! А белые есть? Есть и белые. Цоп-цоп, цайда-брайда, рита-умалайда-брайда, чики-умачики-брики, рита-усалайда. Ясни, ясни, на небе звезды, мерзни, мерзни, волчий хвост! Правая сторона.[122]

This indiscriminate cataloguing of banalities, 'high' and 'low' literature, intimates the absurd cultural situation in Soviet Russia with its promotion of 'high' culture and production of safe, mediocre literature. Thus, Maksim Gorkii's *In the World* (*V liudiakh*)[123] is indiscriminately woven into the narrative with Mikhail Lermontov's *Hero of Our Time*[124] and Dostoevskii's *Crime and Punishment*;[125] nursery rhymes and nonsensical chains are juxtaposed with encyclopaedic entries. In fact, Nymphea's invocation of reality through the street signs is in itself a literary allusion to *Anna Karenina*: to Anna's 'stream-of-consciousness' monologue on her way to the railway station. Paradoxically, enclosed in the text of *School for Fools*, the catalogue re-creates its context: the literary context of the author's reality. This seemingly nonsensical list conceals a story of the remembered self turned into a textual self, actualizing Mandel'stam's words: 'Разночинцу не нужна память, ему достаточно рассказать о книгах, которые он прочел, — и биография готова.'[126]

The textual articulation of the self functions as a medium and a metaphor. As Narcissus leaves a metaphor for his self by the spring, so does the writer — leaving a book as a representation of his transformation. Whether deliberate or incidental, but nonetheless uncanny the proximity of the two store signs — 'ЦВЕТЫ. КНИГИ' ('FLOWERS. BOOKS')[127] — in the passage quoted above is irresistibly suggestive of the analogy between the two metamorphoses.

By placing a double at the core of his work, the artist reminds himself of and ensures his own existence: it is in reflection that he finds his essence. Contrary to Hamilton's opinion, a transformation of a life into an aesthetic object becomes the only possible way to regain that lost self — by transforming that remembered, but vanished, self into a metaphor of itself: a flower, or a book. *School for Fools* becomes a site of reconstruction, bearing a metamorphosis of the teller into the told.

* * * * *

> Narcissus would appear to be opposite from Echo: he persists by denying all except himself; she persists by effacing herself absolutely. Yet they come to the same: it was never himself Narcissus craved, but his reflection, the Echo of his fancy; his death must be partial as his self-knowledge, the voice persists, persists.[128]

The encounter between Narcissus and Echo prefigures his fate. In listening to Echo he refuses to hear her voice, taking it as his own. The retribution comes in the form of another delusion: Narcissus becomes infatuated with an image, which he refuses to take as his own. The tragedy strikes as he realizes his error. And that is where he goes wrong. As Bakhtin (and Lacan and Kristeva) argue:

> здесь не единая и единственная душа выражена, в событие самосозерцания вмешался второй участник, фиктивный другой, не авторитетный и не обоснованный автор; я не один, когда я смотрю на себя в зеркало, я одержим чужою душой.[129]

This dialogue between the 'I' and the other that is within each individual consciousness constitutes what Bakhtin calls 'architectonics': an integrated whole negotiated between 'dannoe' ('given') and 'zadannoe' ('posited as a task to be carried out').[130] The category of the given is the sphere of the other, language and cultural artefacts. The 'posited' category is characterized by incompleteness and the sense that the true meaning of anything always lies outside what is presently available in time and in space. In contrast to the given it is a process not a product. It is how one's own self is perceived from within: incomplete, always in flux, and in need of form. On its own, the 'I-for-myself' cannot generate a coherent narrative, only a vague anxiety and chaotic energy. It is with the intervention of the other supplying the self with impressions and perspectives that the possibility of a story begins.[131]

In his story, Sokolov rewrites the encounter. Giving rein to the nymph, he spares Narcissus his end. She keeps him talking to survive, but, instead, saves him by holding up his image. Thus Echo regains her powers; and Narcissus regains his reality: through his ideality. *School for Fools* is a dialogic monologue, constructed through a persistent Echo. The nymph steals into Sokolov's text, obliterating any difference between reality and its reflection, medium and message, turning the subject of the narrative into its object.[132] Thus origin turns into a metaphor, the context into the text, and the past merges with the present in the echo of one's voice.

Notes to Chapter 1

1. Henri Bergson, *Matter and Memory*, trans. by Nancy Margaret Paul and W. Scott Palmer (New York: Zone Books, 1988), p. 67.
2. Gaston Bachelard, *Water and Dreams: An Essay on the Imagination of Matter*, trans. by Edith R. Farrell (Dallas: Dallas Institute of Humanities and Culture, 1983), pp. 22–23.
3. H. C. Adams, 'The Dancing Mania' (hereafter 'Adams Dancing Mania'), *Religious Manias* (London: Religious Tract Society), 16 August 1884, section 'Sunday at Home', pp. 513–15 (515).
4. Ellendea Proffer quoted in *Canadian-American Slavic Studies*, 40 (2006) (hereafter 'Slavic Studies 40'), 341–49 (p. 344).
5. Slavic Studies 40, p. 344; D. Barton Johnson, 'Literary Biography', *Canadian-American Slavic Studies*, 21 (1987) (hereafter 'Johnson Literary Biography'), 203–30 (p. 213).
6. Andrei Zorin, 'Nasylaiushchii Veter', *Novyi Mir*, 12 (1989), 250–53 (p. 251).
7. Sasha Sokolov, *Shkola dlia durakov* (hereafter 'Shkola') (St Petersburg: Symposium, 2001), p. 46.
8. D. Barton Johnson, 'Background Notes on Sokolov's *School for Fools* and *Between Dog and Wolf*: Conversations with the Author', Slavic Studies 40, 331–39 (p. 334).
9. Slavic Studies 40, p. 342.
10. The deviation from the Library of Congress spelling is intentional in an attempt to convey Veta Acatova's identification with acacia. Similar motifs underlie my spelling of Arcadii Arcadievich Acatov.
11. Shkola, p. 133.
12. Ovid, *Metamorphoses* (hereafter 'Metamorphoses'), trans. by Charles Martin (New York and London: Norton, 2004), p. 104.
13. Shkola, pp. 39–43.
14. Ibid., p. 44.
15. Sasha Sokolov, *School for Fools* (hereafter 'School'), trans. by Carl Proffer (Ann Arbor, MI: Ardis, 1977), pp. 186–88.
16. Shkola, p. 218.
17. See Diana K. Davis, *Through Other Creatures: Modes of Identification in 'A School for Fools' and 'Singing From the Well'* (Ann Arbor, MI: UMI Dissertation Services, 2007), pp. 74–75.
18. Mikhail Bakhtin, 'Avtor i geroi v esteticheskoi deiatel'nosti' (hereafter 'Avtor i geroi'), in *Sobranie sochinenii*, 7 vols (Moscow: Russkie slovari, 1997–2003), I (2003), 69–263 (p. 96). Italics in the original.
19. The narrator's split personality has been regarded by many critics as a symptom of his schizophrenic condition. The etymology of the term schizophrenia points to 'split mind' rather than split personality. In this case schizophrenia is being confused with Multiple Personality Disorder, a psychological condition characterized by the use of amnesic dissociation as a mechanism for coping with an early trauma, which causes the individual to undergo a splitting into personalities that alternate in control over his person. See Ian Hacking, *Rewriting Soul: Multiple Personality and the Sciences of Memory* (Princeton: Princeton University Press, 1995), p. 130.

20. See Shkola, pp. 151–52.
21. Louis A. Sass, *Madness and Modernism: Insanity in the Light of Modern Art, Literature, and Thought* (hereafter 'Sass') (Cambridge, MA: Harvard University Press, 1996), p. 37.
22. Shkola, p. 8, School, p. 4.
23. *New Catholic Encyclopedia* (hereafter 'Catholic Encyclopedia'), 17 vols (New York: McGraw-Hill Book Company, 1967), XIV, 730; Lives of the Saints, p. 545.
24. Catholic Encyclopedia, p. 730.
25. <http://www.catholictradition.org/:Litanies/litany63.htm> [accessed October 2008].
26. *Butler's Lives of the Saints* (hereafter 'Lives of the Saints'), ed. by Herbert Thurston S. J. and Donals Attwater, 3 vols (London: Burns and Oates, 1956), II, 545.
27. Catholic Encyclopedia, p. 730.
28. Shkola, pp. 124–26.
29. Ibid., p. 112.
30. Ibid., p. 118.
31. Ibid., pp. 118–20.
32. Ibid., pp. 50–51.
33. Ibid., p. 231.
34. See Alexander Boguslawski, 'Sokolov's *A School for Fools*: An Escape form Socialist Realism', *Slavic and East European Journal*, 27 (1983), 91–97; Richard C. Borden, 'Time, Backward! Sasha Sokolov and Valentin Kataev', *Canadian-American Slavic Studies*, 21 (1987), 247–63. Ludmilla L. Litus, 'Saša Sokolov's Škola dlja durakov: Aesopian Language and Intertextual Play' (hereafter 'Litus Slavic and East European Journal'), *Slavic and East European Journal*, 41 (1997), 114–34.
35. Sasha Sokolov, 'V dome poveshennogo', in *Trevozhnaia kukolka. Esse* (St Petersburg: Azbuka Klassika, 2007), pp. 25–38 (p. 35); Johnson Literary Biography, pp. 203–05.
36. Many modernist works rely on the trope of madness to create a disjunct narrative, amongst others: Virginia Woolf, William Faulkner, André Breton and Alan Robbe-Grillet, to each of whom Sokolov was compared. Among Russian antecedents, there are Gogol's *The Notes of a Madman*, and Dostoevskii's *The Notes from the Underground* and *The Double*.
37. Richard P. Bentall, *Madness Explained: Psychosis and Human Nature* (London: Penguin Books, 2004), p. 379.
38. John Vernon, *The Garden and the Map: Schizophrenia in Twentieth-Century Literature and Culture* (Chicago: University of Illinois Press, 1973), p. 115.
39. Sass, pp. 121–30.
40. Ibid., p. 178.
41. Shkola, pp. 18–19.
42. Ibid., pp. 182–83.
43. Ludmilla Litus, *Saša Sokolov's 'Skola dlja durakov': Form, Language, Intertext, and Allusion* (hereafter 'Litus thesis') (Ann Arbor, MI: UMI Dissertation Services, 2007), p. 80.
44. Shkola, p. 152; School, p. 133.
45. Shkola, p. 157.
46. See Litus Slavic and East European Journal, p. 116.
47. See Slavic Studies 40, pp. 331–39.
48. Litus thesis, p. 80.
49. Sokolov's obsession with shoes has been discussed in great detail in D. Barton Johnson, 'The Galoshes Manifesto: A Motif in the Novels of Sasha Sokolov', *Oxford Slavonic Papers*, 22 (1989), 155–79.
50. Shkola, p. 27.

51. Ibid., pp. 229–30.
52. Ibid., p. 185. In translation it is rendered: 'GLOVES. And I read the word "gloves" as "love" on the store', School, p. 161.
53. Umberto Eco, *The Infinity of Lists: From Homer to Joyce* (hereafter 'Eco Lists'), trans. by Alastair McEwan (London: MacLehose Press, 2009), p. 49.
54. Shkola, p. 20.
55. Ibid., p. 9.
56. D. Barton Johnson, 'A Structural Analysis of Sasha Sokolov's *School for Fools*: A Paradigmatic Novel' (hereafter 'Johnson Structural Analysis'), *Fiction and Drama in Eastern and Southeastern Europe: Evolution and Experiment in the Postwar Period*, ed. by Henrik Birnbaum and Thomas Eekman (Bloomington, IN: Slavica Publishers, Inc., 1980), pp. 207–237 (p. 230).
57. Sass, pp. 177–207.
58. Shkola, pp. 11–12.
59. Ibid., pp. 28, 136, 217; School, pp. 120,187, 26.
60. Shkola, p. 72.
61. Eco Lists, p. 327.
62. Jorge Luis Borges, 'John Wilkins' Analytical Language', in *The Total Library: Non Fiction, 1922–1986*, trans. by Esther Allen, Suzanne Jill Levine, and Eliot Weinberger (London: The Penguin Press, 2000), pp. 229–32 (p. 231).
63. Eco Lists, p. 353.
64. Shkola, pp. 49–50.
65. Ibid., pp. 67–68.
66. Ibid., pp. 52–53.
67. Iurii Lotman, 'Tekst v tekste', in *Ob iskusstve. Struktura khudozhestvennogo teksta. Semiotika kino i problemy kinoestetiki. Stat'i. Zametki. Vystupleniia* (St Petersburg: Iskusstvo-SPB, 1998), pp. 423–36.
68. Lucien Dällenbach, *The Mirror in the Text* (hereafter 'Dallenbach'), trans. by Jeremy Whiteley and Emma Hughes (Cambridge: Polity Press, 1989), pp. 105–06 (p. 71). Dällenbach's categorization of *mise en abyme* is highly detailed. However, for our purposes it suffices to introduce these two categories of the system.
69. Slavic Studies 40, p. 334.
70. Shkola, p. 102.
71. See Alexandra H. Karriker, 'Narrative Shifts and Cyclic Patterns in *A School for Fools*', *Canadian-American Slavic Studies*, 21 (1987), 287–99 (p. 292); on the re-emerging characters see Fred Moody, 'Madness and the Pattern of Freedom in Sasha Sokolov's *A School for Fools*', *Russian Literature Triquarterly*, 16–17 (1979), 7–32 (p. 31).
72. Shkola, pp. 85–86.
73. Ibid., p. 109.
74. Ibid., p. 106.
75. Ibid., pp. 19–20, italics mine.
76. Ibid., pp. 164–67.
77. School, p. 145.
78. Shkola, pp. 165–66.
79. School, p. 193.
80. Shkola, pp. 37–38.
81. Ibid., pp. 192–93.
82. Linda Hutcheon, *Narcissistic Narrative: The Metafictional Paradox* (hereafter 'Hutcheon Metafiction') (New York: Methuen, 1984), pp. 53–54.
83. Hutcheon Metafiction, p. 23.

84. Alexandra H. Karriker, 'Double Vision: Sasha Sokolov's *School for Fools*' (hereafter 'Karriker Double Vision'), *World Literature Today*, 53 (1979), 610–14 (p. 611).
85. Shkola, p. 12.
86. Avtor i geroi, p. 95.
87. Shkola, pp. 208–14.
88. Karen Rice McDowell, *The Reemergence of Medieval Word-Weaving in Sasha Sokolov's 'Shkola dlia durakov': Invoking the Word* (Ann Arbor, MI: UMI Dissertation Services, 2007), p. 153.
89. See Karriker Double Vision, pp. 611–13.
90. Otto Rank, in his essay 'The Double', demonstrated that the double motif in popular belief and literature is linked with the notion of death, and argued that this fact is in turn linked with narcissism. He was the first one to use the term 'narcissism' in connection with literary criticism. See Otto Rank, 'Der Doppelgänger', *Imago*, 3 (1914) in Louise Vinge, *The Narcissus Theme in Western European Literature up to the Early 19th Century* (hereafter 'Vinge'), trans. by Robert Dewsnap and Nigel Reeves (Lund: Skånska Centraltryckeriet, 1967), pp. 50–51.
91. Shkola, p. 74.
92. Ibid., pp. 156–57.
93. Ibid., p. 228, italics mine.
94. 'Reflection' is translated into Russian as both 'otrazhenie' and 'prelomlenie' — in case of light, for instance — and as used by Sokolov in the quotation above (italicized by me).
95. Shkola, p. 14.
96. Ibid., p. 21.
97. Ibid., pp. 114–16, 126, 175, 229.
98. Ibid., pp. 115–16.
99. Ibid., p. 163.
100. Ibid., p. 231, School, p. 199.
101. Shkola, pp. 235–36.
102. Ibid., pp. 160–61, 261–63, 124–26, respectively.
103. Ibid., pp. 262–63.
104. Giorgio Vasari, *Le vite dei più eccellenti pittori, scultori e architetti*, 2 vols, ed. by Licia e Carlo L. Ragghianti (Milan: Rizzoli, 1971-1973).
105. Walter Pater, 'Leonardo da Vinci' (hereafter 'Pater Vinci'), in *Studies in the History of the Renaissance* (Oxford: Oxford University Press, 2010), pp. 56–72.
106. Sigmund Freud, *Leonardo da Vinci: A Memory of his Childhood* (hereafter 'Freud Vinci'), trans. by Alan Tyson (London and New York: Routledge Classics, 2006), p. 73.
107. Freud Vinci, p. 51, emphasis in the original.
108. Steven Bruhm, *Reflecting Narcissus: A Queer Aesthetic* (Minneapolis and London: University of Minnesota Press, 2001), p. 91.
109. Julia Kristeva, *Tales of Love* (hereafter 'Tales of Love'), trans. by Leon S. Roudiez (New York: Columbia University Press, 1987), pp. 30–37; Heinz Kohut, 'Thoughts on Narcissism and Narcissistic Rage', in *Selected Writings of Heinz Kohut: 1950–1978: The Search for the Self*, ed. by Paul H. Ornstein (New York: International Universities Press, 1978), pp. 615–58.
110. Shkola, p. 44.
111. Ibid., p. 218.
112. Pater Vinci, pp. 69–70.
113. Shkola, pp. 160–61.
114. Tales of Love, p. 37.

115. Victoria Hamilton, *Narcissus and Oedipus: The Children of Psychoanalysis* (London: Karnac Books, 1993), pp. 116–17.
116. Avtor i geroi, p.167.
117. Tales of Love, pp. 23–42.
118. School, p. 43; other instances pp. 212, 228; Shkola, pp. 48, 245, 265.
119. Shkola, p. 257.
120. Ibid., pp. 253–57.
121. Dallenbach, p. 81.
122. Shkola, pp. 185–86.
123. Gor'kii's 'В каюте у себя он сует мне книжку в кожаном переплете, и ложится на койку, у стены ледника. "Читай!"' (in 'V liudiakh', *Detstvo, V liudiakh, Moi universitety* (Leningrad, 1971), p. 280) yields in Sokolov: 'И тогда некий речной кок дал ему книгу: на, читай' (Shkola, p. 185).
124. Sokolov's 'Когда дым рассеялся, на площадке никого не было' resonates with a scene in Mikhail Lermontov *Geroi nashego vremeni*: a duel between Pechorin and Grushitskii.
125. Sokolov's: 'В начале июля, в чрезвычайно жаркое время, под вечер, один молодой человек'. (School, p. 186) is the opening sentence of *Crime and Punishment*.
126. Osip Mandel'shtam, 'Komissarzhevskaia', in 'Egipetskaia marka', *Sobranie sochinenii*, 2 vols, ed. by G. P. Struve and B. A. Fillipov (New York: Inter-Library Association, 1966), II, 137–39 (p. 137).
127. Shkola, p. 185.
128. John Barth, 'Echo', in *Lost in the Funhouse* (New York: Bantam Books, 1980), p. 99.
129. Avtor i geroi, p. 113.
130. Mikhail Bakhtin, 'K filosofii postupka' (hereafter 'K filosofii postupka'), in *Sobranie sochinenii*, 7 vols (Moscow: Russkie slovari, 1997–2003), I (2003), pp. 7–68.
131. K filosofiia postupka, p. 43; Avtor i geroi, p, 131; see also Caryl Emerson, 'The Next Hundred Years of Mikhail Bakhtin (The View from the Classroom)', *Rhetoric Review*, 19 (2000), 12–27 (pp. 17–19).
132. An actualization of the notion of 'the message is the medium' is the narrator's teacher of Russian, nicknamed Vodokachka. The letters that form the word 'vodokachka' (water tower) — V.D.K., pronounced as '*vadaka*' — are the teacher's initials: Valentina Dmitrievna Kaln: 'Пусть та преподаватель совершенно не была похожа на водокачку, — скажешь ты, — зато она необъяснимо напоминает само слово, сочетание букв, из которых оно состоит (состояло, будет состоять) — В, О, Д, О, К, А, Ч, К, А'. Shkola, p. 150.

CHAPTER 2

A Realized Metaphor: The Eucharist Miracles in *Between Dog and Wolf*

Странны, загадочны и трагичны события, происходящие в той захудалой местности, где кроме меня обретали покой и волю Чайковский и Пришвин, Рильке и его переводчик от русской сохи Дрожжин, но где душа человеческая не многим дороже пары сапог. Там протекает Волга, она же Лета, впадающая в тюркское море забвения. Чаевничая ее водою, входя в обстоятельства ее берегов, делаешься навсегда причастен к необъяснимому и нездешнему — в ней и судьбах ей обреченных.[1]

But you see, phonetics is the yeast, the fermenting agent of language. I start with a sound; sound is like a grain from which everything else grows. It's impossible to speak about phonetics separately from meaning. Linguistics captures that notion in the term *zvukosmysl* [sound/sense].[2]

>   Когда межевали свет и тьму
>   Осталась полоса сверхсметных сумерек
>   Лесостепное кочевое волчье
>   Временами бредится мы оттуда родом[3]

It has been argued that *Between Dog and Wolf* reflects Sokolov's real-life experience as a gamekeeper on a hunting reserve in the Tver' (at the time Kalinin) region on the Volga. According to Johnson, the setting provided not only rich linguistic material, which could not be more remote from the urban modernist prose of the previous novel, but also the plot and the characters. Sokolov's predecessor, whose position and dwelling Sokolov had inherited, had come to a bad end. As a result of an incident involving the hunting dogs of a villager, the previous gamekeeper, never popular with the locals, was found drowned. Despite the efforts of an official investigator sent out to clarify the case, the affair remained unresolved. This incident served as the nucleus of Sokolov's novel.[4]

Stripped to its bare bones, *Between Dog and Wolf* is a crime story, and, despite its convoluted presentation, a very simple one. On his way home from a drunken wake a knife grinder kills, in a battle described in the best epic tradition, a gamekeeper's dog, which he takes for a marauding wolf. In revenge, the gamekeeper steals his crutches. The feud escalates and two more of the gamekeeper's hounds are killed, intentionally this time. In the end, the grinder is drowned. The story is projected onto the scenery of the Upper Volga, referred to by its ancient Tartar name, Itil'. It is set sometime in the post-Second World War period, a supposition prompted by an inordinate number of crippled, orphaned, and homeless people, as well as snippets of post-war songs, and references to such phenomena as 'koiko-mesto' ('bed-place', usually in a hospital).[5] The novel, a combination of prose and poetry, comprises three segments, which are distributed over eighteen chapters. The three segments, attributed to the grinder, the gamekeeper, and an authorial persona, represent three perspectives on the events described earlier.

Il'ia Petrikeich Zynzyrela, a wandering knife grinder, whose epistolary exercise opens *Between Dog and Wolf*, is a victim and a 'chronicler' of the events unfolding in the novel. His letter — a complaint on the subject of his stolen crutches[6] — is rendered in the form of *skaz*, and is addressed to a local crime investigator, Sidor Fomich Pozhilykh. The technique of *skaz* designates a type of narrative that focuses on the spoken word, infusing literary discourse (usually first-person) with elements from living speech, often from lower-class, less well-educated, or uncultured narrators. It usually involves peculiarities of style, syntax, or grammar, as well as more obvious instances of sub-standard speech, slang, or dialecticisms.[7] The peculiarity of *skaz* is that it is neither fully oral nor fully literary: it is a literary representation of the oral mindset.[8] In Bakhtinian terms, it is a double-voiced utterance, the effect of which is largely ironic: by appearing to represent, the *skaz* narrator is represented. By highlighting the process of representation, the technique of *skaz* both undermines the stability of narrative authority and shifts the focus from message to medium.

Richly colloquial and folkloric, Il'ia's *skaz* swarms with all sorts of idiosyncrasies and 'inarticulacies'. The solemnity of the occasion — the intrinsic performative element of *skaz*, the 'responsibility' of the narrator before his audience — is undermined by the narrator's self-conscious awareness of language, his entanglement in it. This tension is typically conveyed through malapropisms, paronomastic attractions (mostly popular/poetic etymology), and stylistic infelicities:

> Месяц ясен, за числами не уследишь, год нынешний. Гражданину Сидор Фомичу Пожилых с уважением Зынзырэлы Ильи Петрикеича Заитильщина. Разрешите уже, приступаю. Гражданин Пожилых. Я, хоть Вы меня, вероятно, и не признаете, гражданин, тоже самое, пожилой и для данных мест сравнительно посторонний, но поскольку

точильщик, постольку точу ножи-ножницы, и с панталыку меня вряд ли, пожалуй, сбить, пусть я с первого взгляда и совершенный культяп.⁹

Relying on popular etymology — paramount in Il'ia's narrative — he links the investigator's surname, Pozhilykh (the etymology of which is 'from the elderly ones'), with 'pozhiloi' (elderly). Irony, produced by Il'ia's logical and linguistic 'blunders', usually conceals a pointer, which de-automatizes the expression or the word in question:

> В стрелецкие числа, чтобы опасней, зато бодрей, бобыли обоих мелкоплесовских берегов обустраивают состязания на слабеющем льду. Происходит в кромешной темени, предумышленно без небесных светил, и народ фигуряет кто мудреней и суетится в горелки и взапуски, не зря промоин и трещин. Что чревовато.¹⁰

Il'ia's 'chrevovato', a jamming of 'chrevato' (fraught/pregnant with consequences) and 'chrevo' (womb), is set to trigger an ironic effect of a simple speaker trying to use high-brow words. What emerges from this jumble is that: firstly, the two words are obviously related, and secondly, the combination of the two captures with striking precision the described phenomenon. To skate on thin ice has its consequences, which usually amount to being swallowed by the body of water.

The notorious stylistic and lexical esoterism of the *skaz* sections of *Between Dog and Wolf* has been perhaps the most-discussed topic in the secondary literature and the chief reason for the novel's unreadability and untranslatability. Comprising eight fragments, it alternates with two other distinct segments, one in prose and one in verse.

The prose segment, rendered mostly in the third-person singular or impersonal infinitive constructions, is presented from the point of view of an implied author. This (quasi-) sophisticated discourse constitutes a portrayal of Iakov Il'ich Palamkhterov, hunter, gamekeeper, and poet. The 'authorial' discourse serves as a frame narrative to Iakov's inner monologue, contained within:

> Так, уставясь в окошко в сравнительно поздний час одного из ничтожных и будних дней еще одного промозглого года и пытаясь собраться с мыслями, философствовал герой этой повести. Вита синэ либертатэ нихиль, философствовал он, виверэтэ эст милитарэ. Он был несвеж и немолод.¹¹

It comprises five entries and functions as a centrefold from which other narratives (*skaz* and verse) disperse centrifugally. The structure of the novel, excluding chapter eighteen, presented as *Post Scriptum*, forms a set of convex mirrors. The first and the last chapters are *skaz*, the second and penultimate are prose, the third and the fifteenth chapters are poems, then again two mirroring Il'ia's narratives (4 and 14), the prose narratives (5 and 13), Il'ia's (6 and 12), verse (7 and 11), and Il'ia's (8 and 10). The structure 'folds' in the middle, at chapter nine — a prose entry, thus making it a 'centrefold', which holds the book together.

According to Johnson, in the earliest version of the novel, the point of departure was the figure of Iakov, rather than that of Il'ia, who is considered to be the focus of *Between Dog and Wolf*. This presumption rests on the initial fragment that Sokolov sent to Proffer for the first number of Ardis's new serial miscellany, *Glagol*. The selection focused on Iakov's appearance and his family history, which roughly corresponds to the first prose entry — chapter two in the novel — and ended with a series of reflections on the indeterminacy of identity. The theme of indeterminacy was triggered by the wordplay between the name Iakov and the word 'iakoby' ('as if'), which is used to express doubt about an assertion. The theme also was set forth by the novel's title: *Mezhdu sobakoi i volkom*.[12]

A calque from Latin — *inter canem et lupum* — 'between dog and wolf' is an idiomatic expression that designates twilight: literally, the time of day when a shepherd could not tell a wolf from a dog guarding his flock. It arrived in Russia via France, and remained in use in French: *entre chien et loup*. It appears that its first use in Russian, resulting in 'mezhdu sobakoi i volkom', can be attributed, at least in literature, to Aleksandr Pushkin. It appeared in Pushkin's novel-in-verse, *Evgenii Onegin*:

> Люблю я дружеские враки
> И дружеский бокал вина
> Порою той, что названа
> Пора меж волка и собаки,
> А почему не вижу я.[13]

This stanza, with the exception of the last line, features as the first epigraph to *Between Dog and Wolf*. Interestingly, according to Sokolov, it was Nabokov who pointed out the literary 'origin' of the idiom:

> Карл [Proffer] сказал, что я работаю над романом, который называется 'Между собакой и волком'. О, сказал Набоков, мне очень нравится название. Кстати, спросите Сашу, помнит ли он строфу из Евгения Онегина, где используется это выражение. Я смутно догадывался, что нечто подобное должно быть где-то у Пушкина. Но так как Набоков мне через Карла ясно указал где, я нашел, а потом подумал: не взять ли указанною строфу эпиграфом. И увидел, что это именно то, что надо, чего не хватало.[14]

Thus, it appears that, despite Sokolov's endeavours to get away from Nabokov, the latter's remark influenced the course of the novel greatly. The importance of Pushkin, and in particular his novel-in-verse, to *Between Dog and Wolf* cannot be overstated.

It has been argued that the character of Iakov is 'modelled' on Pushkin's Romantic exile(s) (for there were at least two). Gerald Smith invokes Aleko, the protagonist of Pushkin's poem *Tsygany (The Gypsies)*. Aleko was among the first Russian exiles from civilization in search of inspiration and self-renewal among the unsophisticated and passionate folk of the wilds. The other one is, of course, Evgenii Onegin, the hero of Pushkin's eponymous novel-in-verse, a disillusioned metropolitan sophisticate who retires to the country.[15] It is arguable which 'prototype' is more important to the conception/understanding of Sokolov's hero. Although both of Pushkin's Romanic heroes flee the discontents of civilization, those discontents are strikingly different. Aleko pursues freedom — presumably lacking in the rigidly ordered and artificial society in which he lives — through abandon, passion, and free love, of which he, ultimately, proves incapable. Evgenii, on the contrary, escapes precisely this abandon — of passion, free love, and constant pleasure — to substitute it with diligence, discipline, contemplation, and self-restraint (to the extent to which his aristocratic sensibility would allow it, but then, they say, *in vino veritas*). Another important element to consider is Pushkin's 'identification' with his characters (at least as argued by some of his critics). It is manifest in the name of the protagonist of *The Gypsies*, Aleko — presumably a Roma form of Aleksandr — and in Pushkin's (suggestively) self-reflexive in-text references to his familiarity with Evgenii.[16] Iakov Palamakhterov is a curious hybrid of them all.

Like Pushkin's Romantic exiles, he heads for the wilds. Like Pushkin, he is a poet, in fact, literally so. Iakov's poems, which constitute the third segment of *Between Dog and Wolf*, are riven with stylizations of Pushkin. The most extensive of such instances is Note IX, 'Kak budto sol'iu kto ...' ('As if someone spilt salt on ...'), with an overt reference to the poet himself:

> Бывает так: с утра скучаешь
> И словно бы чего-то ждешь.
> То Пушкина перелистаешь,
> То Пущина перелистнешь.[17]

The poem constitutes a collage of Pushkin's 'Zima. Chto delat' nam v derevne?' ('Winter. What are we to do at this time?'),[18] *Evgenii Onegin*,[19] and *Graf Nulin (Count Nulin)*.[20] Other less explicit references include Note XXV, which echoes *Count Nulin* and chance lines from *Evgenii Onegin*;[21] and Note XXVI, 'Pochtovye khlopoty v mae' ('Postal Errands in May'), which opens with a phrase that parodically reverses the beginning of *Evgenii Onegin* — an allusion intensified by the use of the French word for 'uncle': 'Что это мне oncle мой любезный не пишет, [...]'.[22] Moreover, Pushkin himself makes a 'cameo' appearance in the prose section of Sokolov's novel, which is presented as a materialization of Pushkin's 'Pod'ezzhaia pod Izhory' ('Approaching Izhory'):[23]

> Будучи представителем прокуратуры, Пожилых укладывается около десяти. Он читает в постели столичный журнал, не чурается стихотворений, поэм, и нередко по памяти декламирует то, что запало, запомнилось. В частности — *Подъезжая под Ижоры*, причем Ижоры воображаются большим **деревянным градом на горе**, посреди просторной пожухлой пажити. Через поле, оранжевое, как апельсин, под небом погожего, хоть и не слишком теплого полдня, катит дормез с громоздкими рессорами, сработанными из кованого металла. Пассажир, чернявый и бойкий, с небрежно расчесанными кучерявыми баками, высовывается и, слегка придерживая рукою цилиндр, предается воспоминаниям: *и воспомнил ваши взоры, ваши синие глаза*. Ижоры близятся, и золоченые купола так и блещут. В случае убытия за пределы уезда, особенно если *в жемчужной влажности тумана мерцающе-светло парит смутность странного обмана*, или попросту холодно, надевает непродуваемую *душегрейку и бурки основательного пошива. Переночевав, велит запрягать да поживее. Позвякивает, светает. Эх, прокачу по тряской, ямщик с глазами, как у кролика, в лисьем тулупе, хищно осклабившись волчьей пастью, подмигивает с облучка.*[24]

The passage is a hotchpotch of quotations from 'Izhory' and other typically Pushkinesque poetic vocabulary and imagery, which culminates in a 're-enactment' of a scene from *Kapitanskaia dochka* (*The Captain's Daughter*): Petr Grinev's first encounter with Iemel'ian Pugachev. Introducing into this context a comically familiar image of the poet — black curly sideburns, top hat, and his legendary fidgetiness — Sokolov makes Pushkin 'live up' to his own art. Thus 'substantiating' the poet's art with his literal presence, Sokolov borrows this image to validate his own representation of reality. At the denouement of the scene quoted earlier, Pushkin's artistic reality (grotesquely literalized) 'spills' over into Sokolov's (or rather the implied author's) description of the novel's setting:

> И точно, уж и светает. Справа, в полутора, а то и более, верстах — река. За нею — селенье со множеством бань и барок на берегу. Церковь вся отражается. Отражаются и вороны, роящиеся вкруг колокольни, как черные, вознесенные зефиром портняжные лоскута. Село сие, ежели довериться плану, имеет прозвание долгое и бестолковое. В имени его чудится бухающий ход маховика, оно отзывается, машет издали квадригою крыл, не ведающих иного, высочайшего своего предназначения. [...] И не беда, что в тумане на миг забрезжит сокровенное имя: разобраться доподлинно — Мало-ли-то-Кулебяково, Мыло-ли-Кулелемово — не достает проницательности.[25]

The derivative nature of this scenery is confirmed further through the link between Il'ia's description of his surroundings, which reiterates the passage above, and Pozhilykh's figurations of 'Izhory', quoted earlier:

Воскурили, заспорили и вышли на холод перекурить. Стали мы на пригорке; за нами *град деревянен*, велик, там мужик брандахлыстничает вовсю, а внизу, перед нами, плес — как на ладошке застыл. Оглянитесь, Гурий мастерам заявил, там, на правой руке, будет у нас селение Малокулебяково.[26]

The verse section similarly relies heavily on representations. A compelling example of such derivation of reality is Iakov's Note XXXII, 'Ekloga' ('The Eclogue'), which demonstrates how perception of reality is often pre-conditioned by its representation:

> [...] Эклога
> Слагалась сама. Бормоча,
> Достигнул поленовской риги,
> К саврасовской роще свернул
> И там, как в тургеневской книге,
> Аксаковских уток вспугнул.[27]

The barns and groves come out of Vasilii Polenov and Aleksei Savrasov's paintings, belonging to the school of lyric landscape, which is associated with the realist artistic movement of the nineteenth century, 'Peredvizhniki' (The Wanderers). The ducks fly straight out of Sergei Aksakov's 1852 *Zapiski ruzheinogo okhotnika orenburgskoi gubernii* (*Notes of a Huntsman in the Orenburg Province*). Ivan Turgenev wrote a highly laudatory critical review of Aksakov's book, which was later published as a part of Turgenev's *Collection of Works*. Thus the last two lines of the quatrain can be taken quite literally as Aksakov's ducks indeed constitute an element of Turgenev's book.[28] And finally, these lines constitute a loose 'paraphrase' of Pushkin's stanza from *Evgenii Onegin*:

> Тоской и рифмами томим,
> Бродя над озером моим,
> Пугаю стадо диких уток:
> Вняв пенью сладкозвучных строф,
> Они слетают с берегов.[29]

Other references made in the poem include Mikhail Lermontov, whose line from his poem *Listok* (*A Leaf*): 'Дубровый листок оторвался от ветки родимой'[30] yields: 'Какой-то листок оторвался от ветки родимой меж тем'.[31] A possible reference to Khlebnikov occurs in the penultimate line of the poem: 'Привет вам, родные свояси' ('I salute you, my native region').[32] The word *'свояси'* normally comes in a set expression: 'вернуться во свояси' (to return to one's native region). Like Khlebnikov, who used it as a title for his article, *Svoiasi (Свояси)*, Sokolov takes the word out of its idiomatic context. The very last line of the poem 'Поклон тебе, русский язык' ('I bow to thee, Russian tongue'),[33] evokes Turgenev's poem-in-prose 'Russkii iazyk' ('Russian Language') from his collection *Senilia*:

> Во дни сомнений, во дни тягостных раздумий о судьбах моей родины,
> — ты один мне поддержка и опора, о великий, могучий, правдивый и свободный русский язык!³⁴

The technique of the 'Eclogue' draws on the parodic tradition of cento, a verse composition made up of famous lines selected from the works of the past. A collage of voices, disposed in a new form or order, cento functions as parodic defamiliarization, refracting the intentions of originals. In the 'Eclogue' it is achieved through the juxtaposition of 'polar' opposites such as Khlebnikov and Turgenev, whose discourses produce the most improbable dialogue, and through the superimposition of the sign onto the alleged referent. This principle is captured in the poem's title, 'Eclogue'. The genre of the eclogue suggests a poem written in a classical style on a pastoral subject. Trans-contextualizing a classical verse into his novel, Sokolov creates a comic clash between the poem's claims at bucolic bliss and the novel's setting that starkly communicates a picture of the post-war devastation of provincial Russia. As has been noted, in its evocation of the pastoral, Sokolov's poem is not a parody of the classical genre *per se*, but of the endeavour to compare artistic discourse about reality with reality itself.³⁵ Moreover, it is not a simple parody of the truth-searching, but a parody of a parody: Iakov's undertaking to compare the discourse of cultural 'authorities' with the real world is conceptualized through the evocation of his 'precursors', Don Quixote and Emma Bovary.³⁶

The proper names of the artists and writers in the 'Eclogue' function as concepts, encapsulating the artistic discourses of their bearers. Sokolov's conceptual use of the names of the predecessors carries strong echoes of Khlebnikov's poem:

> О, достоевскиймо бегущей тучи!
> О, пушкиноты млеющего полдня!
> Ночь смотрится, как Тютчев,
> Безмерное замирным полня.³⁷

Rudol'f Duganov in his study of Khlebnikov describes this aesthetic technique as 'onomatomorphous landscape' ('onomatomorfnyi peizazh'), in which the name of an artist represents an integrated picture of the universe as its highest expression.³⁸ For Khlebnikov, the name of an artist constitutes what Iurii Lotman, elaborating on Leibniz's term, called a 'monad': a meaning-generating structure ('smysloporozhdaiushchaia struktura') that functions on all levels of the semiotic sphere.³⁹ Sokolov's use of these 'monads' is closer to what Jacques Derrida in the preface to *Of Grammatology* designated as a 'convenient fiction':

> The names of the authors or doctrines have here no substantial value. They indicate neither identities nor causes. It would be frivolous to think that 'Descartes', 'Leibniz', 'Rousseau', etc are the names of authors, of authors of

movements or displacements that we thus designate. The indicative value I attribute to them is first the name of a problem.⁴⁰

Besides the problem of reality and realism, which is at the basis of *Between Dog and Wolf*, the question is how does one represent it, or in fact, reach for this reality beyond realism.

As the reader is invited to extrapolate from Iakov's contextualization, Iakov comes to the Volga to fathom and share the destinies of its people. His experiences and observations are reflected in his poetry, which constitutes the third part of *Between Dog and Wolf*. It is presented as a journal entitled, with minor variations, 'Zapiski okhotnika' ('Notes of a Hunter'). The title is an overt reference to Turgenev's *Zapiski okhotnika* (*Notes of a Hunter*), best known in English translation as *The Sportsman's Sketches*. Turgenev's *Sketches* are realistic vignettes depicting people, places, and events occurring during the narrator's hunting trips. Iakov's notes similarly represent a recording of his experience as a hunter/gamekeeper among the Volga folk, thus leaving a sense of ambiguity as to whether his verse is based on empirical knowledge, or on the literary representations of hunting in Turgenev. As noted by Smith, Turgenev and Aksakov, both acknowledged in the 'Eclogue', are not the only 'fundamental source of anxiety' about the representation of hunting. Nikolai Nekrasov is another shadow in which Iakov steps in writing about hunting:⁴¹

> Селясь в известной стороне,
> У некоторой бобылки,
> Слагал Записки; [...].
> Я составлял их на ходу,
> Без всяческой натуги —
> То в облетающем саду,
> То в лодке, то на луге.
> Иль на плотах, когда светло
> Бывало до полночи,
> Или в санях, когда мело,
> Слепя мне очи волчьи.
> Слагал, охотился взапой
> И запивал в охотку,
> Пил с егерями зверобой
> И с рыбарями — водку.⁴²

Sprinkled with Pushkinisms (the images of a leafless orchard and the intuitive writing of poetry), this note of Iakov, called 'Preprovoditel'naia', reiterates the motifs of Nekrasov's 'Orina, mat' soldatskaia' ('Orina, Mother of a Soldier'). Nekrasov's poem is a story of Orina, told by a hunter who lodges in her house.⁴³ Needless to say, Orina is the name of Sokolov's heroine, Iakov's mother and Il'ia's wife.

Nekrasov's 'influence' is also manifest in the metrical typology of Iakov's poems, which shows a predominance of the trochaic and ternary meters, used in folkloric models employed by Nekrasov as opposed to the iambic tradition, associated with Pushkin.[44] Another Russian poet who used trochees is Boris Pasternak, whose presence is acknowledged in the second epigraph of the novel. It is a quotation from Pasternak's *Doctor Zhivago*: 'Молодой человек был охотник' ('The young man was a hunter').[45] Pasternak's line, firstly bluntly inconspicuous, not only introduces one of the main characters, but also prefigures the novel's structure: the combination of prose and poetry motivated by the presence of a poet as a protagonist.[46]

Pasternak's organization of poems around the annual cycle in *Doctor Zhivago* is even more pronounced in Sokolov due to their presentation in four clusters rather than in an appendix as in Pasternak. The four clusters, representing the four seasons, have been thought to introduce an element of structure to the chronologically confusing experience of the prose parts.[47] The cycle begins with a portrayal of late autumn in chapter three, entitled 'Zapiski zapoinogo okhotnika' ('Notes of a Drunken Hunter'); chapter seven — 'Zapiski okhotnika' ('Notes of a Hunter') — represents winter; 'Opiat' zapiski' ('More Notes'), chapter eleven, stands for spring. Rounding off the cluster, 'Zhurnal zapoinogo' ('The Journal of a Drunk'), closes with summer/early autumn. The 'realist' effect of this structure is challenged once it is remembered that the object of mimesis is not nature as such but a (Turgenev's/Pasternak's) representation thereof. Apart from the obvious relatedness to Pasternak, Iakov's verse structure, mode, and subject matter draw on the tradition of northern Renaissance landscape painting, namely on Brueghel the Elder's series of the *Months*.

Brueghel's landscape series was inspired by a 1535 series of calendar illustrations by Simon Bening, depicting the annual cycle through the agricultural labours, and based on a famous illustrated manuscript, 'Les très riches heures', made by the Limbourg Brothers in 1411–16.[48] Commissioned in 1565 by a wealthy Antwerp merchant, Niclaes Jonghelinck, and intended as decoration for the interior of the merchant's house, the *Months* portray the progress of the seasons and the rustic activities associated with them.[49] There has been much discussion whether Brueghel's series comprised twelve panels, as was usual, or six, each of which would have represented the activities of two months.[50] In any case, of the series only five panels remain. Three of the paintings — *Hunters in the Snow* (December–January), *Gloomy Day* (February–March), and *Return of the Herd* (October–November) — are in Vienna, where Sokolov saw them in the Kunsthistorisches Museum shortly after his emigration in 1975.[51]

Sokolov's visual experience is reflected in the novel's prose section, which constitutes a series of ekphrases. Three of the five prose chapters are entitled 'Kartinki s vystavki' ('Pictures at an Exhibition') in an explicit allusion to

Modest Musorgskii's piano suite in ten movements. Musorgskii composed his *Kartinki s vystavki* (*Pictures at an Exhibition*) in 1874 in commemoration of his friend, the artist and architect Viktor Hartmann.[52] It is based on Hartmann's art exhibition, which took place in the Academy of Fine Arts in St Petersburg in February 1874, a few months after the artist's death.[53] Musorgskii's composition is structured to represent a stroll through the gallery, rendered through the recurring *Promenade* interludes, with occasional stops to examine an individual picture. Although only six of Hartmann's illustrations relate directly to the suite,[54] *Pictures at an Exhibition* constitutes a musical ekphrasis, defined as 'a series of transmedializations into music of Hartmann's pictorially created world'.[55]

Besides the 'trope' of the exhibition viewing, the device of ekphrasis, and the 'gallery' structure of *The Pictures*, Sokolov borrows the underlying 'teleology' of Musorgskii's work. Alongside Borodin, Balakirev, Cui, and Rimskii-Korsakov, Musorgskii was one of the 'Mighty Handful' ('Moguchaia kuchka'). Created under the patronage of an art critic Vladimir Stasov, it became the hub of a pioneering national style which espoused folklore and the traditions of the peasantry as the new foundation for Russian music.[56] The group was closely connected with and drew inspiration from the Wanderers,[57] an artistic movement which was mentioned earlier in connection with 'Ekloga'. Iakov is set to communicate a similar idea. He comes to the Volga to grasp and represent the lives of its people. Besides his poetic gift, Iakov is an artist, and it is his works that form the textual gallery of the prose chapters. The gallery 'entries' are either demarcated graphically with italics, which signals a title of a painting, or framed by a reference to their pictorial 'origin'. Thus, the picture that opens the 'exhibition', and that constitutes an ekphrasis of Brueghel's *Hunters in the Snow*, is literally framed at the closure of its presentation:

> Что за чудесная, неотмирная такая страна, в восхищении застывает посетитель. Простота и неброскость ореховой рамы лишь подчеркивает очаровательную прелесть пейзажа и колористический блеск лессировки.[58]

Introduced as a hunting report to a 'special committee' ('отчет об охотах в облаву точнее — об обстоятельствах, сопутствующих возвращению охоты с облав'),[59] it evolves into a detailed verbal representation of Brueghel's painting:

> Мы возвращаемся в сумерках. [...] Нас, как правило, несколько зверобоев и до дюжины своры. Декабрь. Чтобы не кидаться в глаза ротозеям и не снижать картины своею неловкой, все еще городскою, походкою, я стараюсь держаться в конце процессии, почему и не вижу ни лиц, ни морд; только чей-нибудь профиль мелькнет на миг. Серые шляпы охотников нахлобучены низко, что называется по уши, и вот

— не различишь и затылков. Один из нас, помимо обычных доспехов — кинжала, ягдташа, копья — обременен общим нашим трофеем: лис затравлен был еще на заре. Полюбуйтесь-ка, кстати, на наших ублюдков и выборзков. Пугающе длинные, гадкие, закрученные по-обезьяньи, будто филипповские кренделя, оставляют ли их хвосты хоть призрачную надежду на благородство кровей. Что утаивать — жалок экстерьер моих гончаков: кожа да кости, и шерсть совершенно свалялась. Впрочем, есть одна пухловатая, рахитичная, с безобразно коротким щипцом — кикимора подстать тому поросенку, которого какие-то простолюдины палят над костром перед входом в таверну, куда, уверив, что вскорости нас догонят, наведались переждать очень сильный порыв лобового ветра некоторые стрелки. Стоит ли говорить о том, что теперь мы находимся на перевале большого холма, обреченного, как и вся местность, рождественскому свежему снегу, и наши фигуры недурно контрастируют с этим фоном. Оставив таверну слева, мы почти миновали ее и начинаем спускаться в долину. Перед нами — давно знакомая панорама. Это — долина реки и город в этой долине при этой реке, и пруды, и скалы вдали, и небо надо всем перечисленным. Это наш край, мы живем здесь, и если одни из нас живут в городе, то другие — в деревне, за изумрудной рекой. Мы легко различаем плотину и мельницу, церковь и возы на улицах, библиотеку, и богадельню, и баню. Видим острую крышу инвалидного дома, точильное заведение, приют глухих и базар. А на льду прудов и реки — масса катающихся. Звонки их голоса и коньки, разгорячены лица. Там — буроватые, напоминающие мех неведомых зверей, купины оголенных кустарников и дерев; сям — прачки, полощущие белье в проруби. Есть еще вмерзшие в лед ладьи, и запруды, и птицы — о, масса птиц — и на ветках, и просто в пространстве, пахнущем сельдереем, — жароптицы, полинялые, выцветшие, или вовсе сменившие свой прихотливый наряд на скромное оперенье сорок и ворон.[60]

Traditionally the rhetorical device of ekphrasis — an inter-media quotation — was used in pictorial poetry. One of the first uses of ekphrasis is commonly traced back to Homer's description of the shield of Achilles in the *Iliad*. The term itself and the first reflection on the device, however, dates to *Imagines* of Philostratus the Elder in the third century — a series of descriptions of pictorial works of art — which Philostratus the Younger, in his own derivative series of similar descriptions, called 'ekphrasis'.[61] Ekphrasis was employed to bring dynamics to a represented model and, in Thomas Mitchell's words, to 'overcome otherness'.[62] Musorgskii's translation of Hartmann's paintings into the language of music is a good example of this 'ekphrastic intention': Musorgskii overcomes the ultimate other (death), transforming his friend's motionless art into the movement of sound.

Sokolov's ekphrasis achieves the opposite effect. By projecting Brueghel's painting onto the landscape, he 'freezes' (the implied author's) reality —

figuratively and literally. The stasis is communicated through the images of the frozen river and pond and the white snowy background (of the hill), against which the hunters are presented as affixed ('фигуры недурно контрастируют с этим фоном') rather than in motion. Also, in the majority of cases, Sokolov's use of ekphrasis is not straightforward, but mediated. Rather than engaging directly with representations, he engages with other representations of these representations. In short, he works with other ekphrases. Besides Musorgskii, there is a range of literary ekphrases that can be traced in Sokolov's text, especially, in his engagement with Brueghel.

It can be argued that Iakov's representation of human suffering,[63] which constitutes one of the main themes of the novel,[64] and which has been identified as the major moral message of many Brueghel paintings,[65] is modelled not directly on Brueghel but on W. H. Auden's ekphrasis in his 'Musée des Beaux Arts'. Running through the images of Brueghel's *The Census at Bethlehem* (1566) and *The Slaughter of the Innocents* (ca. 1564), it culminates in the ekphrasis of *Landscape with the Fall of Icarus* (ca. 1558):

> [...] In Brueghel's Icarus, for instance: how everything turns away
> Quite leisurely from the disaster; the ploughman may
> Have heard the splash, the forsaken cry,
> But for him it was not an important failure; [...][66]

Brueghel's *Icarus* shows a foregrounded landscape busy with detail of life taking its course, in the background of which Icarus falls into the sea (only his kicking legs are visible in the painting). According to Gustav Glück, one of the characteristic features of Brueghel's art is subordination of the centre of meaning to the intensity of minute detail: 'he rarely places the chief event of the story in the visible centre of the picture; he tries rather to conceal it than emphasize it'. For instance, in his painting *Christ Carrying the Cross*, the figure of Christ is lost in the myriad of detail drawing away the viewer's attention from the subject of the painting. This habit has been compared with the tradition of medieval allegory, which demands a close study of the context before coming to the underlying meaning.[67] Like Brueghel's paintings, Sokolov's text requires a careful study of its structure, linkages and references in order to realize its meaning.

Thus Auden's ekphrasis, especially his references to *The Census* and *The Slaughter*, is scattered throughout Sokolov's text. Shimmering through its portrayal of the desolate state of humanity, its images of frozen river and skating, the ekphrasis re-emerges in Il′ia's 'allegory' of existence: in what appears to be an elaboration of Auden's dogs that 'go on with their doggy life':[68]

> Полюбуйтесь, к слову сказать, сколько их [stray dogs] возле нашего заведения в оцепленьи дежурствует. Полагаете — подаяния ожидают? Отнюдь, им надеяться не на что, не заслужили пока. Нет, не подаяния — выдвиженцев ждут. И едва вы начнете изнутри выдвигаться, так

эти псы собачьи катяхи свои леденелые глодать принимаются да языки показывают. Прост расчет их: вероятно, на эти мерзопакости глядя, то ли просто от свежего воздуха, вы и стравите им макароны по-флотски за гривенник. А вы пожадничаете — завсегдатай поблагородней расколется. А ждуны подбегут — и пока суть да муть — все слопают, на морозе парного почавкать не худо ведь. И хмелеют немедля, и свадьбы-женитьбы у них происходят безотлагательно, прямо на людях, и родятся в итоге такие ублюдки, что лучше и не показывайте. Родятся, окрепнут и, как деды и матери — по торной тропе, боковой знаменитой иноходью — марш-марш к тошниловке. Ау, не обрывается здесь у нас поколений-то этих цепь, гремит, побрякивает, и не скроется с глаз наших чайная, стоящая на самом юру. Все мы детвора человеческая, дорогой, и пропустить по стопарю нам не чуждо.[69]

The identification of humans with dogs is developed in the canine and lupine motifs of *Between Dog and Wolf*. It emerges with clarity in the correspondence between Il'ia and the gamekeeper: 'И строчу я ихнему доезжачему — волк. Доезжачий ответствует — выжловка. И пошла у нас летопись';[70] and Il'ia's impression of humanity: 'Чем вокзал ожиданий шибает бестактно в нос? Не сочтите за жалобу, псиной мокрой и беспризорной преет публика в массе своей'.[71] Apart from the theme of the desolate human condition and the eternal return, this passage communicates Brueghel's iconography, characterized by the cyclical structure (the basic principle of the *Months*).

The pattern of the 'eternal return' informs also the structure of Iakov's poems. On the macro-level, the body of the verse section forms a circular arrangement, based on the annual cycle, examined earlier in the chapter. While on the micro-level of individual poems the movement of eternal return is created through a 'shaggy dog tale' structure. This technique harks back to another ekphrastic evocation of Brueghel. William Carlos Williams wrote a cycle of poems, entitled *Pictures from Brueghel* (1962), wherein each poem represents an ekphrasis of a Brueghel painting. In his ekphrasis Williams reconstructs the outline of Brueghel's paintings, as if following the viewer's eye in motion.[72] Sokolov's homage to Brueghel's pictorial technique conceals reflections of/on Williams's representation of Brueghel, in which figures 'Disciplined by the artist | to go round | & round'.[73] Adopting the manner of a 'shaggy dog tale', many of Iakov's poems indeed go round and round:

> И заводский охотник
> Нам рассказывал, что
> Он — заводский охотник,
> Он рассказывал, что.[74]

Note XXV, 'Portret raz"ezdnogo (Vtoroe vospominanie o gorode)' ('A Messenger's Portrait (Second Recollection of the City)') — a lengthy meditation on the essence of a messenger — opens with a question 'Что значит разъездной?' ('A messenger, what does it mean?'), goes on for four pages, and concludes with 'Так вот что значит ...' ('That's what it means ...'),[75] only to begin anew.

One of the most illuminating instances of the self-begetting process is Note XII, 'Filosofskaia' ('Philosophical'):

> Люблю декабрь, январь, февраль и март,
> Апрель и май, июнь, июль и август,
> И Деве я всегда сердечно рад,
> И Брюмерам, чей розовый наряд
> Подчас на ум приводит птицу Аргус.
> Теперь зима в саду моем стоит.
> Как пустота, забытая в сосуде.
> А тот, забытый, на столе стоит.
> А стол, забытый, во саду стоит.
> Забытом же зимы на белом блюде.
> Повой, маэстро, на печной трубе
> Рождественское что-нибудь, анданте.
> Холодная, с сосулей на губе,
> Стоит зима, как вещь в самой себе,
> Не замечая, в сущности, ни канта.[76]

As its name suggests, the poem is a philosophical meditation on the Kantian ambiguity between the subject and the object of perception, achieved through a homonymic play on the word 'kant'. Prompted by the use of the Kantian terminology — 'вещь в самой себе' ('thing-in-itself') — the Russian noun 'kant' (edge/boundary) metamorphoses into the name of Immanuel Kant. Substituting the noun 'chert' (devil), which constitutes an idiomatic expression 'ne videt'/zamechat' ni cherta' ('see/notice nothing'; literary, 'see no devil'), with the word 'kant', Sokolov turns the object of perception and analysis into its subject. Thus, Sokolov's winter, a designated 'thing-in-itself', ends up seeing no Kant:

> Стоит зима, как вещь в самой себе,
> Не замечая, в сущности, ни канта.[77]

The subversion of the roles of the perceiver and the perceived is projected onto the relationship between the inside and the outside, presented through the circular imagery of the poem. The outer space of a winter garden turns into the inner emptiness of a jug — forgotten on a table, which is forgotten in the garden, which is lost (enclosed) in winter's snow. Like Uroboros the poem closes on itself, the inside engulfing the outside, erasing the boundary ('kant') by neglecting it. The poem produces an effect of the Möbius strip, a two-dimensional borderless structure with a continuous single surface. This 'non-orientable' property of the Möbius strip plays a major role in the construction of Sokolov's text, with its deliberate ambiguity between the reflecting and reflected.

A prime example of such 'reversibility' is the poet himself, whose dual nature (of representing and represented) is conceptualized in the juxtaposition of a hunter and his game. The titles of the first and the last prose entries, 'Lovchaia povest'' ('Trapper's Tale), which appear unambiguously to state Iakov's occupation (a hunter and a fox-trapper ('lovets')), gradually reveal a sub-meaning, which re-emerges with renewed intensity in Orina's monologue:

> И заметили, что пацан подглядывает из кустов. *Изловили* его, втащили, насмешничают. Попросила — а дайте я с ним одна. Отошли, им без разницы, картошки начали печь. Поначалу чурался *ловец* мой, такой недотрога был, но приласкала дотошней — освоился.[78]

This scene is an uncanny reverberation of a passage from the first prose entry, 'Lovchaia povest'':

> Ты стоял в чернолесье, незримый. Был ни вечер, ни свет, а на хранилище еще — паруса, и тренеры на моторках хрипели в рупоры приказы гребцам. Взвизгивала, словно чибисы в поле, когда идешь в полумраке через, расставив капканы на лис, дорожа настоящим, обещанным машинистом ружьем. Или когда юнга вел ее под руку к заброшенным стапелям.[79]

The paradox of a trapped trapper, which evokes Nabokov's 'enchanted hunter/ hunted enchanter', is introduced through the motif of fox trapping and is encoded in the reversible nature of the title: 'Lovchaia povest'' is an anagram of 'Volch'ia povest'' (Wolf's tale). The theme of the represented and the representing is developed in one of Iakov's paintings, *Avtoportret v mundire (Self-Portrait in a Uniform)*.[80]

Avtoportret is a complex third degree ekphrastic representation, which fuses and reworks Nikolai Gogol''s novella *Portret (Portrait)* and Oscar Wilde's *The Picture of Dorian Gray*. Both works envision the 'dangers' of art that trespasses the borders of the natural, blurring the artificial and the organic.[81] Painting in these works is an activity that reifies the living body/gaze by recreating it in the non-organic material. Both the gaze of the moneylender in Gogol''s novella and the changes occurring in the portrait of Dorian Gray reveal a split simultaneously in the texture of reality and art.[82] By disrupting the codes and reversing the roles of the represented and representing, these texts illuminate the problem of the ambiguity between the origin and representation, central to Sokolov's text.

The predicament between reality and representation is elaborated in another allusion to Gogol':

> [...] и вскорости стол не узнать. Оттиски, гарнитура — убраны. На их месте — три склянки с пивом, по мере расходу пополняемые из средних размеров боченка, с очевидной значительностью возвышающегося посреди скромн*аго*, пусть и не лишенн*аго* изысканности, выбора блюд:

устрицы; немного анчоусов; фунта полтора зернистой; севрюжья спинка — не цимес, но и невозможно упрекнуть, что дурная; да дюжины три омаров. Цыганы припаздывают.[83]

The scene is a parodic stylization of Gogol', constructed with such characteristic features as an overbearing use of the name–patronymic clusters and obsessive food descriptions. Thus, in a typical Gogolian pseudo-logical sequence, when the last element of the chain does not belong with the rest, which the reader usually fails to notice, Sokolov conflates two meanings, thus creating a comic effect. Enumerating various seafoods, Sokolov concludes the series with 'ne tsimes'. 'Tsimes' is a traditional Jewish sweet dish made of vegetables and fruit, therefore beluga caviar and anchovies are rightly 'no tsimes'. Figuratively, this expression signifies 'not the best of', and most likely Sokolov's intention is to highlight this meaning, yet the original, denotative culinary signification is still evoked.[84] The effect of stylization is emphasized by the pseudo-refined suffixes, highlighted in the quotation, which culminates in the evocation of the dinner episode (hosted by the police chief) from *Mertvye dushi* (*Dead Souls*).[85]

Sokolov's scene, which takes place in a publishing house and features Iakov's great-grandfather, maître-en-page (literally and ironically: a master in the page), Nikodim Ermolaich Palamakhterov, materializes from a page of a reference book, which was published by the aforementioned institution:

Карус Штерн, *Эволюция Мира, Werden und Vergehen*, перевод с немецкаго, Том III Издательство товарищества Мир, Москва, Большая Никитская, 22, Типография товарищества И. Н. Кушнерова и Ко, Пименовская улица, со двора, во дворе немощено, грязь.[86]

The image of the muddy courtyard of the publishing house[87] surfaces in the scatological overtones of Iakov's use of the book. Stern's encyclopaedia — suggestively Iakov's well of knowledge on mimesis (in birds and insects) — is recycled to serve smoking and various 'everyday needs' ('бытовые порывы'):

Так, рассеянно посматривая в окно, или при рассеянном свете коптилки полистывая Каруса Штерна — некогда представительного, солидного, а теперь отощавшего, траченного курительными и бытовыми порывами, но и поныне достойно собой представлявшего единственный том этой сравнительно скромной домашней библиотеки, — философствовал и формулировал Яков Ильич Паламахтеров, неподкупный свидетель и доезжачий своего практического и безжалостного времени.[88]

This interplay between the literal and literary recycling, which discloses the underlying constructive mechanism of Sokolov's text, is developed further in a reference to Lermontov's *Geroi nashego vremeni* (*A Hero of Our Time*).[89] It comes in the form of a distorted quotation, dropped in the last prose entry, chapter sixteen:

На кухонном столе, среди предметов ловитвенной и домашней

> утвари, зачастую он замечал керосиновую лампу. Бывало, во фляге выходило горючее, и фитиль немилосердно коптил. При этом становилось понятно, что в медном чайнике, луженном некогда одним спившимся с круга и дурно кончившим точильщиком, в чайнике с самодельной проволочной ручкой, в котором хранили теперь керосин, не наберется и нескольких капель последнего. *Со мною был чайник,* — глядя, как отрываются от тлеющей ткани и летят вверх по прозрачному приспособлению искры, мямлил Паламахтеров, — чайник, *единственная моя отрада в путешествиях по Кавказу.*[90]

The allusion is evoked by the image of a kerosene container that was once a kettle, made by Il'ia, figuring in the quotation as 'спившимся с круга и дурно кончившим точильщиком'. The reference may be read as an allegory: Iakov's literal recycling of Il'ia's kettle is a metaphor for Sokolov's literary 'recycling' of Lermontov's text, which constitutes another major subtext in *Between Dog and Wolf*.

The title of Iakov's last verse cluster, 'Zhurnal zapoinogo' ('The Journal of a Drunk'), harks back to 'Zhurnal Pechorina' ('Pechorin's Journal'), the second part of *A Hero of Our Time*. Grigorii Pechorin, the protagonist of Lermontov's novel, is another celebrated Romantic hero of Russian literature. While the second part of Lermontov's novel is presented as excerpts from Pechorin's personal journal, the first part constitutes an 'objective' take on Pechorin's character and adventures, narrated by a stylized author. This narrative contains a *mise en abyme* story by an 'eye-witness', Maksim Maksimovich, Pechorin's former companion.[91] Adopting Lermontov's structure, Sokolov presents his hero through the discourse of other(s), a stylized author and a *skaz* narrator, counterbalancing it with the hero's personal observations. Iakov's massacred Latin — 'Вита синэ либертатэ нихиль, философствовал он, виверэтэ эст милитарэ'[92] — echoes Pechorin's musings on freedom: 'я готов на все жертвы, кроме этой [marriage]; двадцать раз жизнь свою, даже честь поставлю на карту ... но свободы моей не продам.'[93] There are other references to Lermontov's text throughout the course of the novel, which serve to evoke the themes of desire, its consummation, betrayal, and ensuing loss/ death of the object of desire.[94]

Like Iakov's poems, the prose segments represent a palimpsest of alien discourses, constituting a postmodern cento. The etymology of the term 'cento' — a cloak made of patches (originally used by Roman soldiers) — is actualized in the *skaz* section of the novel. The image is introduced in the form of Il'ia's 'paraphrase' of Iakov's 'teachings':

> Нечего, учит, приставлять целые заплаты к тряпью рваному — неказисто. А потом — целое-то к чему раздирать. Вот это — про нас, это мы понимаем. Но, признаться и оно ни к чему как-то фактически, ведь имеем ли новое что-нибудь среди хламоты нашенской.[95]

This 'recycling' practice, termed 'recycling poetics' by Hanna Kolb,[96] is a major constructive principle in *Between Dog and Wolf*. As reflected in the present-day recycling emblem it is another manifestation of the Möbius strip as a symbol of the infinite (reiterated in the lemniscates as the standard mathematical symbol of infinity). Its eternal cyclical progression is manifest not only on the literary level of Iakov's intertextual recycling, but also on the literal level in a portrayal of the material recycling in Il'ia's *skaz*. Zaitil'shchina, the main setting of Il'ia's story as indicated by the titles of his narratives, represents its embodiment.

Nothing is produced in Zaitil'shchina. Not even the population itself, which maintains itself by sheltering some wandering strangers or blurring the dividing line between being and non-being. The locals consisting of fishermen and hunters specialize in trapping thin air, as epitomized in Iakov's poem:

> Навскидку я выстрелил. Эхо
> Лишь стало добычей моей,
> И дым цвета лешего меха
> Витал утешеньем очей.[97]

The local centre, Gorodnishche, is decoded in Iakov's poem as 'город нищих и ворья'[98] (the town of paupers and thieves). Its name derives from a jumble of 'gorodishche' — a designation for a fortified settlement in Ancient Rus', or, in the present day, a monstrous town, by analogy with 'chudovishche', a monster — and 'nishchii' (a pauper). The town features a couple of artisans' shops: a cooperative of grinders ('артель индивидов имени Д. Заточника'), and, notably, a recycling cooperative ('артель по сбору всевозможного утиля').[99] It is the hub of a 'recycling' practice, known as 'artel'nyi sposob' (cooperative method). The method, according to Il'ia, is 'Пареной репе подобен, но всякую снасть или живность дозволяет пустить в оборот не единожды'.[100] It involves an endless chain of theft/borrowing and sale: stealing an object and selling it, stealing it again and selling it *ad infinitum*. It is not exclusive to the re-utilization of material objects. Names, for instance, are treated as things, and can be stolen, inherited, and recycled. The case of Nikolai from the village of Ploski is representative:

> А во Плосках из более или менее бегунов обретается юноша Николай, у которого имени собственного не было никогда, верней было, но слишком давно. И когда Николаю Угоднику вышло преображение и он улетел, этот имя его себе урвал — не дал, называется, добру пропасть.[101]

In a deliberate irony, the 'original' name carrier, Nikolai, nicknamed 'Ugodnik' (God's Bishop) — a popular name of St Nicholas (Nikolai Ugodnik) — is a rag-picker, referred to as 'архангел вторичного сырья' ('archangel of recycling').[102]

Recycling — through the change of the owner or function — pervades Il'ia's narrative not only on the 'thematic' level. The paradox of Il'ia's *skaz* is that although it is extremely difficult to get to the bottom of the message — the theft of his crutches — the theft is 'encoded' in the text itself. The technique of *skaz*, with its integration of ready-made language, clichés, hackneyed phrases, and other banalities into aesthetic discourse, is in itself an instance of textual recycling. Drawing on the artistic technique used in the combinatory painting, *objets trouvés*, Pierre Van den Heuvel names this literary technique *'objet volé'* ('stolen object').[103] *Skaz* is indeed a literary *'objet volé'*: a 'stolen' speech *par excellence*.

Thus in the last prose entry, Il'ia's voice is uncannily appropriated by the implied author:

> Яков Ильич обращается к незнакомцу, говоря почему-то не своим языком и не известно чьим языком: спасибо вам, благодарствуйте, шапчонку-то мою прикрепили, а то еду и прямо ума не приложу, где шапка, а она вот она, оказывается, где — к вешалочке прикреплена, премного обязан, я здоровия вам пожелаю вполне, а что мы с Крылобыльчиком к артельщику так отнеслись — так не гневайтесь, мало ли чего не бывает в быту. Конечное дело, погорячились, набедокурили, с кем не случается, но ведь и он же хорош со своей позиции; лампу краденую штормовую мы простили ему как списанную, но где это видано — гончаков изводить; думал, если он инвалид, то и дозволено ему все? Нет, границы у нас некоторые и для калечных намечены, пусть и шире, да еще и кляузы начал строчить, ябеда мелкая, будто мы его костыли утянули, словно иных егерей не имеется. И голос, и слова, и манера — все отдает неестественностью и елеем в речи его, все чуждо ему в его монологе.[104]

Attributed to Iakov, who self-consciously adopts the tone and language reminiscent of Il'ia's *skaz*, the monologue discloses a possible source of the latter's voice: Makar Devushkin, a character of Fedor Dostoevskii's novel-in-letters, *Bednye liudi* (*Poor Folks*).[105] Here, again, Sokolov resorts to a complex intertextual chain by bringing into play Dostoevskii's text, which is an acknowledged 'parody' (imitation) of Gogol''s style.

Kolb compares Sokolov's 'recycling' technique with the principle of *Gschnas* used by Sigmund Freud in his interpretation of dreams,[106] linking it (Sokolov's recycling practice) with the use of 'ready-mades' in the avant-garde art of the early twentieth century. In doing so Kolb disregards an important point. The concept of 'ready-made', which implies a presentation of a utilitarian object as an aesthetic phenomenon, was introduced by Marcel Duchamp. At a 1917 New York art exhibition Duchamp scandalously attempted to present a urinal as an art object, complete with a signature of the artist — Duchamp's pseudonym, R. Mutt — and a title: 'A Fountain'. In this endeavour to 'shock the bourgeoisie', Duchamp and the avant-garde generally sought to disturb the rigid notion of art. In Russia, a similar practice was central to the avant-garde artists and writers, who promoted reality as an aesthetic object. This aestheticization of the mundane continued with conceptualism, an artistic movement that appeared in Russia in the 1970s. Although the motives remained the same — to blur the boundaries between art and life — the accent had shifted: if modernism invited everyday objects to become art, postmodernism was left to deal with the consequences of life as an aesthetic construct. Thus, by employing cultural, linguistic, and ideological stereotypes, conceptualists alienate these formulae from the reality that they seem to denote, reducing a symbol to a sign and thus exposing the exhaustion of language and the absurdity of the ideology that created them.[107]

Sokolov differs from both the avant-garde aestheticization of the real and the conceptualist disclosure of the hyper-real. Firstly, reality is a priori presented in a reflected form through a series of artistic representations. Secondly, in his engagement with these signs, Sokolov does not simply abstract them from their 'original' function or context, but grounds them in their original medium: language. In fact, the novel opens with such grounding: 'Месяц ясен, за числами не уследишь, год нынешний' ('The month/moon is clear, the dates are hard to follow, and the year is present').[108] A pun, produced through a play on the homonym 'mesiats', throws off the reader, forcing him to reflect on the plurality of signifieds covered by a single name. By using the adjective 'iasnyi' (clear), with its indication of both clarity as colour and a level of intelligibility, the narrator provokes a *double entendre*, thus revealing the basis of the notion of time: the abstract category of time is grounded in a spatial (albeit heavenly) body. Such grounding pervades Sokolov's text. Perhaps the most illuminating instance of this praxis is the novel's title: *Mezhdu sobakoi i volkom*.

In *Evgenii Onegin*, whence the phrase derives, the idiom is used as a temporal metaphor, which has been slightly defamiliarized through its translation into Russian. Sokolov goes further and translates this temporal metaphor into a metonymical expression of space. By taking its constitutive parts literally, he brings to the fore the literal meaning of the words against the background of the figurative sense, thus communicating an image of space between the two animals. Namely, *Between Dog and Wolf* is a story of a murder that resulted from the victim's inability to tell a dog from a wolf. Such literalization produces an impression of the novel's generation from its title, which led Johnson to call *Between Dog and Wolf* 'realized metaphor' — a text that derives from its title.[109] The device of 'realized metaphor', which informs Sokolov's text on multiple levels, is positively rampant in the *skaz* section, presented as its narrator's peculiar understanding of (with) language. A good example of such understanding is the phrase 'otbrosit' kon'ki', ('to kick off one's skates'), which means 'to die' in modern Russian.

In Gorodnishche, where everyone seems to be constantly skating, the expression loses its metaphorical aspect, becoming a simple fact: once you are dead, you do not skate.[110] Another instance of such grotesque realization is the idiom 'videt' chto-libo v grobu', which expresses the ultimate degree of unconcern with the matter under consideration. Thus, the Zaitil'e gamekeepers, when Il'ia requests them to return his stolen crutches, laconically reply: 'Зрели мы тебя в гробу с твоими костылями'.[111] The metaphor is grounded later in the novel as they do see the crutches in a casket, as a replacement of an absent corpse:

> Гурия как хоронили — помните? [...] а еще перед самым выносом ради солидности вящей предприняли мы что-нибудь подобное посунуть во внутрь, а буде объявится сам, то заменим. На беду ни подобного, ни бесподобного не выяснилось ничего и ни у кого бы то ни было — все, чертяки, свояк свояку проспорили, каждый каждого по миру пустил. Но случись во светелке на лежаке один недоподлинный гость из приблудных, которому с перебору вступило в речь и сделалось нехорошо и расслабленно. Личностью, дабы не беспокоила, обратили его к стене, на восток, принакрыли рогожею, и ответить, кто есть таков — со стороны бывало бы затруднительно; да никто особенно и не вдавался, у нас ведь попросту: отрубился, сопишь в обе дырки — ну и соизволь почивать, кто бы ни был, лишь бы не озорничай. Инвентарь же — его, не его — как докажешь? — торчал непотребно в красном углу, под Скорбящей. Значит, снасти-то эти и сунули, и снесли — как в назидание, так и в виду их не слишком, но на безрыбьи — подобности. Теперь на досугах невольных мозгую: не из-за тех ли опор егеря Илюху-то ухайдокали, а он — гончаков, и не он ли, следовательно, на лежанке тогда почивал. Так мозгую и перетак, а все сходится: не иначе — точильщиковы клюшки в тот раз погребли, пойти, вероятно, сказать.[112]

This is a key moment of the story, as regards its content, form, and message. Firstly, it solves the riddle of the lost props, which constitutes the prime reason for Il'ia's outpourings. Secondly, it captures the dynamics between the sign and the referent, the origin and its representation explored in the novel, which is based on the topology of the Möbius strip. Rather than merely representing its referent, the sign acts as an uncanny double, which simultaneously negates and supplements. Thus Il'ia's crutches, a metaphor for Gurii's dead body signifying its absence, metonymically signify Il'ia's presence in death.

In Zaitil'shchina, where signifiers are not signs of things but *are* things, naming is a magical activity: the link between the name and its bearer is not metaphorical but metonymic, based on proximity rather than similarity. This spatial 'dimension' of metonymy is grotesquely realized in the name of a character called Kaluga, who is 'nicknamed' Kostroma on the basis of both names deriving from the toponyms of provincial Russian towns in the Volga area. Metonymy is present in the names of most characters, who function as reservoirs of the endless traces of signification inherent in their names. They literally 'enact' their names, which are usually of mythical, legendary, or biblical provenance. In fact, most characters in Il'ia's narrative are uncanny doubles of Christian saints, travestied as a bunch of vicious drunks and thieves.

Thus, a wretched rag-picker Nikolai Ugodnikov, by virtue of his name, is identified with St Nicholas, the miracle worker (Nikolai Ugodnik, in Russian Orthodox tradition). He undergoes a transfiguration by consuming an inordinate quantity of alcohol, as recorded in one of Iakov's verses, 'Preobrazhenie Nikolaia Ugodnikova (Rasskaz util'shchika)' (Transfiguration of Nicholas Bishop (A Story of a Rag-picker)).[113] Petr (Peter) and Pavel (Paul), two generations (uncle and nephew) of moonshine brewers, call themselves apostles.[114] Sokolov's version of George the Dragon Slayer, Egorii, is endorsed with the epithet 'khrabryi' (brave), in an allusion to the Russian Orthodox saint 'Egorii Khrabryi', because he accepts his pals' challenge to steal a tree pole and use it to hang himself.[115] The local ferrymen bear names of the St Thomas and St Jeremy (Foma and Ierema).[116] The name Iakov acquires especially strong religious connotation through the surname attached to it in Il'ia's section: Alfeev. Iakov, one of the twelve apostles, is the son of Alphaeus — 'Алфеев сын'.[117] Il'ia, through the constant biblical references, is identified with Christ. Thus, in chapter twelve (a number pregnant with meaningfulness in the novel ridden with biblical allusions), Il'ia delivers a 'sermon' ('исповедь-проповедь') on Christmas Eve at the local tavern, urging his celebratory pals to confront their temptations by amputating their limbs:

> ежели хоть единая длань соблазняет тебя — не смущайся: немедленно отсеки. Потому что куда прекраснее отчасти во временах благоденствовать, нежели целиком в геенне коптеть.[118]

Needless to say, he is maimed, having lost his limb on the railway tracks. Therefore, he optimistically concludes with: 'Все мы усекновенные, и грядущее наше светло'.[119]

In addition to his links with the New Testament, Il'ia overtly associates himself with Elijah: 'пророк, час один светлый своровивший в июле-месяце у христиан'. In another allusion to the Old Testament, he considers unleashing fire on his pals: 'Пламень, в принципе, надо б на вас низвесть, но пока погожу'.[120] Apart from its biblical origins, his name carries a number of folkloric and literary echoes.

Il'ia Muromets, a Bogatyr' (a term of Turkish origin, designating an ancient Russian knight) from the Russian *bylina*, is, for instance, another 'prototype'. Like Il'ia from Gorodnishche, Il'ia from Murom was an invalid, a parallel established in the lamentations of the former on the loss of his crutches: 'Не могу же я из-за первых, по мере их неприсутствия, тридцать лет, как тезка из Мурома, сиднем сидеть'.[121] The improbable analogy of the wretched old knife-grinder with the legendary Bogatyr' is 'redeemed' in a grotesque re-enactment of the 'Ledovoe poboishche' (Battle on Ice): Aleksandr Nevsky's epic 1242 battle on the Chudskoe Lake. Il'ia's victory over a wild beast (Iakov's hound Mumu, as it turns out), which takes place on the frozen river, is described in the language of the Ancient Rus' epic, mixed with allusions to Lermontov's 'Mtsyri' ('The Novice'), and comically underscored by a reference to Turgenev's eponymous short story featuring the sorry end of Mumu.

> Но от твари дремучей мастеру смерть принимать неприлично, [...] Не отдамся на угрызение, стану биться, как бился тот беглый парнишка в чучмекских горах, торопливо дыша. [...] Что кручинишься, Волче, налетай, коли смел. [...] Супостат изначально упорство выказал, вертелся лишь, как на колу, скуля, но не вынес впоследствие — рванулся, Илью завалил, [...] и валялись мы оба-два дикие все, белесые, ровно черти в амбаре. А вдруг лампада моя угасла, рука моя ослабела — чекалка утек. И взяла меня дрема хмельная, лежу испитой, распаренный — судачек заливной на хрустале Итиля. И пускай заползает заметь в прорухи одежд, пускай волос сечется — мне сладостно. Положа руку на сердце, где еще и когда выпадает подобное испытать, ну и виктория — хищника перемог.[122]

Other speculative sources of Il'ia's origin are folk and fairy tales. The link is established through the narrator's protean surname, oscillating between Zynzyrella, Dzindzirela, and Zhinzhirela. All three versions constitute a corruption of 'Cinderella', the name of the heroine of Charles Perrault's eponymous 1697 fairy-tale. It is revealed in one of the gamekeepers' abusive messages to Il'ia, addressed to 'I. P. Cindirela'.[123] Sokolov's novel borrows and reworks some key elements of *Cinderella*,[124] which, typically of *Between Dog and Wolf*, undergo a monstrous literalization. Thus Cinderella's loss of a glass (or fur) slipper takes a gruesome form of a lost leg and, subsequently, its substitute, the crutches. The Freudian reading of Cinderella's lost slipper as a symbol of lost virginity — through the association of a shoe with feminine genitals,[125] intensified by the wordplay between 'vair' (precious red squirrel fur) and 'verre' (French for 'glass') — receives an uncanny twist in Sokolov's text.

In one of the narrative layers, Il'ia is a cobbler who makes fox-fur slippers for the simple-minded neighbour girl, Orina's successor, seducing her in the process.[126] In another story layer (in Orina's *skaz*), it is Orina who has fur slippers made, and ends up paying for them by providing sexual favours to the shoemaker. Later she gives birth to a child, Iakov, whose father is possibly Il'ia. Iakov, in the nth layer of the text, is identified with a young trapper who presents Orina with a fox cub that soon dies on the rail tracks and whose fur is later used to make the slippers. One of Iakov's seasonal occupations as a gamekeeper, as intimated in one of the poems, is making squirrel boots ('belich'i ichigi').[127] The story becomes more convoluted as, at one point in the narrative, Orina, in her attempt to free Il'ia from imminent death (he is tied to the rail tracks by her lovers), confuses him with her dead fox cub.[128] As Il'ia loses his limb in the ordeal — much as Cinderella loses her slipper in Perrault's fairy tale — Orina's delirious vision of a dead fox on the tracks becomes lucid in the context of Sokolov's text: metonymically Il'ia's leg becomes a fox slipper becomes a fox becomes Il'ia. The chain is substantiated further by Il'ia's identification with a fox. He shares his patronymic — Petrikeich — with a fairy-tale fox, revered in Russian folktales as Lisa (Fox) Patrikeevna, and is heard using phrases attributed to a fairy-tale fox: 'как выскочу как выпрыгну [полетят] клочечки по закоулочкам'.[129]

Sokolov's use of names as manifestations of the semantic resourcefulness/ infinity of language was linked with the devices of Derridian deconstruction. As an example of realization of 'archi-writing', Mark Lipovetskii examines Sokolov's play with the name of the river Volga. Sokolov's manipulation of poetic etymology connects the Volga with the wolf (*volk*), reflected in the name 'Volch'ia rechka' ('Wolf River'). The allusion to the mythical Roman she-wolf that suckled the founders of Rome, Romulus and Remus, invokes the mythological significance of the Volga,[130] which in the Russian cultural tradition has always been identified with the River of Life.[131] Indeed, Sokolov's text is fraught with the play of *différance*, usually presented as a case of popular or poetic etymology, which is another means of reality 'substantiation'.

Thus, in his transformation from 'raz"ezdnoi' (a messenger) to 'doezzhachii' (a gamekeeper), Iakov simply follows the trajectory of the words. Both occupations derive from the stem 'ezd' (to ride, to travel), thus a 'raz"ezdnoi' (from 'raz"ezzhat'': to go, ride around), having 'arrived' ('doekhal'), becomes a 'doezzhachii' (from 'doekhat'': to arrive at).[132] Another illuminating example of the Derridian devices is the deconstruction of the word 'zatochnik' (grinder).

In an allusion to *Moleniie Daniila Zatochnika*, a pastiche of a letter to the prince Iaroslav Vladimirovich composed c.1213–1236 by an eponymous imprisoned jester, the name of Il'ia's grinding cooperative bears the name of Daniil Zatochnik. Playing on the multiple meanings of the verb 'zatochit'', signifying both 'to sharpen' and (archaic/poetic) 'to imprison', the narrative facilitates the contamination of the archaic 'zatochnik' (prisoner) with the modern 'tochil'shchik' (grinder). The linguistic quasi-link takes shape in the context of Il'ia's narrative. Like its 'subtext', Il'ia's letter is a cry for justice: an appeal to the state and law representative. Both authors lament their imprisonment: a prison sentence in the case of Daniil Zatochnik, and a home confinement due to the stolen crutches, for Il'ia.

Another manifestation of the transforming power of language is Il'ia's struggle (quite literal, of course) with an 'uzel' (knot): a stubborn knot on his shoelaces that interfered with Il'ia's attempt to join Orina in the pond.

It is linked, through homonymy, with the 'zheleznodorozhnyi uzel' (railway junction), where her infidelities took place:

> Лучше б, однако, поменьше я перепелом бы влюбленным бил, а побольше бы дальше глядел; может, и углядел бы, кроме насущного узла на тесьме, узел грядый и другого немножечко сорта — где сортируют товарняки, узел, значит, чугунки, с различными его семафорами и хитрыми штучками-дрючками вроде смазчиских крючьев и смазчиков самих по себе, ловко без мыла лезущих куда не след. Тот-то узел мне — благо сполохи полыхали — развязать повезло, а с сортировочным — пусть там все ночи полные огня — грянула неразбериха, непостижимая никакому уму.[133]

The chaos ('nerazberikha') into which Il'ia plunges, presented as the effect of linguistic elusiveness, is embodied in Orina: loose, shifty, time- and space-defying. Taking multiple forms, Orina's flowing identity represents, as argued by Hanna Kolb, the three forms of the eternal feminine: virgin,[134] mother, and harlot.[135] Thus, as we gather from her story, embedded in Il'ia's *skaz*, Orina was an orphan brought up by an old rag-picker woman, living on the outskirts of a Godforsaken town. As a young and simple-minded girl, who features in Iakov's recollection of his youth and in Il'ia's life as a cobbler, she was swayed into having sex with a young sailor, 'Al'batrosov' (a generic name for a sailor deriving from a nursery rhyme 'matros-al'batros'), or/and a cobbler/fox-trapper, living in the basement of her barracks. Later she continues along these lines as a train dispatcher, entertaining a gang of train drivers and engineers along the (rail) way. Orina's transition from virginity to womanhood is presented through a play on the dual meaning of the verb 'guliat'', signifying both 'to take a walk' and 'to be promiscuous'.[136]

> Я сначала одна гуляла, ни с кем. Но ведь возраст берет же свое, и матросик увлек: кроме шуток, что страшного-то, говорит. Что ж ты думаешь, настоял-таки на его. [...] Бабуля расстроилась: час от часу не легче, мол, была у нас Оря гулена, а стала гулящая, то ли будет еще, все нервничала.[137]

Soon enough she finds herself with a child ('v polozhenii').[138] Thus, despite her shiftiness, Orina is the only source of creation in the bareness of the Itil'. This role is emphasized in her link with Mariia, a figure identified as Iakov's mother. Orina's life shows a striking resemblance to that of Mariia, also a train dispatcher as we learn from Iakov's inner-monologue in the novel's prose segment. At one point Mariia is called Marina by her train driver lover.[139] A rather common female name acquires a meta-meaning in Sokolov's text: it merges the two women by conflating their names — Mariia and Orina. The motif of motherhood, encoded in the name of Mariia, emerges through other links — of a more secular nature — embedded in the name of Orina.

As with the majority of the characters in the novel, Orina's name is of literary origin. Owing to the prominence of Pushkin in *Between Dog and Wolf*, it has been speculated that the name Orina is a distortion of 'Arina' (Rodionovna, Pushkin's celebrated nurse).[140] Other literary 'sources' include Nikolai Nekrasov's poem, 'Orina, mat' soldatskaia', and Boris Pil'niak's story *Mat' syra zemlia* (*Mother Moist Earth*). Some of the elements from Nekrasov's poem, such as the name of the heroine, her loss of a son, the hunting theme, and the use of embedded narratives (*skaz*), resonate with Sokolov's novel. Pil'niak's story echoes the setting and cruelties of *Between Dog and Wolf*, likewise unfolding in the backwoods of the Volga, and featuring a rape, maiming, and killing of the heroine, named Orina. An association of Sokolov's Orina with the Mother/Earth, triggered by these intertextual links, is confirmed through her link with Mariia. Mariia's identification with the Earth emerges in a striking portrayal of a primal scene, evoking a cosmogony:

> Станет явным заполночь, когда сквозь сон услышишь, как во дворе шепотом забредит дождь-машинист и вся земля, опьяненная, отравленная настоем осени Маша, горестно покорится ему, приемля его настырное мелкое семя.[141]

The Earth impregnated with the water falling from the sky metamorphoses into Mariia (Masha is a diminutive), woefully yielding to the solicitations of a train driver.

Established through these inner- and inter-textual links, Orina's identification with body/space culminates in the image of the motherland. Lipovetskii connects Orina's character — an unfaithful wife and a mother who abandons her child — with the motif of emigration and Sokolov's personal existential context.[142] The allegory of this relationship could be read in a dialogue between Iakov, in his guise of Il'ia's companion, Alfeev, and Il'ia:

> Россия-матерь огромна, игрива и лает, будто волчица во мгле, а мы ровно блохи скачем по ней, а она по очереди выкусывает нас на ходу, и куда лучше прыгнуть, не разберешь, ау, никогда. Верно, Яша, ау, все мы у нашей краины светлой — как поперек горла кость, все задолжники, во всем кругом виноватые. А обычная мать, он сказал, у меня умерла.[143]

In Lipovetskii's reading, emigration is both a flight from the dark abyss, represented by the mother's body, and a leap into non-being, since Orina/Russia is identified in the novel with Life Everlasting ('Vechnaia Zhizn').[144] However, in *Between Dog and Wolf*, the expression 'Life Everlasting' — a metaphor for death — is death. Disguised as a beautiful stranger that appears from the other side of the river — that is from the other world, represented by Bydogoshch cemetery [145] — Life Everlasting is love incarnate, embodied (pun intended) into Orina's ghost:

> Вы Заитильщину знаете, спорам и прениям здесь предел, хотя б и сравнительный, положить невозможно: заспорили про любовь — кто, мол, она, мадама эта, всецело прекрасная. Всяк свое утверждал; одни — подобно Василию Карабану — что Вечная Жизнь зашла погостить, одни — напротив: раздор, недород, события. Я же, будучи пас, не встреваю, держу нейтраль. Но Вам — Вам признаюсь, правда, не для передачи другим, а то и так тут Илью за горохового шута держат. Для чего, с какой немыслимой стати упросила очкариков меднаук, чтоб мозги мне запудрили — не разберу. [Orina was announced dead after the train accident.]¹⁴⁶ Ныне же кается, ищет по всей реке: не среди ли вас тот, которого. Врут, что нет, потому что сами по уши втюрившись: не знаем, о ком печешься, но побывать с тобой каждый не прочь. И Гурий туда же, даром что чудь. Ненаглядная, умолял, плес наш не узок — широк, и где ютится сей юноша, я не имею понятия, сознаю лишь, что если бы заглянула на немного ко мне, то трен моей сути, узкий, как точеное лезвие, стал бы широким, как этот плес. Перебыла, поговаривают, с ним накануне решительного его заезда с главным псарем всего ничего, но и оно очутилось просителю боком. Беспокоюсь: погибель она моя суженая, и меня она, Оря, ищет, Фомич, тоскуючи. И не знаю, какие взять меры — пропасть ли без вести, или с повинной к ней приковылять самому.¹⁴⁷

As established by the novel's title, the conflation of time and space results in a condition: a twilight zone of total relativity, where 'ласка перемешана с тоской'.¹⁴⁸ By merging the spatial image of the mother/land and the temporal image of Life Everlasting in the figure of Orina, Sokolov erases the line between the categories of time and space, dissolving them into a condition of love (and death, love's double in Sokolov).

Another site of such fusion is the river. The obvious symbolism of the river as the embodiment of time is crystallized — literally — into a solid reflecting surface, in which time becomes a reflection of space. The Itil' is usually portrayed ice-clad, its flow arrested, or immobile: 'вода мимо нас идет — как пишет, идет — как стоит'.¹⁴⁹ As a result, time on the Itil' coincides with space and therefore, like space, all time is simultaneous. As noted by Hanna Kolb, Sokolov makes interesting use of the Bakhtinian notion of chronotope. Once again, taking things literally, he designates each space with its own time:¹⁵⁰

> давай с тобой не время возьмем, а воду обычную. А давай. И останови впечатление, тормошит, в заводи она практически не идет, ее ряска душит, трава, а на стрежне — стремглав; так и время фукцирует, объяснял, в Городнище шустрит, махом крыла стрижа, приблизительно, в Быдогоще — ни шатко ни валко, в лесах — совсем тишь да гладь.¹⁵¹

Thus, by simply changing places, Il'ia, for instance, can reverse or forward the sequence of events: 'Принял я это к сведению и заездил на будущем челноке в позапрошлое'.¹⁵²

The effect of simultaneity of time is also conveyed through the river's ancient name. By superimposing the ancient hydronym onto the present, Sokolov collapses time layers onto a single plane. The process of temporal levelling is furthered through the strong mythical overtones invoked in the image of the Itil'. An incomplete anagram of Lethe ('*Leta*', in Russian), also appearing in *School for Fools*, the Itil' is a grotesque image of the source of oblivion and comfort, generously offering its 'commodities':

> для тебя мне, Илюша из Городнищ, ничего, если разобраться, не жаль; например, воды — хоть залейся; и такое же положение с ракушками — кушай и не считай. А камышек — хочешь под голову, хочешь — на шею дам, отдыхай тогда на здоровье хоть до Страшнеющего Суда.[153]

Through the interplay between the notions of rest (rest as sleep versus eternal rest), Sokolov merges the waters of the Lethe and the Styx, turning the river of memory and forgetfulness into the boundary between life and death.[154] The mythical image is supported by the Itil' version of Charon: a ferryman Foma Pogibel', whose name in English yields something like Thomas Demise. Sokolov's merging of the two mythical rivers results in the state of absolute relativity between the existing and the non-existing. Following the topology of the Möbius strip, the Itil' collapses its two banks into one perpetual other side, as its other name, 'Volch'ia reka' (the Wolf's river), suggests.[155] This relativity or reversibility of the Itil' is illuminated by Il'ia's observation:

> Кстати, послушайте, не знаю, как Вы, исследователи, — мы, точильщики и егеря, полагаем Заволчьем такие места, которые за Волчьей лежат, с которого бы берега ни соблюдать.[156]

Zavolch'e also incorporates spatial, temporal, and psycho-ethical aspects, manifest in its alternative name: Zaitil'shchina. Zaitil'shchina is both space, an area beyond the Itil' (as in 'Smolenshchina', the region around the town of Smolensk) and a time period (as in 'Pugachevshchina', the time of Emel'ian Pugachev's rebellion). If the former is conspicuous (it is the setting of Il'ia's story), the latter aspect is introduced later and is defined as 'the time of trouble': 'Именно с того дня есть — пошла эта смутная Заитильщина, то есть те нелады, ради коих и разоряюсь на Канцелярии.'[157] The fusion of temporal and spatial elements results in a condition associated with lust and thievery (as a consequence of lust for others' property), which informs all levels of Sokolov's text:

> Но возлюбили также и даму пришлую, и любите беззаветно, которая вам никто, и это тоже наравне с безобразиями и татьбой нареку Заитильщиной.[158]

This state of things is epitomized in the relationship between Il'ia and Iakov.

It is modelled on the myth of Oedipus, which, as argued by some of Sokolov's critics, constitutes the only constant in the text.[159]

In an allusion to the familial foot flaw of the Labdacides — a name originating with Labdacus (lame), a grandfather of Oedipus, whose own name stands for a 'swollen foot' — Iakov and Il'ia are both lame. Victims of war and a train accident respectively, they meet in a hospital, which they leave sharing a pair of felt boots (one boot each), thus disclosing, according to Johnson, a possibility of their relatedness.[160] This possibility culminates in Il'ia's title of 'отец-может-быть' (may-be-father).[161] At the end of the novel, it is confirmed that Iakov murders Il'ia.[162] Both of them love the same woman appearing in a multitude of guises, but ultimately identified with Orina. In this Oedipal — symbolic — conflation of vertical (temporal) and horizontal (spatial) axes, via the medium of the mother, Sokolov physically grounds time in space.

The Oedipal predicament between the two protagonists informs the narrative plane of the novel. It is conceptualized as a juxtaposition between speech, traditionally associated with time necessary to utter a word, and text, identified with the immobility of space (a relationship that is captured in Il'ia's view of the river: 'вода мимо нас идет — как пишет, идет — как стоит').[163] This dialectic between the aural/oral and visual/written at work in *Between Dog and Wolf* is prefigured by Pasternak's line, which serves as its epigraph.

The sentence 'Молодой человек был охотник'[164] is borrowed from part five of *Doktor Zhivago*, entitled 'Proshchanie so starym' ('Farewell to the Old Days'). In this episode, which takes place on the train, Iurii Zhivago encounters a young man, with whom he shares a compartment. The young man is a hunter, as we have already established, and a passionate talker. The unsettling feeling, triggered by the man's intense gaze, overly articulate speech, and lapses into occasional withdrawals, is explained next day. He is deaf, and in order to hear and therefore speak, he needs to see and read the lips of his collocutor.[165] By virtue of his link with Pasternak's hunter,[166] Iakov can be associated with the visual aspect of language. It is also reflected in his artistic aspirations, manifested in the 'picture gallery' of the prose section.

While the prose part, with its focus on the visual, is clearly for reading/seeing, Il'ia's section may become less impenetrable if received aurally, which will make its language play come 'alive'. According to Boris Eikhenbaum, *skaz* as a form 'retains a far greater residue of the primitive oral art, where all tales were improvisations, and plots were just an outline to be elaborated as the storyteller went along'.[167] The unmistakable focus in Il'ia's *skaz* on oral culture — through numerous allusions to fairy tales and epics — and language, especially its aural qualities illuminated through paronomasia, is juxtaposed with the literariness and visuality of the prose and verse fragments. Iakov's link with writing is also manifest in his identification with a character named Pavel, Sokolov's version of St Cyril, one of the inventors of the Cyrillic alphabet.

Thus Pavel sent his uncle Piotr across the river to procure a missing letter for the 'azbuka', in the meanwhile bombarding him with his letters:

> Петр [грамотей один слободской] письмо берет, распечатывает, а в нем написано что-то. Дядя Петь, дорогой ты мой, там написано, дрожжи я уже не надеюсь, что привезешь, но надеюсь пока что, что в торговом отрыве от наших мест ты не жил на продувное фу-фу и про азбуку мечтал дерзновенно.[168]

This episode is reiterated in Iakov's Note XXVI, 'Pochtovye khlopoty v mae':

> Павел Петру в Городнище из Быдогощ, скажем, пишет,
> Дядю дрожжей закупить молит браговарных,
> 70 Букву какую-то непременно найти его умоляет,
> В душу лезет, пристал с ножом к горлу,
> Дяде в кубарэ не дает надудлиться малость.
> Петр Павлу в Быдогоще из Городнища отрезал:
> Букву эту, милок, сам себе ищи неустанно,
> 75 Деньги ж, даденные мне тобой, я профиршпилил,
> Знай поэтому, что дрожжи тебе завезу ой ли.[169]

The re-emergence of the letter is framed within Iakov's lament on the absence of a (the) letter from his uncle:

> Что это мне oncle мой любезный не пишет,
> Времени, что ли, опять у него совсем нету.
> Странно, посулил ведь — напишу тебе непременно;
> Вот, свидетельствуйте, не пишет и не едет ни мало.
> 5 Очи, за реку глядя, проглядел я все, право,
> Хоть бы пиктограмму он предпослал, родственник милый,
> Так-то, мол, и так-то, такие-де у меня планы,
> Иначе же и кинуться куда — ума не приложишь,
> Вечно с дядей таким шиворот-наоборот происходит.[170]

Contrasted with speech, writing is linked with death because, unlike speech, it is definitive: terminal. This deathliness of the visual form is captured in Iakov's futile attempt to capture life in his drawings:

> Рисовать тяжелый, невнятный и неряшливый лик Марии и нередко вместо желаемого портрета неопытному рисовальщику — получать изображение как бы ее маски, и маска хотела проснуться, ожить, но мучительное летаргическое бессилие оказывалось сильнее вялых ее желаний — не просыпалась.[171]

The terminal character of writing was maximized with the arrival of print that intensified the conversion of the sound into the permanence of visual space.[172] An allusion to this aspect may be the 'typographical' episode in the prose segment — a stylization of Gogol', discussed earlier — presenting Iakov as a direct descendant (a great-grandson of the maître-en-page) of the world of print. Iakov's own employment of cultural ready-mades in his narratives echoes the way in which typography produces a text out of pre-existing objects (types), which are arranged in space accordingly.

The manifold association of writing with death has a long history; from a biblical reference to writing — 'The Letter kills, but the Spirit gives life'[173] — to Jacques Derrida's assertion that '[w]riting in the common sense is the dead letter, it is the carrier of death. It exhausts life'.[174] This premise has a direct bearing on Sokolov's novel and is captured in a travesty of the conception of the Cyrillic alphabet: 'Гэ-букву, Петр делится, выдумали без хлопот, она у нас наподобие виселицы, читай, потому что на виселице эту букву и выговоришь одну: гэ да гэ.'[175] The sound of asphyxiation, phonetically presented as 'гэ' (gah), through a metonymic link with the gallows (its locus and cause), results in a visual symbol 'Г', imitating the shape of the gallows. Thus the sound is literally tied to, and executed by, its visual sign. This allegory materializes in the image of Il'ia fixed to the railway tracks by Orina's lovers:

> В день дорожной получки, в аванца ль день чекалдыкнул в пристанционном шалмане с путевиками-пропойцами — и ревную в купине с железом наперевес. *Как выскочу, как выпрыгну* с секирой — ага, уличаю, ага! А они — *ату меня, ату*. Ну, крепись, кричат, задрыга сякой! Четверо догоняют и сбили влет. И топтали, интересуясь: что, законно попутали мы тебя, *бляха-муха*? Попутали, плачу, околыши, застукали, молоточки в петличках, как есть законно. Рвусь — ан цепкие. Измордовали, что Сидорова, измызгали и — гляжу — повлекли, несчастливого, по серому шлаку да вниз мурлом. И втащили на насыпь, *мизгирики*, к рельсу проволоками колючими принайтовливают, неуемные. Льза ли, гаврики, я страдал, что я — *лисенок* вам, что ли, какой. Цепкие, грабками хваткими к шпалам воньким совсем пригнетают, дышать не дают кавзерно. Прикрутили, как валенок к снегуру Норвегии — вдоль и намертво, пассатижами, и слиняли, бояки. Жутковато и мне — жду скорого.[176]

The identity of the perpetrators is intimated through the 'hunting' vocabulary and Il'ia's analogy with a fox, highlighted in the quotation. The references to spiders ('mizgiriki') and flies ('bliakha-mukha', literally 'a whore/fly'), likewise highlighted, are illuminated through an earlier passage in the same *skaz* entry:

> Жил да был во дыре уключины *мизгирь*-крестовик. Все он днище, как небо высокое, паутиной оплел. Насекомых отлавливал я и в тенеты к нему кидал. Как же душу он тварям этим, бессовестный, вынимал аккуратно, ужасы. Паша, грядый, Паук ты мой, Петр племяннику из деревни писал, я не видел скушней события, чем январь без дрождей, доставляй — кровь из носу. Сердцем верю, он продолжал, сердцем знаю — не подведешь, но умишко слаб, соблазняется: не привезешь ведь; ахти нам в таком разе, пьяницам.[177]

The parallel between the two episodes is conveyed through the recurrent images of the insects: flies and spiders. Although a fly as such is not specified in the latter quotation, its 'pairing' with the spider is unmistakable due to an association with *Mukha-Tsokotukha*, a children's story-in-verse by Kornei Chukovskii.[178] The sexual connotations, invoked by the images of the spider's trunk, are confirmed by the context: a boat was a shelter in Orina's first sexual encounters. Pavel, who appears as a spider trapping flies in order to take out their 'souls' by means of his 'trunk', overlaps with Iakov, as was demonstrated earlier, thus bringing their relationship back into its Oedipal context.

As in *School for Fools*, the railway theme is a recurrent trope in *Between Dog and Wolf*. Everything that partakes of it is a symbol of violence, mutilation, or death. As in the first novel, these elements are associated with sex, a link that receives a further development in *Between Dog and Wolf*, locking death with birth.

The railway track is the place where Orina meets her lovers, conceives Iakov (as revealed by Il'ia's bitter words: 'Юдоль твоя путевая, мыслилось, сама же ты — непутевая, [...] даже Яшку тебе на шпалах изобрели'),[179] and dies. This association of the railway track with fertilization harks back to the symbolism of the agricultural activities of ploughing and seed-planting. In Zaitil'e, a Soviet version of the rural utopia — a barren land populated by rootless wanderers — the plough metamorphoses into a train, with a train driver as a sower, whose role is illuminated in the 'cosmogonic' episode, quoted earlier. As the earth retains the traces of the plough — or its 'industrialized' version, the railway track — cutting though its surface, so does Orina. She is 'marked' by her lover, who, in order to obtain her 'consent', marks (or threatens to mark) her belly with cigarette burns.[180] The sexuality of violence, manifest in marking and cutting through a surface, is also inherent in the violence of textuality.[181]

As noted by Walter Ong, the etymology of the concepts and vocabulary associated with writing belongs to such activities as cutting and dismembering: 'scribe' originates from the Proto-Indo-European root *skeri* — to cut.[182] Notably, Il'ia, who loses his leg in the train accident, is maimed. His literal attachment to the source of death is reflected on the literary level: his *skaz* is a letter, written/reproduced posthumously, and thus is by default corrupted by literacy/death. However, the paradox is that, despite its kinship with death, the letter ensures the endurance of sound, which, unlike a visual sign, is evanescent: it expires as soon as it is produced, and to endure it must be embodied. Ong views writing as a sort of redemption, a possibility of the resurrection of speech into limitless living contexts by its living readers.[183] There is a playful reference to this possibility in Il'ia's farewell lines to his addressee, the investigator Pozhilykh:

> Вот такие у нас новинки, Фомич. Извиняйте, оказывается, за зряшное беспокойство, бывайте, являйтесь себе кем являетесь, и — счастливого Вам воскресения, так сказать.[184]

The enigmatic 'be whoever you are'– 'являйтесь себе кем являетесь' — is disturbingly suggestive: Sidor Fomich Pozhilykh is whoever *you* are, turned into a character for novelistic convenience. In a Borgesian revelation, the reader of Il'ia's outpourings finds himself fictionalized into the investigator, facing a happy 'voskresenie', a word which signifies both Sunday and resurrection in Russian. Il'ia's spirit is 'resurrected' through its consumption by the reader. This transubstantiation is performed through the evocation of the Holy Communion, in which text becomes wine, which becomes blood (and flesh).

The analogy between text and wine is established early on in the prose section:

> Посему, кряхтя и путаясь в полах амзтараканского, отзывающегося полнейшей ветошью халата, страдая от холода, источаемого замшелыми каменьями погреба, содрогаясь от омерзения при виде многочисленных многоножек и увещевая икоту перейти на безропотных страстотерпцев Федота и Якова, выкатим на свет Божий бочку повествования — и выбьем, наконец, затычку.[185]

The allegory of the barrel of wine evolves into the prominent theme of drinking and moonshine brewing, which constitutes another aspect of the realization of Pushkin's stanza in the epigraph: 'Люблю я дружеские враки | И дружеский бокал вина | Порою той, что названа | Пора меж волка и собаки'.[186] The allegory has been interpreted as a travesty of literary production and consumption, with readers as wine drinkers, writer as a cooper/wine maker, and text as wine/barrel.[187] It receives a further elaboration in a dialogue between Iakov and Il'ia:

> Не превратно ль, доказывает, вино сего года в старую бочку лить, разорвет оно ее по всем швам, искарежит вещь и, что обиднее, само вытечет. Добрый, добрый совет, возразить нечего. Единственно — не про нас, не про нашу Заитильщину небогатую он, ибо как бы это нам винища столь себе раздобыть, чтобы всю бочку — без разницы, новую там или б/у — затарить враз, на какие, с разрешения усомниться, таковские.[188]

Iakov's allegorical presentation of the literary dilemma of content and form, old and new, is literalized by Il'ia's reminder of the material paucity of Zaitil'shchina, where the notion of the new is absurd and everything is recycled. The alphabet, which is literally collected from rubbish, is a compelling manifestation of the derivative state of things: 'Дэ — как дом, бэ — как вэ почти, вэ же почти как бэ, а вот жэ — та загадочна'.[189] The origin of the 'enigmatic' letter 'Ж' is Il'ia's broken grinding wheel:

> брошенное оземь нищим одним — не сокровище ль для иного. Присмотрись повнимательней, разве не искомое тобою легло во прахе тошниловки сей, кинутое Илией в небрежении. Петр егеря урекает,

стыдя: игры ты над моим скудоумием изволишь играть, черта ли нам с Павелом в механизма очильного бросовом колесе, да и неизвестно еще, разрешит ли хозяин его забрать, может оно ему самому надобно. Крылобыл ученого учит в кубарэ на горе: я чужое имущество не хочу тебя учить подбирать, это ты сам умеешь, я тебя иному учу. Загадками ты говоришь, Петр Крылобылу сказал, загадками учишь, сказал Крылобылу Петр, ох, загадками. Выпили они затем. И прочие, за исключением Вашенского корреспондента, тоже приняли; последний же лишь облизнулся. Вот, сказал Крылобыл, рукавом занюхивая, что это за звук раздается у нас над Волчьей, когда кто-либо из наших точильщиков заработает на точильном станке, не же-же-же ли? Ну. Оттого я и спрашиваю, продолжал Крылобыл Петру: колесо от станка точильного, лежащее во прахе тошниловки сей и вывернутое шиворот-наоборот, не есть ли вид буквы искомой. Публика посмотрела и ахнула — ха, вылитое оно.[190]

Il'ia splits his wheel as he falls into a ditch guided by a blind man.[191] The scene is a reworking of Jesus' prophecy of the Pharisees, in which he called them blind: 'Let them alone. They are blind leaders of the blind. And if the blind lead the blind, both will fall into the ditch'.[192] There is an implicit reference to the parable elsewhere in Il'ia's *skaz*:[193] 'руки даже перед едой, фарисейничая, умыть норовим, но в основном все одно — бедокурим, не в рамках приличия состоим'.[194]

According to Matthew's Gospel, when the Pharisees were offended by Jesus' transgression of the custom of the elders to wash hands before eating, he accused them of hypocrisy in their observation of the law: 'Not what goes into the mouth defiles a man; but what comes out of the mouth, this defiles a man'.[195] The Pharisees were renowned for their extremely pedantic attitude to all matters pertaining to the Law of Moses. Upon the pretence of maintaining the Law intact, the Pharisees adhered to the minutest details, burdening and thus controlling their followers by numerous instructions, through which the Law itself was lost. Jesus, who opposed such a formalistic view of religion, preached that true faith consisted not in forms, but in substance, not in outward observances, but in an inward spirit.[196]

Reflecting on their name — 'Pharisee' is the Aramaic form of the Hebrew word 'perushim' ('separated') — Derrida links the Pharisees with the concept of writing as externalization, displacement:

> Writing is the moment of the desert and the moment of Separation. As their name indicates — in Aramaic — the Pharisees, those misunderstood men of literality, were also 'separated ones'. God no longer speaks to us; he has interrupted himself: we must take words upon ourselves. We must be separated from life and communities, and must entrust ourselves to traces, must become men of vision because we have ceased hearing the voice from within the immediate proximity of the garden. [...] Writing is displaced on

the broken line between lost and promised speech. The *difference* between speech and writing is sin, the anger of God emerging from itself, lost immediacy, work outside the garden.[197]

The trauma of separation of the voice from its sacred source — the disappearance of the voice through its taking form — is encoded in Il'ia's evocation of the biblical parable. He is the voice that is literally broken as a result of his following the blind, and thus fulfilling the prophecy. The sound of his (living) grinding wheel in motion, resounding above the river, takes the form of a letter once the wheel is split in two: separated. However, as was noted before, the letter in Sokolov is as much life-giving as it is death-bearing. The letter 'Ж' is pregnant with life-giving associations: it is the first letter of the Russian feminine noun 'life' ('жизнь') as well as 'woman' ('женщина'), the life-giver. As a symbol of femininity, 'Ж' emerges with ironical clarity in the sign for the 'Ladies' Room', suggesting the only place where a woman remains a woman in the Soviet monosociety.[198] The life-infusing nature of the sign 'Ж' is also suggested by its pairing with yeast, the other object of Pavel and Piotr's quest:

> Плачется слезно Петр в кубарэ товарищам: помогите советом, уж гибну я. Послан Павелом в Городнище не то покупать, а может быть и продавать, знаю только — по смерть меня командировать выгодно, и что нету сейчас ни товару, ни денег, а тем более необходимых ему дрожжей. Теребит с того берега: мол, как хочешь, а от пустопорожнего возвращения воздержись. Ну, дрожжей браговарных, возможно, у кого-нибудь и удастся заимообразно изъять, а вот жэ-букву где раздобыть, заколодило нам на ней, просветителям.[199]

The idiosyncratic combination of the letter 'Ж' and yeast — in Russian 'дрозжи', pronounced 'дрожжи' — initially appears to be based purely on the onomatopoeic attraction produced through the duplication of the sound 'zh'. However, in view of the associative resourcefulness of the letter, by converging yeast, which is used in both breadmaking and moonshine brewing, with the sign of femininity and life (a kind of a Russian Yin), 'supplied' through the intercession of the Spirit (Il'ia), Sokolov transforms reading and drinking into the Eucharist miracle of resurrection.

The final 'grounding' of the allegory of wine drinking occurs in the 'Post scriptum', entitled 'Zapiska, poslannaia otdel'noi butylkoi' ('A Note Sent in a Separate Bottle').[200] Here the reader is summoned as a receiver of a message in a bottle, and invited, in his literary decoding, to 'get to the bottom of things' by literally getting to the bottom of the bottle. Merging literary and literal consumption, Sokolov suggests the role of the reader in the text, who becomes an integral part of its production. Other instances of the manipulation of the role of the reader include the device of ekphrasis in the prose section, where the reader becomes a visitor of Iakov's art gallery, and his role as the local investigator, who is cunningly referred to as 'исследователь' ('researcher') rather than 'следователь' ('investigator').²⁰¹ This role of the reader surfaces in Iakov's poem, 'Arkhivnaia' ('The Archival'), in which the reader, turned archivist-researcher, is reading about him reading:

> [...] Однажды и в пенсне
> Нагрянет архивист.
> Во мне он станет рыться,
> Копаться, разбираться
> В каракулях — найдет:
> Рисунок и портрет,
> В кунсткамеру билет,
> И среди остальных —
> Записку эту вот
> И о себе прочтет.²⁰²

This instance of self-reflexivity that captures the split of the reader into the object and subject of perception re-enacts the act of externalization/alienation inherent in writing, which is linked with memory and forgetting.²⁰³

The dedication to *Between Dog and Wolf* reads 'приятелям по рассеянью',²⁰⁴ a phrase that allows multiple interpretations thank to the semantic resourcefulness of the word 'rasseianie'. While the noun 'rasseianie' signifies 'dispersal', its adjectival derivative, 'rasseiannyi', means 'absent-minded' or 'forgetful'. Thus the dedication can be read as a reminder of the author's exile, as a remembrance of a life that is dissipated, and the novel as an act of remembering, which re-emerges in Il'ia's *skaz*: 'да и воспоминания рассеянья не сулят; память не в дебет, брат, в кредит'.²⁰⁵ 'Rasseianie', which derives from the verb 'seiat'' — to sow, is also a calque of 'dissemination'. In Derridian terms, dissemination is a movement within a text that disrupts the stability of any singular perspective or reading through the unleashing of meanings:

> [Dissemination] endlessly opens up a *snag* in writing that can no longer be mended, a spot where neither meaning, however plural, nor *any form of presence* can pin/pen down [*agrapher*] the trace. Dissemination treats — doctors — that *point* where the movement of signification would regularly come to *tie down* the play of the trace, thus producing (a) history. The security of each point arrested in the name of the law is hence blown up.²⁰⁶

The translator of Derrida's *Dissemination*, Barbara Johnson, comments that behind Derrida's term *point* lies Lacan's notion of the *point de capiton* (a stitch in upholstery or quilting), substituted for the Saussurian 'signified'. Dissemination, then, is what produces a disruption (a 'snag') in Lacan's theory, aiming, according to Derrida, to 'pin down' the history of a subject.²⁰⁷

The dispersal of meaning in *Between Dog and Wolf* is one of the underlying creative mechanisms, achieved through intertextuality and wordplay (mostly paronomasia and poetical etymology). In fact, Sokolov's '*toch*il'shchik' (grinder), an agent of the movement of dissemination, offers his own reading of *point* ('*toch*ka'). As a derivative of the verb 'tochit'' (to sharpen/to grind), it signifies 'sharpening'. As a 'russification' of the German term 'Punkt' (point) it becomes a 'point of collection' ('priiemnaia tochka'): 'И откроют при фабричке точку, но не коньков, а приемную'.[208]

In his meditation on dissemination Derrida writes: 'Whether in the case of what is called "language" (discourse, text, etc.) or in the case of some "real" seed-sowing, each term is indeed a germ, and each germ a term'.[209] The comparison of discourse to seed sowing finds its way into Sokolov's novel, presented as a reworking of Jesus' *Parable of the Sower*:

> И еще один случай произошел. Сеял, якобы, сеятель. Неясно, где — на Рунихах, на Лазаревом ли Поле, у Бабкина ли Креста. [...] Сеятель же одно зерно при дороге бросил, другое на камни какие-то уронил, третье в чертополох, и лишь четвертое более или менее удачно поместить ему удалось. Итого, одно зерно кречет усвоил, второе — коршун, иное — перепела. А вы как думали? Им продовольствоваться хочешь-не хочешь, а тоже крутись. Зато четвертое взошло с грехом пополам и выдало ни с того ни с сего урожай непомерный — сто зерен. Почитал я ту книгу охотникову и осознал: перемелется.[210]

In the parable, according to the Gospel of Matthew,[211] a teacher (Jesus) is allegorized as a sower, and a blessed mind (ear that hears, eye that sees, and heart that understands) is likened to the fruitful ground. The theme is reiterated in the Gospel of John, a quotation from which serves as an epigraph to Dostoevskii's *The Brothers Karamazov*: 'Most assuredly, I say to you, unless a grain of wheat falls into the ground and dies, it remains alone; but if it dies, it produces much grain'.[212] The sentence resonates with Derrida's wordplay in his reflection on the process of dissemination, quoted earlier, in which he explores the polysemous nature of the word 'term'. Thus each word (term) is a seed and each seed is a term — a dead/line (literally) and the moment of birth, in the sense of, for instance, a pregnancy term. Contextualized within Zosima's speech, it has been read as a key to Dostoevskii's novel:[213]

> На земле же воистину мы как бы блуждаем, и не было бы драгоценного Христова образа перед нами, то погибли бы мы и заблудились совсем, как род человеческий перед потопом. Многое на земле от нас скрыто, но взамен того даровано нам тайное сокровенное ощущение живой связи нашей с миром иным, с миром горним и высшим, да и корни наших мыслей и чувств не здесь, а в мирах иных. Вот почему и говорят философы, что сущности вещей нельзя постичь на земле. Бог взял семена из миров иных и посеял на сей земле и взрастил сад свой, и взошло все, что могло взойти, но взращенное живет и живо лишь чувством соприкосновения своего таинственным мирам

иным; если ослабевает или уничтожается в тебе сие чувство, то умирает и взращенное в тебе. Тогда станешь к жизни равнодушен и возненавидишь ее.[214]

This rootlessness, which results from the loss of the link with the other, higher world, is also the subject of *The Parable of the Sower*, discussed earlier: 'yet he has no root in himself, but endures only for a while. For when tribulation or persecution arises because of the word, immediately he stumbles'.[215] As an internal and external exile from Soviet Russia, Sokolov certainly is familiar with the feeling of rootlessness, or 'deterritorialization', both in spatial and in temporal terms.[216] His dedication — 'to friends in dispersal' — may be a reference to this experience of rootlessness, and the novel is an attempt at reinstating Zosima's sacred link between the immanent and the transcendental: 'тайное сокровенное ощущение живой связи нашей с миром иным, с миром горним и высшим'. The other world for the émigré Sokolov is represented by Russia: not empirical Russia but its timeless image grounded in its space and its language. Its embodiment in the novel is Orina, the mysterious 'ЖЕнщина' who is dead but who keeps coming back. A shadow, she appears in the text only in reflected form: as a memory of her in Il'ia's *skaz* and in Iakov's texts (poems and his inner-monologue). She is given a voice only once, at the very core of the novel: her *skaz*, embedded in Il'ia's *skaz*, represents a third-degree reflection. This elusiveness of her character is sublimated through Orina's ubiquitous presence in the text in a myriad of guises.

Such versatility and simultaneous presence led Barbara Heldt to call Orina an emblem of Sokolov's 'drifting text'.[217] Indeed, the persistent reproduction of her image, which screams of her actual absence, is analogous to writing that implies the absence of the speaker. Both text and Orina constitute a supplement to an absent origin. The correlation between their roles as emanations of some lost origin resonates with Derrida's reading of Rousseau's *Essay On the Origin of Languages* in his *Of Grammatology*. For Derrida, Rousseau's description of writing as a mere supplement to speech in the sense of a substitute for nature conceals an unconscious association between writing and masturbation.[218] Thus Il'ia's and Iakov's unrequited love for Orina/Mother/land is 'supplemented' through its displacement into the text.

For Derrida supplement is an addition and a substitution at the same moment: 'One cannot determine the center and exhaust totalization because the sign which replaces the center in its absence — this sign is added, occurs as a surplus, as a *supplement*'.[219]

The notion of surplus in Derrida's definition of supplement resonates with the Bakhtinian 'surplus of vision' ('izbytok videniia') connected with the ontological condition of outsidedness, which allows one to 'complete' — give form to — the object of perception.[220] To achieve this surplus and thus give form to his experience of reality as inherently disjunct and elusive, Sokolov resorts to reflections of this reality. Looking through the eyes of the other — Auden, Brueghel, Musorgskii, Pushkin, Turgenev, and so on — he is able to create distance between himself and his experience, necessary for its externalization. Sokolov recovers the world by reducing it to the word, evoking Khlebnikov's 'все лишь ступог [neologism comprising 'stupat''- to step, and 'porog'-threshold] к имени, даже ночная вселенная'.[221] Thus reflection of reality becomes reflected reality, based not on imitation, but on displacement, in which language does not so much communicate as embody what is absent: it becomes an artefact of reality.

Reflected through the other space, other time, other's eyes and words, *Between Dog and Wolf* is a twilight zone in which the gap between fiction and reality, between times and spaces is transcended through language. The lost context emerges from the text, reduced to the materiality of the letter, to the surface of the page, and to the very moment of reading. After all: 'In the beginning was the Word'.[222]

Notes to Chapter 2

1. Sasha Sokolov, 'Na sokrovennykh skrizhaliakh' (hereafter 'Sokolov Skrizhali'), in *Trevozhnaia kukolka* (St Petersburg: Azbuka-klassika, 2007), pp. 39–48 (pp. 46–47).
2. Ivan Podshivalov, 'A Conversation with Sasha Sokolov: Moscow, 1989' (hereafter 'Slavic Studies 40'), trans. by Ludmilla Litus, *Canadian-American Slavic Studies*, 40 (2006), 352–66 (pp. 357–58). Originally published in *Moskovskii Komsomolets* (20 August 1989).
3. Aleksei Tsvetkov, *Edem* (Ann Arbor, MI: Ardis Publishers, 1985), p. 39.
4. D. Barton Johnson, 'Background Notes on Sokolov's *School for Fools* and *Between Dog and Wolf*: Conversations with the Author' (hereafter 'Slavic Studies 40'), *Canadian-American Slavic Studies*, 40 (2006), 331–39 (p. 335).
5. Vadim Kreid, 'Zaitil'shchina', *Dvadtsat'dva*, 19 (1981), 213–18 (p. 214); Hanna Kolb, 'The Dissolution of Reality in Sasha Sokolov's Mezhdu Sobakoi i Volkom' (hereafter 'Kolb'), in *Reconstructing the Canon: Russian Writing in the 1980s*, ed. Arnold McMillin (London: Harwood Academic Publishers, 2000), pp. 193–223 (p. 199); Leona Toker, 'Gamesman's Sketches (Found in a Bottle): A Reading of Sasha Sokolov's *Between Dog and Wolf*' (hereafter 'Toker'), *Canadian-American Slavic Studies*, 21 (1987), 347–67 (p. 357).
6. Sasha Sokolov, *Mezhdu sobakoi i volkom* (hereafter 'Sobaka') (St Petersburg: Symposium, 2001), p. 12.
7. Jeremy Hicks, *Mikhail Zoshchenko and the Poetics of Skaz* (hereafter 'Hicks Skaz') (Nottingham: Astra Press, 2000), p. 34.
8. Hicks Skaz, p. 77; Boris Eikhenbaum, 'Leskov i sovremennaia proza' (hereafter 'Eikhenbaum Leskov'), *Literatura: Teoriia, kritika, polemika* (Chicago, IL: Russian Study Series, 1969), pp. 210–25 (p. 215)
9. Sobaka, p. 11.
10. Ibid., p. 13.
11. Ibid., p. 38.
12. Slavic Studies 40, p. 337.
13. Aleksandr Pushkin, *Evgenii Onegin* (hereafter 'Evgenii Onegin') (Moscow: Gosudarstvennoe izdatel'stvo detskoi literatury Ministerstva prosveshcheniia RSFSR,

1960), pp. 135-36.
14. Victor Erofeev, 'Vremia dlia chastnykh besed ...', *Oktiabr'*, 8 (1989), 195-202 (p. 198).
15. Gerald S. Smith, 'The Verse in Sasha Sokolov's *Between Dog and Wolf*' (hereafter 'Smith'), *Canadian-American Slavic Studies*, 21 (1987), 321-45 (p. 329).
16. Smith, p. 329.
17. *Sobaka*, pp. 50-52.
18. Aleksandr Pushkin, 'Zima. Chto delat' nam v derevne?', in *Sobranie sochinenii*, 6 vols (Moscow: Pravda, 1969), I, 310-11.
19. Aleksandr Pushkin, 'Evgenii Onegin', in *Izbrannye proizvedeniia* (hereafter 'Onegin'), 2 vols (Moscow: Khudozhestvennaia literatura, 1970), II, 5-158 (see pp. 77, 80, 126).
20. Aleksandr Pushkin, 'Graf Nulin', in *Izbrannye proizvedeniia*, 2 vols (Moscow: Khudozhestvennaia literatura, 1970), I, 336-45 (p. 338).
21. Smith, p. 334.
22. *Sobaka*, p. 161.
23. Aleksandr Pushkin, 'Pod'ezzhaia pod Izhory', in *Sochinenia*, 3 vols (Moscow: Gosudarstvennoe izdatel'stvo khudozhestvennoi literatury, 1962), I, 272:

>'Подъезжая под Ижоры,
>Я взглянул на небеса
>И вспомнил ваши взоры,
>Ваши синие глаза'.

24. *Sobaka*, pp. 130-31, bold italics mine.
25. Ibid., pp. 130-31.
26. Ibid., p. 18, italics mine.
27. Ibid., pp. 220-21.
28. Ivan Turgenev, '"Zapiski ruzheinogo okhotnika Orenburgskoi gubernii". S. A-va. Pis'mo k odnomu iz izdatelei 'Sovremennika', in *Sobranie sochinenii*, 12 vols (Moscow: Khudozhestvennaia literatura, 1979), XII, 159-72; Ivan Turgenev, 'O "Zapiskakh ruzheinogo okhotnika" S.T. Aksakova', in *Sobranie sochinenii*, 12 vols (Moscow: Khudozhestvennaia literatura, 1979), XII, 150-58.
29. Onegin, p. 131.
30. Mikhail Lermontov, 'Listok', in *Izbrannye sochineniia*, 3 vols (Moscow: Russkaia kniga, 1996), I, 78.
31. *Sobaka*, p. 221.
32. Ibid.
33. Ibid.
34. Ivan Turgenev, 'Russkii iazyk', in *Polnoe sobranie sochinenii i pisem*, 28 vols (Moscow and Leningrad: Nauka, 1967), XIII, 198.
35. See Kolb, p. 216; Toker, p. 365.
36. While Cervantes is evoked through the recurring images of mill wings, an overt allusion to Flaubert is in the prose segment, suggesting Iakov's identification with him: 'И очнуться в египетском саркофаге, в охотничьем шалаше, в башне господина Флобера', p. 187.
37. Velimir Khlebnikov, *Tvoreniia* (Moscow: Sovetskii pisatel', 1986), p. 54.
38. Thus, according to Duganov, the name of Dostoevskii ('dostoevskiimo' is Dostoevskii combined with 'pis'mo'- his writing) represents the dark and gloomy nether world of the earth; Pushkin ('pushkinoty' is Pushkin plus 'krasoty'- things beautiful) stands for the higher spheres of light (sun), harmony, and beauty; and Tiutchev, whose poetry is filled with birds (nightingales) and astral bodies, is a symbol of the mysterious nocturnal universe. Rudol'f V. Duganov, *Velimir Khlebnikov: Priroda tvorchestva* (hereafter, 'Duganov') (Moscow: Sovetskii pisatel', 1990), pp. 96-101.

39. Iurii Lotman, 'Kul'tura kak sub"ekt i sama-sebe ob"ekt', in *Izbrannye stat'i*, 3 vols (Tallin: Aleksandra, 1993), III, 369.
40. Jacques Derrida, *Of Grammatology* (hereafter 'Derrida Grammatology'), trans. by Gayatri Chakravorty Spivak (Baltimore and London: The Johns Hopkins University Press, 1976), p. liv.
41. Smith, p. 329.
42. Sobaka, pp. 225–26.
43. Nikolai Nekrasov, 'Orina, mat' soldatskaia', in *Sobranie sochinenii*, 4 vols (Moscow: Pravda, 1979), II, 91–95 (p. 91).
44. Smith, pp. 329–30. Called a 'civic' poet ('grazhdanskii poet'), Nekrasov was among the first poets to advocate the notion of art as *ancilla populi*. Thus the people with their needs and strivings became the centre of Russian poetry, introducing a major break with the classical — aesthetical — poetic tradition epitomized by Pushkin.
45. Boris Pasternak, *Doktor Zhivago* (hereafter 'Pasternak Zhivago') (Moscow: Knizhnaia palata, 1989), p. 126, trans. mine.
46. Smith also mentions Karolina Pavlova's *Dvoinaia zhizn'* (*The Double Life*); Vladimir Nabokov's *Dar* (*The Gift*): See Smith, p. 321.
47. Smith, p. 325.
48. Walter S. Gibson, *Bruegel* (hereafter 'Gibson Bruegel') (London: Thames and Hudson, 2002), pp. 147–48.
49. Gustav Glück, *Pieter Brueghel the Elder* (hereafter 'Glück Brueghel') (London: A. Zwemmer, 1951), plate 22.
50. Gibson Bruegel, pp. 147–56.
51. According to Johnson and Andrei Zorin, Brueghel's *Hunters* served as a stimulus to the ensuing re-creation of Sokolov's life in the Upper Volga. See D. Barton Johnson, '*Mezhdu sobakoi i volkom*: O fantasticheskom iskusstve Sashi Sokolova' (hereafter 'Johnson Vremia'), *Vremia i my*, 64 (1982), 165–75 (p. 170); Andrei Zorin, 'Nasylaiushchii Veter' (hereafter 'Zorin'), *Novyi Mir*, 12 (1989), 250–53 (p. 253).
52. The complete title of the work is *Kartinki s vystavki: vospominanie o Viktore Gartmane* (*Pictures at an Exhibition: Remembrance of Viktor Hartmann*).
53. Michael Russ, *Mussorgsky: Pictures at an Exhibition* (hereafter 'Russ') (Cambridge: Cambridge University Press, 1992).
54. Ibid., p. 16.
55. Siglind Bruhn, 'A Concept of Paintings: "Musical Ekphrasis" in the Twentieth-Century' <http://www personal.umich.edu.> [accessed 30 November 2008].
56. Mikhail Zetlin, *The Five: The Evolution of the Russian School of Music*, trans. by George Panin (New York: International Universities Press, 1959).
57. Musorgskii, for instance, found *Burlaki na Volge* (*Barge Haulers on the Volga*), a painting of Il'ia Repin, particularly inspiring. See Modest Musorgskii, 'Letter from 13 June, 1873', in *Izbrannye pis'ma* (Moscow: Gosudarstvennoe muzykal'noe izdatel'stvo, 1953), p. 91.
58. Sobaka, p. 36.
59. Ibid., p. 34.
60. Ibid., pp. 34–36.
61. Murray Krieger, *Ekphrasis: The Illusion of the Natural Sign* (Baltimore: Johns Hopkins University Press, 1992), pp. 7–8.
62. W. J. T. Mitchell, *Picture Theory: Essays on Verbal and Visual Representation* (Chicago and London: University of Chicago Press, 1994), p. 156.
63. The deterministic image of human suffering and the universal indifference to this suffering emerges especially clearly in the poems 'Tochil'shchik (razgovor s kritikom) ('The Grinder (A Conversation with a Critic)') (Sobaka, p. 45) and 'Zagovor' ('A Spell')

(Sobaka, pp. 95–96). In the latter Brueghel is inscribed literally into the texture of the poem. Brugge, the Dutch name for Bruges, a Flemish town (in Belgium presently), and what seems to be an imaginary location, Lepp, yield Bruegel P(ieter):

> 'И от плоского Брюгге до холмистого Лепп,
> От Тутаева аж — до Быдогощ
> Заводские охотники, горланя: гей-гоп! –
> Пьют под сенью оснеженных рощ'. (Sobaka, p. 96)

64. Drawing attention to the correspondence between Sokolov's and Brueghel's imagery — a range of monstrous cripples and paupers — Andrei Zorin notes parallels in their treatment of the subject: 'Инвалиды у Саши Соколова, как, собственно, и у Брейгеля, менее всего взывают к нашим патерналистическим чувствам милосердия и сострадания'. Zorin, p. 253.
65. James A. W. Hefferman, *Museum of Words: The Poetics of Ekphrasis from Homer to Ashbery* (hereafter 'Hefferman') (Chicago and London: University of Chicago Press, 1993), p. 148.
66. W. H. Auden, 'Musée des Beaux Arts', in *The English Auden. Poems, Essays and Dramatic Writings, 1927-1939*, ed. by Edward Mendelson (London and Boston: Faber and Faber, 1977), p. 237.
67. Glück Brueghel, p. 11; Kenneth C. Lindsay and Bernard Huppé, 'Meaning and Method in Brueghel's Painting', *The Journal of Aesthetics and Art Criticism*, 14.3 (1956), 376-86 (pp. 377–80).
68. Compare Auden's 'Children who did not specially want it to happen, skating / On a pond at the edge of the wood'. Auden, p. 273.
69. Sobaka, p. 208.
70. Ibid., p. 178.
71. Ibid., p. 83.
72. Hefferman, pp. 152–69.
73. William Carlos Williams, 'The Wedding Dance in the Open Air', from 'Pictures from Brughel', in *Selected Poems*, ed. by Charles Tomlinson (London: Penguin Books, 2000), p. 217.
74. Sobaka, p. 214.
75. Ibid., pp. 157 and 161.
76. Ibid., p. 97.
77. Ibid.
78. Ibid., p. 138, italics mine.
79. Ibid., pp. 32–33.
80. Ibid., pp. 36–37.
81. This anticipation of the artistic technique of collage is manifest especially strongly in Gogol', who actually writes about inserting extra-textual objects into the canvas: 'Это было уже не искусство: это разрушало даже гармонию самого портрета. Это были живые, это были человеческие глаза! Казалось, как будто они были вырезаны из живого человека и вставлены сюда'. Nikolai Gogol', 'Portret', in *Sobranie sochinenii*, 8 vols (Moscow: Terra-knizhnyi klub, 2001), III, 61–110 (p. 70).
82. See Ekaterina Bobrinskaia, *Russkii avangard: granitsy iskusstva* (Moscow: Novoe literaturnoe obozrenie, 2006), p. 240.
83. Sobaka, p. 80, italics mine.
84. Kindly pointed out to me by my PhD supervisor, Dr Maria Rubins.
85. See Nikolai Gogol', 'Mertvye dushi', in *Povesti. Mertvye dushi* (Moscow: AST Olimp, 1996), pp. 269–530 (p. 423).
86. Sobaka, pp. 72–73, italics in the original.

87. The episode opens with Nikodim Ermolaich admonishing the publishing house workers for rolling printing paper, which was just delivered, in the mud of the yard. See Sobaka, p. 73.
88. Ibid., p. 82.
89. Mikhail Lermontov, *Geroi nashego vremeni* (hereafter 'Lermontov Geroi') (Moscow: Goslitizdat, 1941).
90. Sobaka, pp. 227–28, italics mine. Cf. Lermontov's: 'Я пригласил своего спутника выпить вместе стакан чая, ибо со мной был чайник — единственная отрада моя в путешествиях по Кавказу', in Lermontov Geroi, p. 17.
91. The multiplicity of perspectives allowed Lermontov to draw a complex picture of a self-reflexive hero, tortured by his attempts to challenge perceptions of him by others: 'Во мне два человека: один живет в полном смысле этого слова, другой мыслит и судит его'. Lermontov Geroi, p. 174.
92. Sobaka, p. 38.
93. Lermontov Geroi, p. 161.
94. In particular it regards the episode in the first prose entry, where these themes are triggered by allusions to Kazbek — a mountain peak in the Caucasus, and Kazbich, one of the characters from the first chapter of Lermontov's novel, 'Bela'. See Sobaka, p. 32
95. Sobaka, p. 109.
96. Kolb, p. 211.
97. Sobaka, p. 221.
98. Ibid., p. 105.
99. Ibid., pp. 11 and 15.
100. Ibid., p. 113.
101. Ibid., p. 18.
102. Ibid., p. 106.
103. A similar practice is employed by the *nouveaux romanciers*, who insert advertisements, post cards, graffiti, and so on, in their narrative texts. Pierre van den Huevel, *Parole Mot Silence: Pour une poétique de l'enonciation* (Paris: Librairie José Corti, 1985), pp. 261–62.
104. Sobaka, p. 230.
105. Makar Devushkin as a 'source' of Il'ia's speech was pointed out by Arnold McMillin, who drew an analogy between Sokolov's text and Dostoevkii's novels (on the basis of the centrality of the themes of jealousy, revenge, and murder). See Arnold McMillin, 'Aberration or the Future: The Avant Garde Novels of Sasha Sokolov', in *From Pushkin to Palisandriia: Essays on the Russian Novel in Honour of Richard Freeborn*, ed. by A. McMillin (London: Macmillan, 1990), pp. 229–43 (pp. 236–37).
106. *Gschnas* is a game played at the bohemian parties of Vienna. It involved 'constructing what appear to be rare and precious objects out of trivial and preferably comic and worthless material (for instance, in making armour out of saucepans, whips of straw and dinner rolls)'. An ironic effect was produced by the contrast between the original context and an object's new use. Sigmund Freud, *The Interpretation of Dreams*, trans. by James Stachey (Harmondsworth: Penguin, 1991), p. 310, in Kolb, pp. 210–11.
107. Vladimir Aristov, 'Observations on Meta', in *Re-Entering the Sign: Articulating New Russian Culture*, ed. by Ellen E. Berry and Anesa Miller-Pogacar (Ann Arbor, MI: University of Michigan Press, 1995), pp. 219–26 (p. 224).
108. Sobaka, p. 11.
109. D. Barton Johnson, 'Saša Sokolov and Vladimir Nabokov', *Russian Language Journal*, 41 (1987), 153–62 (p. 155).
110. Sobaka, p. 13.
111. Ibid., p. 166.

112. Ibid., pp. 234-35.
113. Ibid., p. 106.
114. Ibid., p. 200.
115. Ibid., p. 140.
116. Ibid., p. 92.
117. Matthew 10:3.
118. Sobaka, p. 175.
119. Ibid.
120. Ibid., pp. 54 and 176.
121. Ibid., p. 195.
122. Ibid., pp. 172-73.
123. Ibid., p. 178.
124. D. Barton Johnson, 'Sasha Sokolov's *Between Dog and Wolf* and the Modernist Tradition' (hereafter 'Johnson Modernist Tradition'), in *The Third Wave: Russian Literature in Emigration*, ed. by Olga Matich and Michael Heim (Ann Arbor, MI: Ardis, 1984), pp. 208-17 (p. 211).
125. See Ellis Havelock, *The Psychology of Sex* (New York: Random House, 1936); William Rossi, *The Sex Life of the Foot and Shoe* (Ware: Wordsworth Editions, 1989).
126. Johnson Modernist Tradition, p. 211.
127. Sobaka, p. 46.
128. Ibid., p. 204.
129. Ibid., pp. 203 and 176.
130. One of the alternative names of the Volga in the novel is: 'Volch'ia reka' (The Wolf's River).
131. Mark Lipovetsky, *Russian Postmodernist Fiction: Dialogue with Chaos* (hereafter 'Lipovetsky'), ed. by Eliot Borenstein (Armonk, NY: M. E. Sharpe, 1998), p. 145.
132. See E. A. Iablokov, '"Nashel ia nachalo dorogi otsiuda — tuda" (o motivnoi structure romana Sashi Sokolova "Mezhdu sobakoi i volkom")', in *Literatura 'tret'ei volny': sbornik nauchnykh statei*, ed. by V. P. Skobelev (Samara: Samarskii universitet, 1997), pp. 202-14 (p. 209).
133. Sobaka, pp. 25-26.
134. In Kolb's 'classification' it is 'saint' rather than 'virgin', a category that seems more appropriate to my analysis.
135. Kolb, pp. 203-04.
136. See Barbara Heldt, 'Female Skaz in Sasha Sokolov's *Between Dog and Wolf*' (hereafter 'Heldt'), *Canadian American Slavic Studies*, 21 (1987), 279-85 (p. 280).
137. Sobaka, pp. 134-36.
138. Ibid., p. 134.
139. Ibid., p. 31.
140. Toker, p. 353.
141. Sobaka, p. 32.
142. Lipovetsky, p. 144.
143. Sobaka, p. 83.
144. Lipovetsky, p. 144; see Sobaka, pp. 206-07.
145. Sobaka, pp. 145-46.
146. Ibid., p. 205.
147. Ibid., pp. 206-07.
148. Ibid., p. 106.
149. Ibid., p. 141.
150. Kolb, pp. 200-02.

151. Sobaka, p. 195.
152. Ibid., p. 196.
153. Ibid., p. 28.
154. See D. Barton Johnson, 'Sasha Sokolov's Twilight Cosmos: Themes and Motifs', *Slavic Review*, 45 (1986), 639–49 (p. 646).
155. The river's name is contextualized within Sokolov's play on 'волчья /ловчая', discussed earlier in connection with Iakov.
156. Sobaka, p. 61.
157. Ibid., p. 169.
158. Ibid., p. 176.
159. Johnson Vremia, p. 171; Arnold McMillin, 'Aberration or the Future: The Avant-Garde Novels of Sasha Sokolov' (hereafter 'McMillin Avant-Garde'), in *From Pushkin to Palisandriia: Essays on the Russian Novel in Honour of Richard Freeborn*, ed. by A. McMillin's (London: Macmillan, 1990), pp. 229–43 (p. 237).
160. D. Barton Johnson, 'Sasha Sokolov: The New Russian Avant-garde', *Critique: Studies in Contemporary Fiction*, 30 (1989), 163–78 (p. 170).
161. Sobaka, p. 84.
162. Ibid., pp. 231, 235–36.
163. Ibid., pp. 141.
164. Pasternak Zhivago, pp. 126.
165. Ibid., pp. 126–30.
166. Perhaps it is worth recalling that Iakov's dog, Mumu, killed by Il'ia, in Turgenev belonged to the deaf and dumb Gerasim, which may be regarded as another link with Pasternak's deaf character.
167. Eikhenbaum Leskov, p. 215, translated in Hicks Skaz, p. 85.
168. Sobaka, p. 53.
169. Ibid., p. 165.
170. Ibid., pp. 161–62.
171. Ibid., p. 32.
172. Walter Ong, *Interfaces of the World: Studies in the Evolution of Consciousness and Culture* (hereafter 'Ong Interfaces') (Ithaca and London: Cornell University Press, 1977), p. 281.
173. Corinthians 3:6.
174. Derrida Grammatology, p. 17.
175. Sobaka, p. 54.
176. Ibid., pp. 203–04, italics mine.
177. Ibid., pp. 199–200, italics mine.
178. The story features a fly captured and tortured by a spider and eventually rescued by a heroic mosquito.
179. Sobaka, p. 194.
180. Ibid., p. 135.
181. Derrida quoting from Freud's *Inhibitions, Symptoms, and Anxiety*: 'As soon as writing, which entails making a fluid flow out of the tube onto a piece of white paper, assumes the significance of copulation, or as soon as walking becomes a symbolic substitute for treading upon the body of mother earth, both writing and walking are stopped because they represent the performance of a forbidden sexual act.' (Jacques Derrida, 'Freud and the Science of Writing', in *Writing and Difference* (hereafter 'Derrida Difference'), trans. by Alan Bass (London and New York: Routledge Classics, 2009), pp. 246–91 (p. 288–89)).
182. Ong Interfaces, p. 240.
183. Ibid., p. 257.

184. Sobaka, p. 236.
185. Ibid., p. 38.
186. Evgenii Onegin, pp. 135–36.
187. Kolb, p. 212.
188. Sobaka, p. 109.
189. Ibid., p. 54.
190. Ibid., pp. 55–56.
191. Ibid., pp. 54–55.
192. Matthew 15:7–14.
193. This parable is, notably, a subject of one of Brueghel's paintings, *The Parable of the Blind*.
194. Sobaka, p. 170.
195. Matthew 15:7–14.
196. William Smith, 'Pharisees', *Smith's Bible Dictionary* (1901): <http://www.christnotes.org/dictionary.php?dict=sbd&q=pharisees> [accessed March 2009].
197. Jacques Derrida, 'Edmond Jabès and The Question of the Book', in Derrida Difference, pp. 77–96 (p. 83), italics in the original.
198. The theme of the lavatory in the Soviet context of communal flats as the only space in which a person retains his privacy (individuality) and human dignity was poignantly developed by Il'ia Kabakov in his installations.
199. Sobaka, pp. 53–54.
200. Ibid., pp. 237–38.
201. Ibid., p. 61.
202. Ibid., pp. 100–01.
203. 'Writing is that forgetting of the self, that exteriorization, the contrary of the interiorizing memory, [...] It is this that Phaedrus said: writing is at once mnemotechnique and the power of forgetting'. Derrida Grammatology, p. 24.
204. Sobaka, p. 8.
205. Ibid., p. 23.
206. Jacques Derrida, *Dissemination* (hereafter 'Derrida Dissemination'), trans. by Barbara Johnson (London: Athlone Press, 1981), p. 26.
207. Barbara Johnson, in Derrida Dissemination, n. 26, pp. 26–27.
208. Sobaka, p. 111.
209. Derrida Dissemination, p. 304.
210. Sobaka, pp. 109–10.
211. Matthew 13:2–23.
212. John 12:24.
213. See Mikhail Epshtein, *Slovo i molchanie: Metafizika russkoi literatury* (Moscow: Vysshaia shkola, 2006), p. 139.
214. Fedor Dostoevskii, 'Brat'ia Karamazovy', *Sobranie sochinenii*, 15 vols (Leningrad: Nauka, 1991), IX, 360.
215. Matthew 13:21.
216. 'Deterritorialization' is a term coined by Gilles Deleuze and Felix Guattari, who used it to designate the freeing of labour-power from specific means of production. See Gilles Deleuze and Félix Guattari, *Anti-Oedipus: Capitalism and Schizophrenia*, trans. by Robert Hurley, Mark Seem, and Helen R. Lane (London: Continuum, 2004). In the socio-cultural context deterritorialization refers to a severance of ties between culture and place, which occurs through the removal of subjects and/or objects from their place in space and time. See Mark Lipovetskii's discussion of this phenomenon in connection with Sokolov's text in Lipovetsky, pp. 236–37.

217. Heldt, p. 279.
218. Derrida Grammatology, p. 144.
219. Derrida Difference, p. 365, italics in the original.
220. Mikhail Bakhtin, 'Avtor i geroi esteticheskoi deiatel'nosti', in *Sobranie sochinenii*, 7 vols (Moscow: Russkie slovari, 1997–2003), I (2003), pp. 69–263 (p. 95).
221. Velimir Khlebnikov, *Stikhotvoreniia. Poemy. Dramy. Proza*, ed. by R. V. Duganov (Moscow: Sovetskaia Rossiia, 1986), p. 16, quoted in Duganov, p. 102.
222. John 1:1.

CHAPTER 3

~

A Lie That Tells the Truth: Mediation of Reality in *Palisandriia*

> Indefinable, unshakeable, it is the heroism of people not called upon to be heroes. It will find new ways to react both with and against public tastes, it will selfishly and selflessly shriek on, entertaining the self and the spectator in one mad gesture, oblivious of what it is required to do. Camp is always in the future; that is why the present needs it so badly.[1]

> я возлагаю надежду на искусство фантасмагорическое с гипотезами вместо цели и гротеском взамен бытописания. Оно наиболее полно отвечает современности. Пусть утрированные образы Гофмана, Достоевского, Гойи и Шагала и самого социалистического Маяковского и многих других реалистов и не реалистов научат нас, как быть правдивыми с помощью нелепой фантазии.[2]

> И наступила пора окончательных мемуаров, последней, мандельштамовской прямоты.[3]

The first impression *Palisandriia* leaves is that of implausibility and 'bad taste' — a hard-to-digest fusion of arcane language, bombastic grandeur of form, and bawdy content. This concoction is presented as a memoir of Palisandr Dal'berg, great-nephew of Lavrentii Beriia and grandson of Grigorii Rasputin. The memoir is introduced by a biographer's note and consists of a prologue, four 'books', and an epilogue. It is peopled with a host of famous and infamous historical figures, mostly Russian/Soviet (although not exclusively), which are presented through the eyes of Sokolov's quirky narrator. It captures the narrator's life in its totality, from childhood, which falls in the Stalinist years (echoing Sokolov's own), to the moment of death sometime in the 2050s according to the biographer's foreword. The story is set in or around Moscow, codified as Emsk yet easily recognizable through the unmistakable landmarks such as the Kremlin and the Novodevichii Convent. The singularity of place is broken in the last chapter, 'The Book of Embassy' ('Kniga poslaniia'), which unfolds as a global journey before its return to the point of departure in the epilogue.

The story of Palisandr openly follows the trajectory of an epic/mythic hero: his noble birth, exile, and return as a saviour. In fact, the device is 'bared' in the in-text acknowledgement of the 'historical parallelism':

> Нахохлясь, проследовал в библиотеку и, взгромоздись на насест стремянки, листаю рекомендованное. И что же? В такие-то и такие-то веки такие-то и такие-то сироты знатного происхождения, [...] были направлены за рубеж на предмет увнучения или усыновления и по отъезде из милых отчизн отлучены от них навсегда. В изгнанье влачили элегантную бедность. Тихий, вкрадчивый ужас исторического параллелизма покрыл мою кожу мурашками.[4]

The epic character of the journey of Palisandr, who 'прошел по-наполеоновски славный путь от простого кремлевского сироты и ключника в Доме Массажа Правительства до главы государства и командора главенствующего ордена',[5] is announced in the novel's title, *Palisandriia*, by analogy with *Odiseia* (the Russian translation of the *Odyssey*). Another allusion to the legendary blind bard is Palisandr's wearing what he calls 'Homeric' glasses ('gomericheskie'): dark glasses for the blind.[6] The Homeric subtext is also acknowledged through evocations of Joyce's *Ulysses*, another work that took the epic as its organizing principle.[7]

The hero's context is appropriately mythologized, drawing heavily on the underlying myth of the Soviet utopia: the Great Family residing in a prehistorical paradise presided over by a patriarch/God.[8] Orphaned at an early age, Palisandr is brought up in the Kremlin by a host of guardians: Stalin, Beriia, Khrushchev, Brezhnev, and Andropov amongst others. The Kremlin is presented as a sovereign state within the country, run by the ruling Order of Watchmakers (Келейная организация часовщиков), which consists of Palisandr's father-protectors. It appears as a celestial order, projected onto a timeless, vaguely Slavic background. From this Slavicized version of Mount Olympus the Order of Watchmakers controls the earthly fates of people.

The mythical essence of the Soviet project was first addressed by Andrei Siniavskii in the late 1950s. In his treatise *Chto takoe sotsialisticheskii realism?* (*What is Socialist Realism?*), published in *Tamizdat* in 1959, Siniavskii appealed for the production of a Communist *Iliad* (which was answered a quarter of a century later by Sokolov's post-utopian *Odyssey*):

> It seems the very term 'socialist realism' contains an insoluble contradiction. A socialist, i.e. a purposeful, a religious, art cannot be produced with the literary method of the nineteenth century called 'realism'. And a really faithful representation of life cannot be achieved in a language based on teleological concepts. If socialist realism really wants to rise to the level of the great world cultures and produce its *Communiad*, there is only one way to do it. It must give up the 'realism', renounce the sorry and fruitless attempts to write a socialist *Anna Karenina* or a socialist *Cherry Orchard*.

When it abandons its effort to achieve verisimilitude, it will be able to express the grand and implausible sense of our era.[9]

The scandalous power of Siniavskii's essay lies in the fact that it is not a condemnation of Socialist Realism, but an invitation to a conscious (if ironic) aesthetic appreciation. This project has been subsequently realized by sots-art, which, in recognizing the complexity of Stalinist art, took Soviet reality for what it was or aspired to be: an object of art.

The artistic phenomenon of sots-art emerged in the 1960s, when it was unofficially known as 'retrospectivism', 'soviet pop', or 'totalitarian conceptualism'.[10] The term 'sots-art' was coined in 1972 by its key figures, artists Vitalii Komar and Aleksandr Melamid, while preparing the festive decorations for a pioneer camp. Contrary to some superficial conceptions of sots-art, it is not a parody of Socialist Realism. Komar and Melamid define it as a 'reflection of the reflection' — a meta-commentary with the elements of self-parody 'because we are all products of this system and contain its features'.[11] It is viewed as a final stage of Socialist Realism, representing its self-transgression.

Sots-art was initially conceived as a Soviet counterpart to American pop-art, whereby a response to the supremacy of consumerism in Western society was replaced by a reaction to the dominance of ideology in the Soviet Union. Both artistic phenomena constitute a reflection on the aesthetics (means) and philosophy (ideology) of a utopian project that attempted to subordinate reality to a system of ideas/images that were supposed to transform it and lead to the creation of a simulacrum. Utilizing the images and icons of Socialist realism, sots-art deconstructs its intentions by placing these ideologemes in seemingly incongruous, and yet encoded contexts. Such trans-contextualization reveals the primary symbolic structures that underlie Soviet mythology and that are used by the system to demonstrate its sacred origin.[12] Representing a grotesque realization of these ambitions, sots-art discredits them by drawing on their absurdities and contradictions.[13]

Palisandriia is considered to be a textual analogue of sots-art,[14] and it has been argued that the novel is written in the same stylistic key as Komar and Melamid's painting *Comrade Stalin and the Muses* (1981–82).[15] This painting, executed in Social realist style, features Stalin in his Generalissimo uniform surrounded by Classicist muses draped in diaphanous garments. In Sokolov's text, the Classicist and Soviet modes are represented linguistically, through what has been described as 'decadent cultural' and 'military' registers.[16] This oxymoronic union, informing the linguistic and stylistic layers of the text, is also supported by the tension between the solemn and the sublime form of the novel, and its scabrous content. The apotheosis of this fusion is the protagonist: alopecia-stricken, cross-eyed, seven-fingered androgynous sexual pervert, modelled on the epic/Soviet positive hero.

Palisandriia is essentially what Katerina Clark defined as a 'ritualized biography', whereby the public and private ends overlap so that the hero's personal life becomes a historical allegory. Clark argues that by the mid-1930s the obligatory quality of party-mindedness (*partiinost'*) did not merely entail using politically correct attitudes or themes, but 'it required of the novel a "lifelike" incarnation of political values, organized "correctly"'.[17] Thus every Socialist realist work became an allegory representing ritual disguised as a distillation of the Marxist-Leninist version of historical progress: a rite of passage whereby the protagonist — the 'positive hero' — is initiated into the Great Family of the Soviet state.[18] In this political myth, orphanhood played a major role, as Clark argues, because:

> [A] child without a father is to that extent a child without identity. And in the great tale of Soviet society, whether told within fiction or without, all are orphans until they find their identity in the 'great family'.[19]

The 'identity' of Sokolov's orphan is constructed from a number of myths. One of the chief constructive myths, alluded to in the novel's subtitle, *Intsest kremlevskogo grafomana (Incest of the Kremlin Graphomaniac)*,[20] is presented as a severe case of gerontophilia — a result of a childhood trauma.

In his medieval incarnation, Palisandr was sexually corrupted by his stepmother, his maternal aunt. He relives the act of defilement in all his subsequent incarnations, experiencing it as the return of the repressed. The incestuous nature of Palisandr's liaisons is facilitated not only by his gerontophilia, but also by his being related to most of his lovers. As an adopted son of the Kremlin, he possesses multiple mothers — wives of his numerous guardians. To complete the emerging picture, Palisandr is guilty of patricide. He kills (or attempts to) at least two of his 'fathers': he participates in the practical joke that led to Stalin's death, and he attempts to assassinate (in a fit of jealousy) another patriarch, Brezhnev. Investing his hero with the Oedipus complex, and planting him in the epicentre of Soviet power, Sokolov seems to suggest the incestuous under-layer of Soviet history.[21]

An Oedipal reading of Soviet ideology was attempted by Mikhail Epshtein.[22] Epshtein argues that Soviet 'materialism-atheism', which has more in common with a mother cult than a philosophical system, combines worship of nature with a form of theomachy that rejects worship of the heavenly Father:

> Materialism, when coupled with atheism, is nothing but the conscious projection of this childish [Oedipus] complex: the son striving to take his mother away from his father by killing the father or, better yet, simply by announcing his death. [...] In reality, the son kills his father, not to worship his mother religiously, but to master her sexually. In the same way materialism-atheism dethrones God the Father not for the sake of the maternal superiority of Nature, but for the son's superiority over his mother.[23]

The triumph of materialism in Soviet Russia paradoxically resulted in the subjugation of matter to the spirit of ideology. Mother Nature/Russia was demoted from her role of authority on the vertical scale onto the horizontal axis of wife or sister, dominated by her son turned patriarch. Sokolov's representation of Russia as Titian's Danaë in anticipation of Palisandr's/Perseus arrival is illuminating: 'Впереди, за хребтами и реками, вальяжно раскинувшись на многострадальном ложе своих исконных пространств, искусно убранном скромными полевыми цветами, ждала нас Россия (Даная!)'.[24] Re-emerging from his rite of passage, the hero re-enters the mother/land on a train — his phallic 'extension' — the symbolism of which is familiar from Sokolov's other texts.

The embodiment of the demoted maternal archetype is Shaganeh, Palisandr's elderly beloved. In a parodic inversion of Pushkin's novella, *Kapitanskaia dochka* (*The Captain's Daughter*), she is introduced as 'kapitanskaia mat'' (Captain's mother).[25] Her archetypal role also emerges in her 'duties' as the 'Mother Superior' of the Novodevichii convent and her overt link with the Roman wolf.[26] According to the legend, a she-wolf coming down from the hills to quench her thirst found two infants crying and suckled them. These were the future founders of Rome, Romulus and Remus. Eventually, they were nursed by Acca Larentia, the wife of a shepherd, Faustulus, who found the infants and took them to his house. The fusion of Acca Larentia with the wolf may be explained by the fact that Acca was known as '*lupa*', which meant both she-wolf and harlot in ancient Rome.[27] The 'lupine' motif re-emerges in the name of Moulin de Saint-Loup — Palisandr's abode in exile — which translates literally as 'Mill of St Wolf'. The Italian word for a brothel, '*lupanar*', which both Novodevichii and Moulin de Saint-Loup technically are, also derives from the word '*lupa*'.

Another key to the mythical 'origin' of the Soviet project is its identification with the myth of Cronos. It has been argued that it constitutes the proto-image of the father-and-son relationships developed in the novel and an allusion to the Stalinist purges.[28] Sokolov plays on the confusion of Cronos and Chronos,[29] presenting the ruling state as 'Chronochiate' (Хронархиат).[30]

Cronos, one of the Titans, was fathered by Uranus upon Mother Earth. Uranus, hating his offspring, forced them back into Mother Earth (the Underworld, in mythical presentation). When Mother Earth was about to burst, she persuaded Cronos along with other Titans to attack his father. Armed with a sickle (!), Cronos struck Uranus when he was asleep, castrating him, and released the Cyclopes from the Underworld.

Ironically, one of Palisandr's heroic deeds involves exhumation of his compatriots. He returns to Russia from his exile bringing a vast collection of dead émigré Russians. The symbolism of the hero's act — reinstalment/ reconciliation of the past with/in the present — is gruesomely supplemented by the physicality of its realization. It also seems to draw on a similarly ambitious project to 'resurrect all fathers' proposed at the turn of the twentieth century by a Russian thinker, Nikolai Fedorov.

The 'philosophy of the common task' ('filosofiia obshchego dela'), as Fedorov designated it, consisted of the creation of technological, social, and political conditions that would result in the artificial resurrection of everyone who has ever lived. Fedorov viewed this project as a realization of the Christian promise of the resurrection of the dead at the end of time. However, believing only in material — physical — existence, he dismissed the Christian theses of the afterlife, and the immortality of the soul. Thus, he held that immortality of the body could be achieved through proper social organization and modern technological means.[31]

Fedorov's project has been viewed as a reaction to an inherent contradiction in nineteenth-century socialist thought. Promising full social justice, socialism linked this promise with the idea of progress, which implied that the benefits of this justice would be enjoyed only by future generations. The resurrection of all the dead, which would end the discrimination perpetrated against the dead for the benefit of the living, appeared as the only solution to this historical injustice. Fedorov's ideas re-emerged in the Soviet programme of space exploration. The founder of the Soviet space programme, Konstantin Tsiolkovskii, believed in the possibility of the technological resurrection of the dead. The first space vehicle he designed was intended to transport the resurrected dead to other planets where they could settle.[32] Thus, communism was to be established in space and time.

Sokolov's hero is the grotesque embodiment and agent of this race against time. His immortality (Palisandr is addressed by his orderly as 'Your Eternity')[33], his education at the Funeral Division of the Kremlin School of Manual Training for Noble Orphans,[34] his interest/investment in the burial business, and, finally, Palisandr's fondness for old women, bordering on necrophilia — all attest to it. In fact, Palisandr is known as Lemur, a nickname he receives in the Novodevichii. In Roman mythology, lemurs are restless spirits of the dead who were denied a proper burial. In Goethe, who was inspired by an ancient tomb near Naples featuring skeleton-like creatures,[35] lemurs are Mephistopheles' servants, digging the grave for Faust.[36] In Sokolov, lemur is merged with l'Amour, French for Cupid.[37] This synthesis of love and death is ultimately another manifestation of the same drive to annul time: by 'engaging' with the older women the hero erases the boundaries between the past and the present. In fact, the novel opens with an act of suspension of time as Beriia, the 'Cardinal Guardian of the Present', commits suicide by hanging himself on the clock of the Kremlin Spassky Tower. It initiates the period of Timelessness.

Palisandr's problematic relationship with Chronos begins when, in a reference to Laurence Sterne, the weight of a pendulum clock falls on his nose. Given the sexual connotations of Sterne's 'trope', which also underlie Gogol's short story, *The Nose*,[38] the episode conveys a fear of castration: a symbolic castration by time — anxiety illuminated through the allusion to the myth of Cronos. As a consequence of this incident, Palisandr develops a hatred/fear of clocks and other markers of time such as reflecting surfaces.[39] Thus to cheat time he learns to 'neutralize' his reflections. In a reversal of Dorian Gray, who warded off time by magically projecting decrepitude onto his representation, Palisandr preserves himself by 'training' his reflections to ignore him as he disguises himself with various masks (executor's, carnival, medical) and 'Homeric' glasses, mentioned earlier: 'Тогда справедливость восторжествовала, ибо мои отражения больше не узнавали меня, а я не узнавал в них себя. И следовательно, мы не узнавали друг друга'.[40]

Palisandr's hatred of reflective surfaces disguises his fear of death. The association of the mirror with death has been linked with the myth of Narcissus, beckoned to death by his reflection.[41] In Palisandr's case, it is not the fear of his reflection as such that strikes him; it is the disappearance thereof in the murky depth of the pool. It emerges in his 'first' encounter with the mirror at the Saint-Loup,[42] which he craftily avoided for most of his lives: 'Тогда — открылось. Тогда — зазияло овально. Тогда — засквозило глубокой голубизною осеннего омута — провалом винтового лестничного пролета — о, о — тогда'.[43] The encounter communicates an image of falling into an abyss — of a pool or a stairwell. The stairwell as another agent of death is introduced through a reference to a Russian writer, Vsevolod Garshin (1855–88), who committed suicide by throwing himself down a stairwell in his house in St Petersburg.[44] The symbolism of falling into the abyss, which haunts the text, is conveyed not only through the images of beckoning vortexes, but is also presented graphically: as a grapheme 'o', which leaves no ambiguity as to the origin of the phobia.[45] The recurrent use of the word 'then' ('togda') links this passage with Palisandr's picture of the structure of the universe, which he compares to *cervix uteri*, reminiscent of an old-fashioned gramophone speaker horn:

> Вселенная по Эйнштейну загибается, будто труба у этого граммофона. Или как шейка матки. Спирально. И если довериться Фрейду, то следует кануть в нее обратно — концептуально завихриться в ней — затеряться в загибах ее относительности — и тогда — тогда.[46]

In fact, the novel opens with an image of death as a return to the womb as Beriia winds his way up a spiral-shaped staircase to commit suicide. He literally steps outside time, squeezing through the clock keyhole:

> Не мешкая, он взвинтил себя винтовой внутрибашенной лестницей до отказа и с маху толкнул входную, броней одетую дверь. Та

вела в каземат механизма. [...] Так называемая ремонтная скважина циферблата, имевшая форму замочной, предназначалась для выхода на циферблат. Лаврентий Павлович подошел и открыл ее.[47]

The sexual connotations of the key and the keyhole are established in Palisandr's position in the Novodevichii convent as a key master — 'лицо, начальствующее над всеми монастырскими скважинами'.[48]

This quasi-Freudian vision of death as a fall into the womb surfaces in a condition called 'astrophobia',[49] literally a fear of stars, which inspired the title of Michael Heim's English translation:

> Но вряд ли было что во Вселенной ужасней, губительней и месмеричней ночного, полного дальних солнц, колодца. Ведь, отразившись в нем вместе с ними, вы словно бы начинали падать в его пролет, будто в космос. *Падать и пропадать из виду, утрачивая себя, свою бесценную индивидуальность и бессмертную душу. Падать и становиться одной из миллионов падающих в беспредельность звезд.* Кремлевский колодец! Ему безусловно не было дна, и он еженощно манил артиста своею волшебной кромешностью.[50]

The loss of identity/individuality as an existential prerequisite in Soviet Russia is alluded to in the pathogenesis of Palisandr's 'astrophobia'. Stars themselves come to the fore: not the 'distant suns' of the universe, but the tangible red stars of the Kremlin, the symbol of Soviet totalitarian power, multiplied in the star-studded military shoulder straps:

> Трудно поверить: вот мы ехали утром в кибитке, и я смотрел на ваши погоны без всякого страху. А прежде, в бытность ребенком, опекуны навещали меня исключительно в штатском — чтоб не травмировать. Но я был классический астрофобик, и дурнее всего мне делалось от ночного ясного неба.[51]

In *The Origins and History of Consciousness* Erich Neumann writes that sexuality, associated with the unconscious and embodied in the figure of the Great Mother, constitutes the prime threat to the ego. The Great Mother symbolizes the collective will, in which the individual is sacrificed for the primordial drive of the species for procreation. 'The intoxicating effect of the Great Mother' on the ego leads to effeminacy and castration, by being transformed into her, or to madness and death, by being dismembered.'[52] The examples quoted earlier — the fall, disappearance, and the loss of self and its individuality — communicate an archetypal fear/act of being devoured by the Great and terrible Mother.

As in all Sokolov's works, the sexual act and desire are associated with death. The 'progression' of the representation of death (and sexuality) in Sokolov's oeuvre begins as an expression of vacuity (absence) in *School for Fools*, evolves into the notion of promiscuity (fecundity and indiscriminate acceptance) in

Between Dog and Wolf, and re-emerges in the image of *Vagina dentata*[53] and the act of ingestion in *Palisandriia*. *School for Fools* is filled with the shadows of the narrator's desire, (dis)embodied in Veta, Roza, and Sheina — dead or missing (at least partially, as in Sheina's case) — culminating in the image of a chalk-pale ('melovaia') woman, a metaphor for death. In *Between Dog and Wolf* it is Life Everlasting indiscriminately beckoning victims in her search for the destined one. And, finally, in *Palisandriia*, it is the Terrible Mother (substitute), who appears as an improbable form of a Russian nesting doll, *Matrioshka*.

Matrioshka is a diminutive of Matriona, a name that derives from the Latin for mother: 'Mater'. The doll contains several replicas of itself within,[54] which are meant to represent a family, wherein younger generations are 'safely kept' within the parental body, engulfed. For Palisandr it is a symbol of reincarnation and the survival of the human race:

> Расписная матрешка, — набрасывает Командор в дневнике, — воплотила в себе убежденность нашего мужика в неистребимости рода людского'. И ниже; 'Матрешка — это оптимистическая трагедия об инкарнации, карме, детотворении. Это, наконец, очаровательная человеческая комедия, выполненная из обыкновенной российской липы'.[55]

The reference to *Optimisticheskaia tragedia* (*The Optimistic Tragedy*) (1933), a play by Vsevolod Vishnevskii about the post-October Revolution events, alludes to the birth of the Soviet State. The reference to Balzac's multi-volume collection of interlinked novels, *La Comédie humaine* (*The Human Comedy*), connotes multiplicity. Notably, Palisandr's memoir is constructed in accordance with the '*Matrioshka*' principle:

> Приятно добавить, что многотомье 'Воспоминаний' не столько роман, сколько целый не то чтобы цикл, а каскад романов, плавно переходящих друг в друга естественными уступами: не успевает один закончиться, а следующий уж начался. Произведение выстроено по принципу пресловутой матрешки: роман в романе, роман в романе, and so on.[56]

The polysemantic nature of the Russian word 'roman', which can signify both 'a novel' and 'a love affair', allows for multiple readings. 'Roman v romane' can be read in parallel (as 'a novel within a novel' and 'a love affair within a love affair') or diagonally (as 'a novel in a love affair' and 'a love affair in a novel'). All four equations are explored in the novel. The parallel dimension is represented by the self-reflexivity of Palisandr's memoir with its *mise en abyme* structure, and the incestuous nature of his relationships. The diagonal dimension is actualized through the blurring of life and fiction wherein each fiction is a romance and each romance is fiction.

Palisandr's memoir — 'kaskad romanov' — is a series of romances. Factually, Palisandr is conducting a love affair with Russian history, literally embodied in a range of historical or quasi-historical figures: Catherine the Great; Grigorii Rasputin's grandmother, Agrippina; Fanny Kaplan, who attempted to assassinate Lenin; Stalin's wife, Nadezhda Allilueva; Brezhnev's wife, Viktoriia.[57] In fact, Clio, the muse of history, is overtly mentioned among his sexual victims, identified with one of his aunts ('mnogoiurodnye tetki'):

> Превратно истолковав их доверие, вы совершили массовое растление престарелых. [...] Ах, музы, музы, все они — наши сестры, горькие и заезженные существа вроде нас — незлобивы, отходчивы. А Клио, о которой вы отзывались не слишком почтительно, уверяя нас, будто ее кобыла стоит на кремлевской конюшне и некоторые учащиеся вашего ремесленного училища келейно используют ее в низменных интересах, — [...] Клио тоже простит.[58]

Clio's association with horses as in the passage above constructs a link with Mazhorette, a passionate horse lover, whom Palisandr confuses with his maternal aunt, the original source of his defilement:[59] 'Портрет блудницы [Mazhorette] не будет полным, если не подчеркнуть, что она проводила каникулы в Эпсоме, городе скаковых испытаний кобыл, каковых испытаний она завсегдатай'.[60] As the embodiment of History, Mazhorette represents corrupting and distinctly non-Russian forces which were imposed from without. The foreignness of this ruinous influence is alluded to through her name[61] and her nickname: 'dama iz Amsterdama' (a dame from Amsterdam). Her presentation as a spiral and vertical entity, associated with (historical) time, is clearly contrasted with the horizontal notion of 'eternal' Russia as space, pictured as the everlasting pasture in the 'Danaë' passage, quoted earlier. This emphasis on the foreign provenance of the temptress could be read as a nod to the notion that emerged during the de-Stalinization period, wherein the Petrine westernization of medieval Russia, the October Revolution, and Stalinism were regarded as the evil foisted upon Russia as part of a western conspiracy.[62] This historico-political corruption is subjectivized in *Palisandriia*, where the protagonist becomes a victim of Mazhorette's sexual and psychological sadism. This 'domestication' of history reaches grotesque proportions in *Palisandriia*, where it becomes interchangeable with genealogy, with a strong incestuous streak in it.

The hero's role as a lover of History re-emerges in a parodic realization of the idiom 'the steed of History'. In one of his existences he is an equine lover of Catherine the Great.[63] Thus investing his sexual life with pan-historical significance, Palisandr merges the transcendental and the immediate spheres.

The 'transcendental' dimension of his liaisons is illuminated in the 'cosmogonic' portrayal of one of his 'sessions' with Mazhorette, where the latter is identified with the universe[64] and Palisandr's phallus with *axis mundi*: 'Фрейд прав. Зизи [his euphemism for penis] есть та самая ось, на которой вертится вся Вселенная'.⁶⁵ The image is supported by Palisandr Dal'berg's association with a tree — 'palisandr' or 'palissandrovoe derevo', a rosewood tree of the Dalbeghia family⁶⁶ — a traditional phallic symbol of the universal pillar which connects heaven and earth. Thus buttressed by the multiple evocations of the primordial myth, incest becomes the original creative act. Contextualized within the 'proto-myth' of the novel — the myth of Cronos — the symbolism of releasing the captives, the castration of the father, and lying on/with the mother points to the archetypal rite of the separation of sky (Uranus) and earth, which makes full creation possible.

Incest is the foundation — 'a canvas' — on which Palisandr the Chronicler weaves the threads of his/stories: a point where the individual/immanent and the universal/transcendental meet:

> Так, если у Джойса в 'Уллисе' все действие укладывается в двадцать четыре часа, то в нашем случае речь идет о минутах, в течение коих длится инцестуальный коитус. Им книга начинается, вместе с ним и заканчивается. Совершая его, автор успевает не только утешить соблазнившую его престарелую родственницу, но и проанализировать причинно-следственную цепочку приведших к нему событий историко-политического и бытового характера. По сути этот ярчайший во всей словесности — шире — во всей мировой культуре — акт человеческой близости представляет собою не что иное, как грубую свежевытканную основу — холстину для изображенья на ней многокрасочной панорамы той грандиозной эпохи, что так чутко совпала со старостью Командора, — эпохи сплошных страстей и коллизий. Террор и войны. Митинги и совещания. Похищения и совращения. Все сколько-нибудь забавное и замечательное имеет здесь свое место. Искусный словесный ткач, П. Прелестный всегда сочетает общественное и личное таким образом, что первое выгодно дополняет и оттеняет второе. И vice versa. События, люди, предметы всегда находят себе у П. параллель или пару и так или иначе переплетаются и вплетаются в ткань панно, образуя узоры симметрии, аналогии и метафоры.⁶⁷

Both Olga Matich and Karen Ryan read *Palisandriia* as a trivialization of history and conclude that it demonstrates Sokolov's position that literature should not be confused with politics and history.⁶⁸ Indeed, Sokolov's text can be viewed as a reaction to the tradition of Russian 'literaturocentrism', a counterpart to logocentrism — the scapegoat of (Western) postmodernism.

As has been noted, Russian postmodernism is not, or not only, based on the deconstruction of Logos.⁶⁹ Owing to the tradition of despotism in Russia's political system, literature historically played the role of the opposition to the state. The juxtaposition of poet versus Tsar has been the central aspect of Russian culture for at least a couple of centuries. In the later part of the last century, coinciding with, or indeed triggered by, the collapse of the Soviet

Empire, this edifice began to show cracks. *Palisandriia*, like other sots-art works, is a text that surveys the cracks and lays bare the bricks underneath. This process began with Sokolov's earlier texts, especially *Between Dog and Wolf*, with its extensive intertextual play and its focus on language. If this work engaged mostly with ancient and classical literature, *Palisandriia* takes issue and forms a polemical exchange with the dissident culture, with its literary and historical self-indulgence.[70] Indeed, a few dissident writers and memoirists feature in the text, including such figures as Nina Berberova, Svetlana Allilueva, Aleksandr Solzhenitsyn, and Eduard Limonov.

An illuminating example of Sokolov's concern with the sacred status of literature is a fusion of two writers with strong nationalist/political views: Aleksandr Solzhenitsyn and Vladimir Soloukhin (1924–97), a Soviet writer who strived for the preservation of the 'authentic' cultural legacy. By playing on the title of one of Soloukhin's books, *V poiskakh ikony* (*In Search of an Icon*), Sokolov reveals the ambiguous nature of the cultural artefact and deflates (Solzhenitsyn's) claims to the ultimate truth.[71] Sokolov's chronicler openly polemicizes with a range of dissident 'insider' accounts, offering his own version, which is presented as the ultimate truth. Thus attacking Abdurakhman Avtorkhanov's 1976 *Zagadka smerti Stalina: zagovor Beriia* (*The Mystery of Stalin's Death: Beria's Plot*), Palisandr writes:

> Что же касается так называемой загадки смерти собственно Сталина, то спешу заверить любителей помистифицировать публику вроде некоего Авторханова Абдурахмана, оставившего Отчизну в годину ее затруднений и настрочившего несколько псевдоисторических детективов, что там, где есть факты, загадкам — бой.[72]

In his version of the event, it is faithful Ruslan, a guard dog from Georgii Vladimov's 1979 eponymous novel *Vernyi Ruslan* (*Faithful Ruslan*), who incidentally kills Stalin.[73]

On the textual level 'trivialization' of the dissident attempts at faithful historical presentation is achieved through the implantation of snippets of these 'documents' directly into the chronicle.[74] Thus the titles of the first and last 'Books' of the chronicle — 'Kniga izgnaniia' (The Book of Exile) and 'Kniga poslaniia' (The Book of Embassy) — derive from a poem by Nina Berberova, a Russian émigré writer and poet:

> Я говорю: я не в изгнанье,
> Я не ищу земных путей,
> *Я не в изгнанье, я — в посланье,*
> Легко мне жить среди людей.[75]

As a result of this trans-contextualization, the original, which is meant to provide extratextual validation to Palisandr's memoir, is exposed as an equally artificial construct. In/validating his/story through intertextual, rather than extratextual evidence, Palisandr undermines the claims of any 'first-hand' account to exclusive authenticity and objectivity of perspective. Thus incorporating the title of Vasilii Grossman's post-Stalinist novel, *Vse techet* (*Everything Flows*), and switching from symbolic code to the lowly sphere of practical life, Sokolov questions its attempt at objective representation:

> За годы потянувшегося за тем безвременья и сменившей его эволюции из прохудившихся кранов нашей твердыни воды утекло — на редкость. Вот и сегодня, внаброс окрыляя себя крылаткой, паки и паки влачишься в Комендантскую башню живым меморандумом: '*Все течет!* Пришлите специалистов!' А комендант лебезит, заискивает, дескать, о да. Ваша Вечность, уже высылаем, уж выслали. Однако Улита все едет, и факт остается фактом: беспечности кремлевских водопроводчиков можно лишь позавидовать.[76]

Reconstructing the context, Sokolov replaces it with a text. Emsk is a jumble of Nikolai Gogol''s town 'N' and Omsk, a city in Western Siberia and Dostoevskii's place of exile. Arkhangelskoe, Palisandr's prison outside Emsk, features 'Balkonskii's oak tree'.[77] The name of the quasi-home of The Princess Romanova, Moulin de Saint-Loup, derives from Proust's *In Search of Lost Time*.

In his refusal to distinguish between historical fact and fiction, Sokolov suggests that both historiography and art unavoidably narrativize the past; we receive and know it already as a text. History is defined as a typically Kantian *Ding an sich*, filled with scrupulously dated but unknown and unknowable events. It is envisioned as a chain of people writing about these events and people writing about those who write, or about those who write about those who write:

> И все-таки в целом история есть типичная кантовская вещь в себе. Если не замечать известной апокалиптичности ее интонаций, если не апоплексичности их, то прежде всего отмечаешь тот неслучайный, быть может, факт, что она преисполнена скрупулезно датированных, но незнакомых и непознаваемых происшествий. Взятые по отдельности, они озадачивают; вкупе — обескураживают. [...] Я лично решил для себя полагать и могу поклясться, что история есть процесс непрестанной, хоть плавной, ломки. Одно неизменно сменяло другое, другое — третье, а пятое, как говорится, — десятое. И всегда были люди, народы, публично питавшие друг ко другу симпатию или неприязнь; а где-то поблизости всегда оказывались какие-то люди, писавшие касательно этих взаимоотношений; и не переводились люди, писавшие об этих писавших, а также писавшие о писавших насчет писавших.[78]

Constructed as a dialogue with the 'testaments' to the Soviet epoch, Palisandr's memoir offers its own portrayal of history — deliberately outlandish, sublime, and fiendishly idyllic:

> Вот — правительственный пикник в Нескучном; я сплю в коляске; Абакумов, сидя на корточках, раздувает угли для шашлыка; Ягода играет с Ежовым в шашки; Фрунзе с Якиром склонились над картой местности; Орджоникидзе откупоривает гурджаани. Я люблю это старое фото не только за то, что оно навевает мне детские грезы, но и за то, что кроны запечатленных на нем деревьев отбрасывают на траву пятнистую тень, и если забыться, то можно подумать, что действие происходит на леопардовых шкурах.[79]

In this quirky snapshot both the dissident and the official versions are exposed as fantastic. The idyllic picnic scene implodes as it is transported into a ridiculously foreign context, turning into kitsch and laying bare the absurdity of the official version of Soviet history (magnified by Sokolov's 'unreliable' narrator). The alleged first-handedness of the dissident version with its claims at authenticity and agonizing immediacy is also considerably tarnished once framed within Palisandr's idiosyncratic vision.

In this apology for 'Soviet reality' Sokolov's hero reconstructs the mechanism of sublimation. In familiarizing and embellishing the ugly and the frightening, he draws on the Freudian notion of the uncanny (*Unheimlich*), reversing the process. Through their transformation into members of the family, the ominous figures of Beriia, Stalin, and other members of the Soviet government are made intimate: homely (*Heimlich*). Such a transformation results in the uncanny effect produced through the tension between the readers' 'objective' knowledge of historical 'facts' and their subjective aestheticized representation. Soviet history becomes an artefact — a family album comprised of photographs taken on special happy occasions. It becomes a perspective.

Apart from a particular way of considering something, perspective is an artistic technique of representing an object or a person in correct relation — size and position — to other things in the picture. Working in a non-painterly medium, Palisandr resorts to a kind of ekphrasis, producing an illusion of depth and distance on the temporal level. As an object of representation, the Soviet period is framed by a wide temporal margin. Owing to the longevity and ubiquity of the chronicler, the document bears witness to history from the early Middle Ages to 2044, according to the epilogue. This chronological margin provides the author (real or stylized) with perspective: a meta-position that Bakhtin defined as 'outsideness', the basic formula of an aesthetically constructive attitude. Proposing his own criterion of truth, Sokolov's graphomaniac chronicler replaces ideology and chronology with a pan-aesthetic perspective as a method of perception and evaluation of the world:

> Я — хроникер текущего времени, Петр Федорович. Хронограф. И дабы запротоколировать его, не пренебрегаю никакими условностями. Вернее — искусствами. Сочиняю, рисую, слегка музицирую. Не чужд

и хореографии. Словом — артист, Петр Федорович, артист. Ничего не попишешь.⁸⁰

In adopting this aesthetic existential position Palisandr resembles the nineteenth century's surrogate for the aristocrat in matters of culture — the dandy. In Charles Baudelaire's definition, dandies

> have no other calling but to cultivate the idea of beauty in their persons, to satisfy their passions, to feel and to think. [...] Dandyism does not even consist, as many thoughtless people seem to believe, in an immoderate taste for the toilet and material elegance. [...] It is first and foremost the burning need to create for oneself a personal originality, bounded only by the limits of the proprieties. It is a kind of cult of the self which can nevertheless survive the pursuit of a happiness to be found in someone else — in woman, for example; which can even survive all that goes by in the name of illusions.⁸¹

Historically, a dandy is a man who places particular importance on physical appearance, refined language, and leisurely hobbies, pursued with the appearance of nonchalance in a cult of self. Palisandr's hyper-aesthetic stance, the exquisite refinement of his speech (in spite of the bawdy content, his memoir is devoid of any crude language), and his cultivation of style and of the sublime make him a veritable dandy. There are multiple references to the premises and expressions of dandyism in *Palisandriia*, from Sokolov's 'inversion' of *Lolita* (Humbert Humbert is, of course, a consummate aesthete) to references to Proust's novel (the figure of Saint-Loup is one of most striking evocations of a dandy in literature),⁸² to allusions to the dandy's love of fine art and wines:

> Хорошо, запершись ввечеру у себя в мезонине с бутылкою старого дебюсси, перебирать, ворошить персональные карточки, медленно наливаясь той самой, знакомой всякому собирателю, рыцарской скупостью и хмелея в грезах о новых сериях и раритетах.⁸³

In principle, there is no difference between Debussy, the composer, Alfred de Musset, the poet and novelist (presented in the novel as 'Albe de Musset' ('Альб де Мюссе'), wine enjoyed by Mazhorette while seducing a priest),⁸⁴ and some other French product of high culture — wine in this case — as long as it connotes something arcane and forbiddingly decadent, and is recognized as such. If we look beyond the semiotics, dandyism is a form of resistance to philistinism — 'poshlust' as Nabokov put it — lust for easy gratification, or an illusion thereof.

Palisandr's pseudo-dandyism draws on the aesthetic sensibility called Camp that appreciates an object for its bad taste and ironic value.⁸⁵ Or, as Susan Sontag defined it in her *Notes on Camp*: Camp is 'a good taste of bad taste'.⁸⁶ That is why, as Sontag argues, it is not so much an artistic trend in itself as 'an irrepressible, a virtually uncontrolled sensibility':⁸⁷ a capacity to consider the style of others. According to Sontag, in the postmodern age of white noise and mass culture ('epokha pobedonosnogo plebsa',[88] to use Palisandr's words) such a sensibility is the answer to the problem of aestheticism and authenticity. Making no distinction between the unique object and the mass-produced object, 'the connoisseur of Camp' revels in 'the coarsest, commonest pleasures, in the arts of the masses'.[89]

> Как портретист П. [Palisandr] не жаловал мелкие планы — хотелось монументального, броского. Он возлюбил ниспускаться обрывистыми берегами некоторых водоемов к полоскальным сооружениям и создавать групповые портреты прачек, работающих в самых непритязательных позах. Судьбы простонародья с его эстетикой неэстетичного, с грубоватыми шутками — волновали всемерно. А как пейзажист — разрабатывал темы осени: мотивы сентябрьских шквалов, октябрьской индевелости и ноябрьского первоснежья, характеризующегося изысканной хрупкостью очертаний и черт.[90]

Among the examples of Camp Sontag lists art nouveau with its fusion of the organic and the artificial — light fixtures as plants and rooms as grottoes — and pre-Raphaelite painting and poetry with their focus on androgyny. In fact, the androgyne is argued to be one of the most typical expressions of Camp sensibility as the epitome of marginality.[91] Philip Core in his book on Camp, whose title I borrowed as a part of this chapter's name,[92] raises the question of the difficulty of defining Camp. Instead he proposes to explain it through its expressions: people, film, art, and so on. Sokolov's protagonist could have easily made Core's list of Camp objects/subjects: part plant, part human androgyne, a consummate aesthete, a sexual idol, Stalin's darling and Catherine the Great's lover, Palisandr is a direct descendant of historical 'aristocracy', among whom are the likes of Mary Stuart, Winston Churchill, Grigorii Rasputin, and Lavrentii Beriia.

The concept of Camp is closely related to Kitsch, an artistic practice that, in order to ennoble itself and its consumer, imitates the high art exhibited in the museums.[93] The label Kitsch has been applied to Socialist realism due to its 'validating' itself by quoting classical art and superimposing its form on the proletarian subject. Boris Grois wrote about the totalitarian art of the Stalin period, which he compared to an icon, that it is read by the audience on the basis of the appropriate codes rather than its artistic value.[94] Indeed, this substitution of the aesthetic category for the ethical category, according to Herman Broch, constitutes the essence of Kitsch.[95] This division into quasi-art, identified with Kitsch as something intended to arouse an emotional effect rather than permit disinterested contemplation, and art proper comes from Schopenhauer.[96] In his *The World as Will and Representation* Schopenhauer outlines the difference between the sublime and the charming/attractive. While the former invites pure contemplation, the latter stimulates the consumer's senses:

Since opposites throw light on each other, it may be here in place to remark that the real opposite of the sublime is something that is not at first sight recognized as such, namely the *charming* or *attractive*. By this I understand that which excites the will by directly presenting it to satisfaction, fulfilment. The feeling of the sublime arises from the fact that something positively unfavourable to the will becomes the object of pure contemplation. This contemplation is then maintained only by a constant turning away from the will and exaltation above its interests; and this constitutes the sublimity of the disposition. On the other hand, the charming or attractive draws the beholder down from pure contemplation, demanded by every apprehension of the beautiful, since it necessarily stirs his will by objects that directly appeal to it. Thus the beholder no longer remains the pure subject of knowing, but becomes the needy and dependent subject of willing. [...] In historical painting and in sculpture the charming consists in nude figures, the position, semi-drapery, and whole treatment of which are calculated to excite the lustful feelings in the beholder. Purely aesthetical contemplation is at once abolished, and the purpose of art is thus defeated.[97]

Camp has been defined as an 'experience of kitsch of someone who knows that what he is seeing is kitsch'.[98] As a form of appreciation of Kitsch, Camp differs from it precisely in that it introduces a degree of neutrality towards content: an attitude of ethico-aesthetic detachment. Unlike Kitsch, Camp is self-conscious and ironic. While Kitsch attempts to present the frivolous as serious, Camp transforms the serious into the frivolous. Such elevation of gravity is one of the major mechanisms in *Palisandriia*. It is usually achieved through the contamination of solemnity and pathos with erotic and scatological motifs. For instance, the pathos of the Romantic notion of love is made grotesque and pathetic through the prism of a gerontophiliac obsession. Generally, eroticism, bordering on pornography, is used to undermine any claims of seriousness. It is achieved through a deconstruction — realization — of the myth of Oedipus, which serves as the model for the link between sexual domination and political power, extensively explored in *Palisandriia* and in sots-art as a whole. It typically takes the form of Kitsch, associated with the late nineteenth-century trend known as *art pompier* with its voluptuous nudes, or through the invocation of the Freudian unconscious.[99]

As was mentioned earlier in connection with sublimation and the uncanny, Freud makes a few appearances in *Palisandriia*. One of the illuminating examples of this presence is Sokolov's positing of philosophical concepts — Nietzsche in this case — in a Freudian context: Palisandr's position as the convent's key master, the sexual connotations of which were mentioned earlier, is defined as 'a symbol of secret power and the will to power':

'Вы — ключник, любезнейший, осознайте. Вы — по древней традиции — есть лицо, начальствующее над всеми монастырскими скважинами. Причем не только, и даже не столько в прямом, сколько, знаете ли, в переносном смысле'. Жест, которым Оле проиллюстрировал свою мысль, был малоприличен. И граф продолжал: 'Да, ваша должность двусмысленна, тем и трудна, я знаю. Зато она символична, почетна. Зато вы служите не каким-нибудь клерком на побегушках вроде любого из нас, неудачников, а вы служите символом сокровенной власти и воли к ней.'[100]

The apotheosis of the libidinal corruption of power is the hero's decision to assassinate Brezhnev as an outcome of the politics of desire, rather than politics proper. 'Hired' by Andropov to do away with the current ruler Brezhnev, Palisandr, after a long hesitation, resolves to undertake the challenge in a fit of jealousy: Brezhnev is a new lover of his Shaganeh. The reduction of political power to sexual drive is also achieved through the de-stabilization of the conventional linguistic and contextual forms as in the episode of Beriia's suicide:

> Часовой содрогнулся и конвульсивно отдал часовщику последнюю честь.
> 'Отдыхайте', — махнул рукою Лаврентий. Доброта генерал-генерала не знала мер никогда, и войска любили его, как умели.[101]

The ironic effect stems from the semantic ambiguity of the expression — 'otdat' posledniuiu chest'' — which literally signifies 'to give the last salute/honour'. Placing an adjective 'posledniaia' (last) in the set phrase 'otdat' chest'' (to give a military salute), Sokolov collapses the military form with the romantic pathetic expression 'poteriat' posledniu chest'' (to lose one's honour — often by yielding to sexual advances). The double-entendre effect is strengthened by the image of the guard's convulsing body and the troops that loved Beriia as best they could.

Such 'eroticization of power' is ubiquitous in *Palisandriia* and is employed not only because of its ability to scandalize. It also plays a 'compensatory' role, thus 'fulfilling' one of the major premises of Socialist realism, as argued by Komar and Melamid:

> Эротика выполняет также своеобразную иронически-компенсаторную функцию, доводящую до воображаемого апогея цели и задачи самого метода социалистического реализма, призванного, по замыслу великих, побуждать зрителя к доблестному выполнению отображаемых в монументальных полотнах трудовых, героических и прочих действий и, следовательно, заключающего в себе, по мнению Комара и Меламида, черты единственного побуждающего, то есть порнографического жанра. Повышенная 'чувственность' их стиля как будто бы и компенсирует эту недореализованную незыблемым творческим методом 'призывную' функцию.[102]

Modelling his protagonist on 'the Holy of Holies of socialist realism',[103] the Soviet positive hero, Sokolov 'realizes' its potential by shifting the focus from ethical goals to the aesthetic domain, epitomized by erotic love. Palisandr is a Stakhanovite of the labour of love. His success with women reduces the pursuits of Don Juan (who takes the form of a sixteenth-century playwright, Lope de Vega in another nod to Freud and his analogy between writing and sex)[104] to embarrassment.[105]

Sokolov's use of 'faction' is another way to lift the veil of solemnity. His 'historical' characters constitute a collage of stereotypes and urban myths, specially chosen for their absurdity. Thus the image of Catherine the Great in *Palisandriia* derives from one of the urban myths about the Empress's death. In a mixture of the legend and Tolstoy's *Kholstomer* (*Yard-Stick*), Palisandr, who appears as the Empress's equine lover, incidentally and gruesomely causes her death.[106] The name and biography of Shaganeh derive from Sergei Esenin's *Persidskie motivy* (*Persian Themes*), whose image is implicitly invoked in the account of her story.[107] Beriia's stereotype is embodied in the figure of the executioner Larry (Lawrence) Dahlberg, Palisandr's (and Beriia's) fictitious ancestor. Lawrence's bloody occupation reflects Lavrentii's infamous activities, saucily captured in various 'confessional' chronicles, such as Anton Antonov-Ovseenko's *Kariera palacha* (*Executioner's Career*).[108] Stalin, a benevolent and fatherly figure before death, is deified after it, as suggested by Beriia's entreaty, echoing Jesus on the cross: 'Ах, Иосиф, Иосиф, зачем ты оставил нас, генацвале' ('Oh, Joseph, dear Joseph, why has thou forsaken us?').[109] Naturally, the chief mythical figure of the chronicle is the chronicler himself. Spanning the whole array of myths from the primordial forces to the modern positive hero, Palisandr is myth personified:

> А вот для Вас, для Биографа, я — в силу обратности исторической перспективы — несравненно выше любого меня, пусть даже и вознесенного, мрамореющего уже при жизни. Я — миф. И Вы творите его.[110]

One of the major underlying myths of his creation is the myth of Androgyne. While the clues are dropped throughout the narrative, the readers remain none the wiser until the very end (appreciating all the double entendres post factum). Palisandr's androgyny is revealed by, naturally, 'Carl Jung', a doctor at Mazhorette's den.[111] The Jungian theme is developed through the presentation of the anima and animus division. It emerges in Palisandr's brotherly love for an adolescent beggar girl, encountered on the steps of St Basil's Cathedral in Moscow. This Holy Fool figure is identified with Russia as remembered by the hero in his exile. The irony and artifice of this identification are manifest in the literary juxtapositions drawn by Palisandr:

> Россия же — та неизбывна. И вместе с тем никогда я не звало ее ни мамашей, ни бабушкой или там теткой. И не казалась мне родина ни вечерней звездой, ни полдневной в бору кукушкой, ни ранней — ни

свет ни заря — молошницей, каковою она являлась джойсовскому студиозусу в башне на берегу бурнопенного моря Гиннес; она мне всегда рисовалась скуластой болезненной нищенкой с паперти храма Святого Василия, рахитичным подростком с матовыми и подсвеченными светом свечи щеками, с высоким костистым челом и в чьих-то обносках. [...] И пусть мы жили по разные стороны крепостной стены, с годами наша приязнь же крепла, становилась возвышенней и нежней, но в силу моей посвященности женщинам пожилым могла быть лишь платонической. Назовите ее любовью издалека, и Вы нисколько не ошибетесь, ибо до самого отъезда дерзающего лица в послание мы так и не сблизились, не обмолвились словом. А там, в послании, под влиянием похождений во мне — будто старая рана — открылась по ней ностальгия.[112]

Palisandr names her 'Rek', a name that can be traced to the expression 'imiarek': a generic term used in official documents to designate a blank space for a name ('such and such' or 'so and so'). Another interpretation may be connected with 'rech" — speech — which derives from the stem 'rek'.[113] The latter reading surfaces in Palisandr's musings on his loss and their mutual non-being, at least for one another. However, they go on living eternally in the 'region of legends and tales':

> И ты тоже не плачь обо мне, Россия. Не плачь, ведь тебя больше нету. Как и меня. Нас нету. Мы перешли. Отболели. И все-таки — да здравствуем мы, вечно сущие в области легенд и преданий, мы, обреченные вечной разлуке брат и сестра.[114]

In Sokolov, the two halves of the whole are never destined to meet: like Palisandr and his reflections, they do not recognize one another as time has irrevocably changed their features:

> О любовное догробовое томление по девочке Рек, с которой мы более никогда не виделись. Или же — виделись, но не узнали друг друга, поскольку оба неузнаваемо постарели. О старость! Даже и ты отлетела. И — обратите внимание! — все, что случилось, случилось напрасно и зря. А пробрешь — зияла, а жизнь — отболела.[115]

All that remains is the abyss of time and history, whose presence is marked by the grapheme 'o'. Palisandr's internalization of the abyss emerges in his androgynous name: Palisandro — the ending 'o' in Russian nouns typically signifying the neuter gender. The added irony of the name stems from its alleged ordinariness: in Italian and Spanish 'o' is a masculine ending. Thus the symbolic discourse is constantly undermined by the focus on the conspicuously sexual aspect of androgyny.

Mircea Eliade associated such concern with physiology with decadence and viewed it as the 'degradation of the symbol': 'when the mind is no longer capable of perceiving the metaphysical significance of a symbol, it is understood at the levels which become increasingly coarse'.[116] With Sokolov the physiological is indistinguishable from the metaphysical: one is the reverse side of the other. *Coincidentia oppositorum*, symbolized by androgyny, finds an ironic expression in Palisandr's passion for muddy baths, which conceals not only his 'condition', but also where purification equals defilement. The union of the opposites culminates in the grotesque merging of love and death, practised by Sokolov's protagonist. Death is merely 'coitus with Eternity', according to Palisandr: 'Смерти нет, господин Биограф; но существует отдохновенье в тиши залетейских рощ, есть соитие с Вечностью, с Забытьем в образе бедной няни'.[117] The embodiment of this eternal rest on the other side of Lethe, Palisandr's nurse Agrippa, seals the image of death as incestuous act. Eternally undergoing his rite of (maternal) passage, the hero locks death and birth together. The blurred monotony of existence is presented as an endless chain of reincarnations, where various circumstances and contexts finally merge into a slow-motion *déjà vu*:

> Итак, сминая бегонии луга, я все бегу навстречу ее экипажу: теперь — и тогда — и завтра — и всякий раз, как в том возникает необходимость — в любом из человеческих воплощений моих — неукоснительно, всенепременно — я все бегу. И с каждым разом предшествующая 'Мажорет' все менее отличается от последующей, а форейтор — все менее от форейтора, бег — от бега, и луг — от луга, и я — от я. И однажды наступит час, когда все многократно воспроизведенные дежавю со всеми их вариациями сольются за глубиной перспективы в единое ужебыло. И я не смогу себе дать отчета, в каком из бытии моих я бегу вот сейчас, вот сию минуту, и что такое сия минута, и к чему здесь эти бегонии, и при чем тут — а если при чем, то кто — кто этот некто, обозначаемый с Вашего позволения буквой я. Хотя, если честно, я не способен в том отчитаться уже и нынче, и тем не менее все бегу и бегу.[118]

One of the striking images of the eternal return that haunts the novel is the evocation of the genesis of the Soviet utopia:

> Уже подъезжая к вокзалу, на крыше которого колыхался плакат 'Дальберг — совесть нашего человечества', продиктовало последний тезис: 'Культ моей личности всячески пресекать'. И вышло на крытый перрон, где оркестры шумели 'Аве Марию', ставшую позже державным гимном.
> Встречавшее в полном составе Временное правительство — трепетало. Я пристально поздоровалось.
> В крепость ехали по Тверской, ныне проспект Кербабаева. Заложив руки за спину и мерно покачиваясь с носков на пятки, я стояло в открытом авто и экспромтом бросало на ветер речь 'К моему народу'.
> [...]
> 'Да здравствует!' — кричали в ответ и устилали дорогу любезными

моей сердцевине иерихонскими розами. А? Вы помните? И повсюду — по улицам, закоулкам и площадям — по всему ненаглядному Эмску — по всей Москве — штопорили метельные крутни.¹¹⁹

Parodic references to the writing of the theses and the Provisional Government (Lenin's arrival at the Finland Station in Petrograd and his 'April' theses), the denunciation of the personality cult (Stalin and Khrushchev), and the recreation of the general aura of the pre-/post-revolutionary atmosphere produce the effect of *déjà vu*. The uncanny feeling is intensified by the invocation, in the last paragraph, of Aleksandr Blok's revolutionary poem, *Dvenadtsat'* (*The Twelve*), with its images of the snow storm and the figure of Christ crowned with a halo of roses.¹²⁰

This re-enactment of the creation of the Soviet utopia sounds like a warning. In a letter to Don Johnson, Sokolov described his work, when still in gestation, as 'a philosophico-futurological novel with features of the political pamphlet'.¹²¹ Like a few other 'futurological' texts, considered eccentric at the time of their writing and publication, *Palisandriia* turned out to be visionary. Despite the idiosyncrasy of its presentation Palisandr's chronicle, as Petr Vail' and Aleksandr Genis noted, is not far off the actual phantasmagoria of Soviet history.¹²² It also anticipated the collapse of the Soviet regime and the avalanche of changes taking place in the 1990s and 2000s in the former Soviet Union. The novel's reflection of the ensuing (or an attempt at) return of totalitarian rule is equally uncanny in view of current developments: the initial of Sokolov's hero-ruler, shortened by the end of the novel to P., is suggestively prophetic.¹²³

Olga Matich argued that Sokolov's protagonist represents a realization of the utopia: unable to procreate, he reconciles all the opposites.¹²⁴ Holding a similar view, Grois designated Palisandr 'the quintessential postmodernist hero', viewing him as the embodiment of postmodernist universalism and the blurring of differences:

> Палисандр Дальберг в этом отношении — истинный герой постмодерного времени. Модернизм определяется операцией вычитания, постмодернизм — это эпоха сложения, умножения и возведения в степень. [...] Грани между подлинным и неподлинным, своим и чужим, высоким искусством и китчем, индивидуальным и массовым стерлись. Все оказалось в ситуации семейного сходства, в родстве. Поэтому герой постмодернистского времени начал, в отличие от непрерывно ужимавшегося героя авангарда, неудержимо разрастаться в пространстве и времени.¹²⁵

Grois argues that *Palisandriia* demonstrates the illusion of pluralism, revealing it as another ideological construct, used as a path for a utopian escape through a 'negative utopia'.¹²⁶ Plato's ideal androgynous being turns into a monstrous hybrid: a grotesque realization of a utopia, in which all the established polarities enter into the state of confusion. Or a dialogue, which some read in the Chekhovian and others in the Bakhtinian key, wherein utterances either cancel or enrich one another.

The Oedipal individualist of the modernist era is transformed into a postmodernist omnivorous, narcissistic monster. Having swallowed many a myth and cultural language, Palisandr is regurgitating them in graphomaniac frenzy — literally:

> Тогда автор привстало на цыпочки. И, подавшись еще немного вперед, перевесилось и вообразило ее себе во всех ее пошлостях, безобразиях и гнойниках, как если бы это была не жизнь, а какая-то прокаженная сифилитичка, продажная тротуарная дрянь, которую оно когда-то боготворило. Его передернуло. Борт души накренился. О равновесие, инстинктивно робея утратить тебя самым необратимым образом, оно держалось одною рукой за перила, меж тем как иною нащупывало неразличимые в свете перегоревшей лампочки спекшиеся уста свои. Нащупав, оно разомкнуло их. Разъяло и челюсти. *И привычным движеньем бывалого ключника сунуло в разверстую скважину рта ключ двуперстия.*
> Автора вырвало.[127]

Larissa Rudova interprets this obscene gesture as a symbol of disillusionment. Sokolov's hero is an artist abandoned in the vacuum of post-history, where authenticity or creation is no longer possible.[128] Despite a certain degree of disenchantment communicated in the passage, its finale is a creative act in disguise. It is a variation on ejaculation, as suggested by the familiar (highlighted) references to keys, orifices, and the stairwell. For Palisandr, this post-historical timelessness, in which all historical and mythical figures — which amount to the same thing in *Palisandriia* — coexist, is the time to 'dare and create' ('derzat' i tvorit'').[129]

Such 'aesthetics of the obscene' with the focus on perversion, death, excrement, rubbish — things of the end — is a major element of Russian postmodern culture of the 1980–90s. Epshtein designated this type of art 'arrière-garde', nominating Sokolov as its 'mentor'.[130] It is described as an 'art of amorphousness — not of exacting experimentation, but of an all-encompassing and accepting bottom, the last gurgling crater into which the overdone excrements of the earlier majestic forms and grandiose ideas are to fall'.[131] Indeed, *Palisandriia*'s preoccupation with geronto-necrophilia and scatology attest to it. One of the compelling realizations of Epshtein's definition of 'arrière-garde' is the episode ironically entitled 'Casus Cactus' — with all the implications of the stem 'cac'.[132]

As a punishment for an insignificant breach of the rules established by the cruel Mazhorette at the Saint-Loup, Palisandr is locked in a tower and force-fed for several days on end with pea soup. As a result of this exacting diet and the absence of sanitary facilities in the medieval structure, he relieves himself through an embrasure onto the flowerbed (of cacti), once cultivated by his would-be Grandmother, Anastasiia Romanova. The latter stands for both Monarchy and pre-Revolutionary Russian culture, which Palisandr, embarking on his 'embassy' to the West, is to 'inherit' and, evidently, to restore. This process is presented as an intended adoption of Palisandr by the Princess and her husband, Baron Chavchavadze-Ogly. Given the prospective grandson's sexual preferences, the anticipation is filled with excitement, the nature of which is alluded in Palisandr's means of transport to Romanova's estate: an air balloon made of a giant condom.

In his discussion of the arrière-garde, Epshtein argues that, within its aesthetics of scatology, forms that are overdue and decaying make up the fertilizer of the arrière-garde (also aptly referred to as the 'rear guard'), permitting its renewal.[132] In what is presented as the desecration of the past, Palisandr performs an act of renewal, merging, as always in Sokolov, the symbolic with the literal, the visceral. It is the closest he gets to the sacrifice — a defence mechanism of an organism/culture/nation against the abject. The paradox of the abject is that it comes from inside. Sacrifice allows it to be expelled from the inner boundaries and posited as an object, the other, non-I. By stepping outside and attaining a meta-historical, -cultural, -sexual and meta-human position, Palisandr takes on the role of the abject. He becomes the ultimate scapegoat, the reflecting (cess)pool of his context and its various ambitions, from Stalinist to dissident to postmodern. Reiterating their images and contradictions, he discloses their likeness and the inevitability of repetition, illuminated by the imagery of the eternal return.

As the de-Stalinization period demonstrated, it proved impossible to break free from Stalin and the Soviet legacy without reiterating them in one way or another. *Palisandriia* is a reflection on the ethical and aesthetic situation engendered by the disappearance of the historical referent. It demonstrates how Soviet history became an abject, expelled and manipulated through incarnation/verbalization. It also reminds us that, in fact, there is nothing outside this verbalization. In one way or another, the real has to be mediated in order for it to be consciously experienced. It is not a negation of the real or the past, but recognition that historical reality is discursive reality: we receive and know it already as a text — the only artefact remaining. Hence the 'ultimate Mandelshtamian sincerity' ('posledniia mandel'shtamovskaia priamota') of Palisandr's memoir,[133] which lies in its derivativeness from Mandel'shtam and myriad other texts. In its fusing of chronicle with memoir, turning context into text, *Palisandriia* reveals a common denominator of art, history, psychology, and ideology. Sharing the same pool of signs, images, and schemas, they constitute a signifying system which is used to give meaning to the past.

Perhaps *Palisandriia* should not be read as an object of intellection, but as a series of intuitions. These intuitions are means to grasp the real, which manifests itself through them. Since intuitions — too intimate and immediate — cannot be communicated without mediation, Sokolov works with their reflections. Thus his text does not convey ideas but summons images reflecting these intuitions.

There is no space or time without a point of reference. There is no history or past without mediation. Sokolov's chronicler subjectivizes history, time, and space, positioning his own person as the only frame of reference, the ultimate mediator, and thus reaches degree zero where no concept/idea survives. By deconstructing the original myth, the appropriation of this myth, and the ensuing deconstruction of this appropriation, *Palisandriia* transcends the loss, emerging as a pure intuition of the 'man's situation', within or without history: an artistic lie that spills the truth.

Notes to Chapter 3

1. Philip Core, *Camp: The Lie That Tells the Truth* (hereafter, 'Core'), (London: Plexus, 1984), p. 15.
2. Abram Tertz, 'Chto takoe sotsialisticheskii realizm?', in *Fantasticheskii mir Abrama Tertza* (Paris: Mezhdunarodnoe literaturnoe sodruzhestvo, 1967), pp. 401–46 (p. 446).
3. Sasha Sokolov, *Palisandriia* (hereafter 'Palisandriia') (St Petersburg: Symposium, 2004), p. 26.
4. Ibid., p. 381.
5. Ibid., p. 10.
6. 'А когда уставал, надевал очки с фиолетовой оптикой — для слепых, называемые им гомерическими'. Ibid., p. 359.
7. Ibid., pp. 366–67.
8. As argued by Katerina Clark, the trope of the 'Great Family' constituted the essence of Socialist realism: its master plot. Within this scheme Soviet leaders became 'fathers' (with Stalin as the patriarch), the national heroes were model 'sons', and the state is a 'family' or 'tribe'. As a metaphor for society, it provided the state with a set of symbols for legitimizing its increasingly hierarchical structure by endowing it with a sacred 'origin', and ensured the loyalty of its citizens. See Katerina Clark, *The Soviet Novel: History as Ritual* (hereafter 'Clark') (Bloomington and Indianapolis: Indiana University Press, 2000), pp. 114–30.
9. Abram Tertz, 'On Socialist Realism', in *The Trial Begins and On Socialist Realism*, trans. by George Dennis (hereafter 'Tertz') (Berkeley and Los Angeles: University of California Press, 1982), pp. 127–219 (p. 215).
10. Vitalii Komar and Aleksandr Milamid, a manuscript (1989), quoted in Olga Kholmogorova, *Sots-art* (hereafter 'Kholmogorova Sots-art') (Moscow: Galart, 1994), not paginated.
11. Kholmogorova Sots-art, n.p.
12. Boris Grois, *The Total Art of Stalinism: Avant-garde, Aesthetic Dictatorship, and Beyond* (hereafter 'Grois Stalinism'), trans. by Charles Rougle (Princeton: Princeton University Press, 1992), pp. 92–95.
13. One of the major contradictions of Socialist realism is its appropriation of the classical

forms and their superimposition on the proletarian subject, which, in Siniavskii's words, resulted in an 'unnatural liaison [that] produced monsters'. See Tertz, p. 213.
14. Nancy Condee, 'Sot-Art, Conceptualism, and Russian Postmodernism: An Introduction', in *Endquote: Sots-Art Literature and Soviet Grand Style* (hereafter 'Endquote'), ed. by Marina Balina, Nancy Condee, and Evgenii Dobrenko (Evanston, IL: Northwestern University Press, 2000), pp. vii–xx (p. xi); Karen Ryan, 'Sokolov's *Palisandriya*: The Art of History' (hereafter 'Ryan'), in *Twentieth-Century Russian Literature: Selected Papers from the Fifth World Congress of Central and East European Studies, Warsaw 1995*, ed. by Karen L. Ryan, Barry P. Scherr, and Ronald J. Hill (London: Macmillan, 2000), pp. 215–27 (pp. 218–19); Alexander Zholkovsky,'The Stylistic Roots of Palisandriia' (hereafter, 'Zholkovsky Roots'), *Canadian-American Slavic Studies*, 21 (1987), 369–400 (pp. 380–81).
15. Zholkovsky Roots, pp. 380–90.
16. Ibid.
17. Clark, pp. 130–31.
18. Ibid., p. 265.
19. Ibid., pp. 134–35.
20. Palisandriia, p. 451. In Michael Heim's translation the subtitle reads: 'Incest Behind the Kremlin Walls: Note of a Graphomaniac'.
21. Olga Matich, 'Sasha Sokolov's *Palisandriia*: History and Myth' (hereafter 'Matich Russian Review'), *The Russian Review*, 45 (1985), 415–26 (p. 419).
22. Mikhail Epshtein, *After the Future: The Paradoxes of Postmodernism and Contemporary Russian Culture* (hereafter 'After Future'), trans. by Anesa Miller-Pogacar (Amherst, MA: University of Massachusetts Press, 1995), p. 179. The notion of the Oedipus complex as ideological construct was developed in Gilles Deleuze and Félix Guattari, *Anti-Oedipus: Capitalism and Schizophrenia*, trans. by Robert Hurley, Mark Seem, and Helen R. Lane (London: Continuum, 2004), pp. 111–17.
23. After Future, pp. 179–80.
24. Palisandriia, p. 22.
25. Ibid., p. 39.
26. Ibid., pp. 143, 199. Describing their first night of passion with Shaganeh, Palisandr envisions himself as the Tiber bothers (p. 143).
27. Michael Grant, *Roman Myths* (London: Weidenfeld and Nicolson, 1971), pp. 99–106.
28. Ryan, pp. 222–24; Matich Russian Review, p. 419.
29. Later Greeks fused the two into the 'Father Time' with his 'relentless sickle'. See Robert Graves, *The Greek Myths* (hereafter 'The Greek Myths') (London: Penguin Books, 1992), pp. 31–38 (p. 38).
30. Palisandriia, p. 23.
31. Nikolai Fedorov, 'Filosofiia obshchego dela', in *Sochineniia*, 3 vols (Moscow: Akademiia Nauk, Institut filosofii, 1982), I, 53–503.
32. Boris Groys, *Ilya Kabakov: The Man Who Flew into Space from his Apartment* (London: Afterall Books, 2006), pp. 13–19.
33. Palisandriia, pp. 21, 178.
34. Palisandriia, p. 50.
35. Johann Wolfgang von Goethe, *Faust*, 2 vols, trans. by David Luke (hereafter 'Faust') (Oxford and New York: Oxford University Press, 1994), II, 296.
36. Faust, pp. 221–24.
37. See Palisandriia, pp. 41–42.
38. There is an overt reference to this aspect of Gogol''s novella in Palisandriia, p. 164.
39. Palisandriia, p. 162.
40. Palisandriia, pp. 356–59.

41. D. Barton Johnson, 'Saša Sokolov's Palisandrija' (hereafter 'Johnson Palisandrija'), *Slavic and East European Journal*, 30 (1986), 389–403 (p. 396).
42. The irony of the toponym — Saint-Loup is a character of Marcel Proust's *In Search of Lost Time* — as a locus of 'time regained' is developed through an evocation of Proust's title (*V poiskakh utrachennogo vremeni*, in the Russian translation): 'Мы живем в восхитительные века, — витийствовал он. — *Непрестанно ведутся поиски утраченного времени*, ищутся и находятся новые манускрипты, скрижали, бесценные факты отшумевших эпох!'. Palisandriia, pp. 344–45.
43. Ibid., pp. 355–56.
44. Ibid., pp. 24, 460–61.
45. The same graphème appears in Palisandr's saucy encounter with Mme Brezhneva: Palisandriia, pp. 280–81. Also, upon the revelation of his androgyny, the hero's name acquires an 'o' at the end, typical of a neuter Russian noun: Palisandro.
46. Palisandriia, pp. 373–74.
47. Ibid., pp. 15–19.
48. Ibid., p. 41.
49. There could be a link with Urania, the muse of Astronomy, as well as the myth of Uranos and the act of non-birth by being pushed back into the mother.
50. Palisandriia, p. 358, italics mine.
51. Ibid., p. 95.
52. Erich Neumann, *The Origins and History of Consciousness* (hereafter 'Neumann') (London: Karnac Books, 1989), pp. 298–300.
53. 'Toothed vagina'. Erich Neumann defines it as the archetype of the 'Terrible Mother', a maddening enchantress, alluring, destructive, and devouring. Neumann, p. 322.
54. Johnson views Sokolov's use of the image of Matrioshka, in which 'all of the nested generations are intimately concurrent', as a metaphor for conflation of time. See D. Barton Johnson, 'Sasha Sokolov's Twilight Cosmos: Themes and Motifs' (hereafter 'Johnson Slavic Review'), *Slavic Review*, 45 (1986), 639–49 (p. 642).
55. Palisandriia, p. 369.
56. Ibid., p. 369.
57. Ibid., pp. 282, 451, 229–30, 122, 277–80.
58. Ibid., pp. 169–73.
59. Ibid., pp. 27 and 413.
60. Ibid., p. 408.
61. 'Majorette' is the name for a baton-twirler, traditionally associated with a marching band. An auxiliary of the drum major (hence 'Majorette') responsible for conducting the band, she represents a visual component of the performance. The military pomp associated with this word, and the visual spectacle (with its underlying drive to incite) offered by the majorette's role, may have to do with Sokolov's choice of the name.
62. See Johnson Slavic Review, p. 644; Grois Stalinism, p. 77.
63. Palisandriia, pp. 282–83.
64. A similar image is used in his description of history as a fennel-shaped vortex (krugovert' rokovaia), Palisandriia, p. 273.
65. Palisandriia, p. 424.
66. See also Sasha Sokolov, 'Palisandre — c'est moi?', in *Trevozhnaia kukolka* (St Petersburg: Azbuka-klassika, 2007), pp. 48–62 (p. 62).
67. Palisandriia, pp. 366–67.
68. Matich Russian Review, p. 419; Ryan, p. 220.
69. See Mark Lipovetskii, *Paralogii: Transformatsiia (post)modernistskogo diskursa v kul'ture 1920–2000-h godov* (Moscow: Novoe literaturnoe obozrenie, 2008).

70. Olga Matich, 'Sasha Sokolov and his Literary Context' (hereafter 'Matich Slavic Studies'), *Canadian-American Slavic Studies*, 21 (1987), 301–19 (p. 315).
71. Ibid., pp. 118–19.
72. ibid., p. 124.
73. Ibid., pp. 125–31.
74. A thorough analysis of this technique has been produced by Aleksandr Zholkovsky in his study of *Palisandriia*'s intertextual influence in Zholkovsky Roots, p. 372.
75. Nina Berberova, 'Liricheskaia poema', in *Bez zakata; Malen'kaia devochka; Rasskazy; Stikhi (1924–26)* (Moscow: Izdatel'stvo imeni Sabashnikovykh, 1999), pp. 333–41 (p. 341), italics mine.
76. Palisandriia, p. 21, italics mine.
77. Ibid., p. 241.
78. Ibid., pp. 30–31.
79. Ibid., p. 250.
80. Ibid., p. 357.
81. Charles Baudelaire, 'The Painter of Modern Life', in *The Painter of Modern Life and Other Essays* (hereafter 'Baudelaire'), trans. and ed. by Jonathan Mayne (London: Phaidon, 1995), pp. 1–41 (p. 27).
82. See Marcel Proust, 'Within a Budding Grove', in *Remembrance of Things Past*, 12 vols, trans. by C. K. Scott Moncrieff (London: Chatto & Windus, 1961), IV, pp. 36–66.
83. Palisandriia, p. 454.
84. Ibid., p. 399.
85. OED defines Camp as 'ostentatiously and extravagantly effeminate; deliberately theatrical in style or behaviour'.
86. Susan Sontag, 'Notes on "Camp"', in *Against Interpretation and Other Essays* (hereafter 'Sontag') (London: Penguin Classics, 2009), pp. 275–92 (p. 291).
87. Sontag, p. 284.
88. Palisandriia, p. 413.
89. Sontag, p. 289.
90. Palisandriia, p. 185.
91. Sontag, p. 279.
92. Core borrowed the phrase from Jean Cocteau, who described himself as 'a lie that tells the truth'. Cocteau is also an author of a deceptive autobiography that is a definition of Camp, according to Core. See Core, p. 9.
93. The etymology of the word 'kitsch' may stem from the verb *kitschen* — from a dialect of Mecklenburg — meaning 'to make furniture look antique'. Another meaning is 'to collect mud from the street', while there is also the verb *verkitschen*: 'to sell cheaply'.) According to some sources the term 'kitsch' derives from the word 'sketch': in the second half of the nineteenth century tourists in Munich wishing to buy a cheap picture asked for a sketch. This gave rise to the term used to mean vulgar trash produced for purchases eager for facile 'aesthetic' experiences. See Umberto Eco, *On Ugliness*, trans. by Alastair McEwen (hereafter 'On Ugliness') (London: Harvill Secker, 2007), p. 394.
94. Grois argues that '[t]o the audience of the Stalin period it offered the traditional and truly aesthetic experience of terror, since an incorrect coding or decoding could mean death' (Grois Stalinism, pp. 55–56). The question remains whether the terror felt by the spectator can be categorized as an aesthetic experience. It seems that fear, just as devotion and attraction, belongs to the psychological/ethical rather than aesthetic category, which is meant to be an act of pure contemplation: detached and equanimous. The arousal of either negative or positive affect triggers the same effect: the artistic intuition is abused for ideological — ethical — sensual — ends. Aesthetics becomes the means rather than the end.

95. Hermann Broch, 'The Technique of 'Effect'', in *Kitsch*, referred to in On Ugliness, pp. 403–06.
96. Ibid., p. 400.
97. Arthur Schopenhauer, 'The Representation Independent of the Principle of Sufficient Reason: The Platonic Idea: The Object of Art', in *The World as Will and Representation*, 2 vols, trans. by E. F. Payne (New York: Dover Publications, 1969), I, Book 3, pp. 167–267 (pp. 207–08), italics in the original.
98. On Ugliness, p. 411.
99. As Olga Kholmogorova writes in her study of sots-art: 'Так, подобно шоку возникает в [...] соц-арте постоянный эротический фон, подаваемый то в виде салонно-академической пышнотелости, то в духе фрейдийской психологии бессознательного, считавшей сексуально-физиологические мотивы завуалированной доминантой характера отдельных личностей и целых исторических эпох.' See Kholmogorova Sots-art, n.p.
100. Palisandriia, p. 41.
101. Ibid., p. 15.
102. Kholmogorova Sots-art, n. p.
103. Terz, p. 172.
104. De Vega was famed for the unparalleled volume of his literary output, which in Palisandr's equation of writing with sex makes perfect sense.
105. Palisandriia, pp. 180–83.
106. Ibid., pp. 282–83.
107. Ibid., p. 136.
108. Anton Antonov-Ovseenko, 'Kar'era palacha', *Zvezda*, 9 (1988), 152.
109. Palisandriia, p. 16. The theme of Stalin's 'deification' was advanced in Siniavskii's seminal treatise.
110. Ibid., p. 114.
111. Ibid., pp. 418–19
112. Ibid., pp. 446–47.
113. See Johnson Palisandrija, p. 398. Johnson also notes another meaning evoked by the name, etymologically related to 'rech': 'reka' — river — standing for the river of Russian history.
114. Palisandriia, p. 447.
115. Ibid., p. 461.
116. Mircea Eliade, 'Mephistopheles and the Androgyne, or Mystery of the Whole', in *The Two and the One*, trans. by J. M. Cohen (London: Harville Press, 1965), pp. 78–124 (p. 100).
117. Palisandriia, p. 411.
118. Ibid., p. 413.
119. Ibid., pp. 458–59.
120. Also noted by Larissa Rudova, 'Reading *Palisandria*: Of Menippean Satire and Sots-Art' (hereafter 'Rudova Endquote'), in Endquote, pp. 211–24 (p. 222).
121. D. Barton Johnson, 'Literary Biography' (hereafter 'Literary Biography'), *Canadian-American Slavic Studies*, 21 (1987), 203–30 (p. 217) (letter from March 1980).
122. See Petr Vail' and Aleksandr Genis, 'Soslagatel'noe naklonenie istorii: tsvetnik rossiiskogo anakhronizma', *Grani*, 139 (1986), 137–64 (p. 161).
123. I am indebted to this parallel to Dr Peter Duncan (SSEES), who was struck by similarities as regards familial involvement of the other P. in the life of Kremlin dwellers. His paternal grandfather, Spiridon Ivanovich Putin (1879–1965), was employed at Lenin's dacha at Gorki as a cook, and after Lenin's death in 1924, he continued to work for Lenin's wife, Nadezhda Krupskaia. He would later cook for Stalin when the Soviet

leader visited one of his dachas in the Moscow region. Later he was employed at a dacha belonging to the Moscow City Committee of the Communist Party of the Soviet Union, at which the young Putin would visit him.
124. Matich Slavic Studies, pp. 317–18.
125. Boris Grois, 'Zhizn' kak utopiia i utopiia kak zhizn': iskusstvo sots-arta', *Sintaksis*, 18 (1987), 171–81 (p. 178).
126. Grois Stalinism, pp. 102–05.
127. Palisandriia, p. 461, emphasis mine.
128. Rudova Endquote, p. 221.
129. 'Третьего дня без шестнадцати девять настало безвременье — время дерзать и творить'. Palisandriia, p. 92.
130. After Future, p. 93. See also Matich, who describes Palisandr as 'a writer who lives after the end of art, art in the meaning of avant-garde, reconciling Stalin with the dissident writer Vladimov, Jung with Freud, man with woman'. Matich Slavic Studies, pp. 317–18.
131. After Future, p. 89.
132. 'kaka' is a Russian childish form for faeces.
133. After Future, pp. 93–94.
134. Palisandriia, p. 26.

CONCLUSION

> Texts are more important than life, for me. Language is more important than life. So if you deal with language, you are creating not only texts, but also something more important than life. It's been said many times, of course, but it is true that first there was the Word, and God created the Word, the Word is God, and God is more important than life.[1]

> Ideally, however, it is language negating its own mass and the laws of gravity; it is language's striving upward — or sideways — to that beginning where the Word was. In any case, it is a movement of language into pre- (supra-) genre realms, that is into the spheres from which it sprang.[2]

> Утвердить факт своей единственной незаменимой причастности бытию — значит войти в бытие именно там, где оно не равно себе самому — войти в событие бытия.[3]

For Sokolov, words are the origin and the end. In *School for Fools* language becomes the only element that constitutes and controls reality. This is manifest in Nymphea's schizophrenic withdrawal into language as the means to keep the real at bay, lest it overwhelm. The narrative self and the narrative world are formed through reflection, emerging as an echo in response to the Word and embodied in Veta.

The life-bearing function of language in *Between Dog and Wolf* is illuminated through its association with the feminine, exemplified by the letter 'Ж'. The novel begins with the objectification of language and art. Initially presented as objects of reflection, through the techniques of *skaz* and ekphrasis, they emerge as the creative subject of this reflection. As sound becomes yeast, language becomes wine, text becomes the body and the act of reading turns into a communion.[4]

In *Palisandriia* the purification takes a similar route: through the process of indiscriminate ingestion. The main source of creativity remains language, as is attested by Palisandr's fusion of writing and sex and epitomized by his 'Don-Juanesque' competition with Lope de Vega. Another implicit equation of language to life is conveyed through the symbolic resourcefulness of the grapheme 'O', identified with the vagina. Through these associations the act of writing is affirmed as the ultimate creative act and the graphomaniacal hysteria of the regurgitated concepts and meta-narratives turns out to be a purifying and creative process.

Such sacralization of language — its positing as the transcendental centre — is typical of an exile for whom a text stands in for the lost context. The reaction to this cultural phenomenon, which has been defined as 'deterritorialization', is an attempt to transcend specific spatial or temporal boundaries by reaching out for the removed context or cultural object. Mark Lipovetskii describes this (re-)constructed cultural space as a 'creative chronotope', in which 'fiction replacing a lost reality assumes the status of authenticity'.[5] To be more precise, it is not fiction as such — stories do not really figure in Sokolov's art — but language that takes place (of time and space). It is, as in Brodskii's definition of art, 'a spirit seeking flesh but finding words'.[6]

Contrary to some opinions regarding Sokolov's work as a form of escapism[7] or linguistic pyrotechnics,[8] his texts are not means to construct an 'alternative' reality, or escape the given, but an attempt to animate it. Thus *School for Fools* acquires and projects onto the world body through duality and reflection; *Between Dog and Wolf* resorts to representations in its resurrection of the real; *Palisandriia* literally and literarily animates history.

Sokolov's texts are not a denial of the real, but an acknowledgement of its insufficiency. Both *School for Fools* and *Between Dog and Wolf* speak about how the world contains barely anything of what we value in it. It is even more so with *Palisandriia*, a text that openly acknowledges the reflected nature of reality, which withdraws into its reflection as the last refuge. Working within a complex network of reflections, Sokolov offers reality his (writing) hand. For, in order for it to become a meaningful event, reality requires mediation.

For Bakhtin, this mediation constitutes the responsibility of each individual consciousness towards reality. Just as the self, formed through the reflection of the other, this other and the world require realization — objectivization, for Bakhtin — from without. This position of outsidedness constitutes the act of answerability — responsibility — of the 'I' towards the other and the world:

> Существенным (но не единственным) моментом эстетического созерцания является вживание в индивидуальный предмет видения, видение его изнутри в его собственном существе. За этим моментом вживания всегда следует момент объективации, т. е. положение понятой вживанием индивидуальности вне себя, отделение ее от себя, возврат в себя, и только это возвращенное в себя сознание, со своего места, эстетически оформляет изнутри схваченную вживанием индивидуальность, как единую, целостную, качественно своеобразную. И все эти эстетические моменты: единство, целостность, самодостаточность, своеобразие трансгредиентны самой определяемой индивидуальности, изнутри ее самой для нее в ее жизни этих моментов нет, она не живет ими для себя, они имеют смысл и

осуществляются вживающимся уже вне ее, оформляя и объективируя слепую материю вживания.⁹

What emerges from this dialogue is the 'event of being' ('sobytie bytiia'): a form of being which has been animated by an individual perception/participation ('vzhivanie'). This type of being, which Bakhtin refers to as 'participatory consciousness' ('uchastnoe myshlenie'), is situated on the border between the ideal (transcendental) and real (physical) realms. It has been speculated that Bakhtin's concept of 'sobytie bytiia' may derive from Viacheslav Ivanov's theory of myth. This theory presents myth as a manifestation of a supra-sensual reality, an event ('sobytie') that takes place on the border of the immediate and transcendental realms. This event is the point where these worlds meet. Bakhtin's 'event of being' communicates a very similar idea. The world, perceived through the participatory consciousness becomes an event, in which this consciousness participates. Thus, it is not the world that is constituted of events which lie outside consciousness, but it is this consciousness that turns the world into the event.¹⁰

Reality requires deliverance. The unique responsibility of the subject is to deliver it by participating in and reflecting upon it. It is a delicate task since the object is shy. It tends to take the form of a chair or a cup that humbly offers its services without expecting anything back. Or it can take the form of another such commodity: a word, for instance, which is usually confused with some sort of vehicle — perhaps a bicycle — to be taken from point A to point B. However, a question remains:

> А и Б сидели на трубе.
> А упало, Б пропало.
> Что осталось на трубе?

Something remained, and/и that is where the real takes refuge.

All of Sokolov's protagonists are writers. Such self-reflexivity, conveyed through the defamiliarization of the act of writing, illuminates further the role of language in Sokolov's texts. Rejecting the functionality of a vehicle, language becomes an end in itself. Or rather a beginning. By employing the techniques that promote language as an autonomous being — schizophrenic discourse, *skaz*, stylization, and parody — Sokolov achieves the immediacy of the Bakhtinian event of being: the joining point where the individual consciousness and the world meet.

In his notes on Dostoevskii, Bakhtin defines this 'meeting' place as a 'chronotopical point', describing it as an event that is perceived to stand outside the ordinary course of life:

> Действие совершается в хронотопических точках, изъятых из обычного хода жизни и из обычного жизненного пространства, в эксцент-

рических точках, в инфернальных, райских (просветление, блаженство, осанна) и чистилищных точках. [...] Из этих эксцентрических, кризисных, инфернальных точек никогда не сложишь линии биографического или исторического становления. Обычно сцена является сгущением обычного хода жизни, конденсацией временного жизненного процесса, потенцированного ходом и временем жизни; у Д[остоевского] они выпадают из времени, строятся в его разрывах и сломах.[11]

Sokolov's art is also positioned around these breaking points. His characters, inhabiting Bakhtinian chronotopical lacunae, are eccentrics and fools, who oscillate between myth and personal trauma. In their balancing act between physics and metaphysics they seek to transcend their materiality, and end up finding redemption in the body of language. One legendary Holy Fool is considered by Bakhtin to be the prime example of this redeeming act:

> Великий символ активности, отошедший Христос, в причастии, в распределении плоти и крови его претерпевая перманентную смерть, жив и действенен в мире событий именно как отошедший из мира, его не-существованием в мире мы живы и причастны ему, укрепляемы. Мир, откуда ушел Христос, уже не будет тем миром, где его никогда не было, он принципиально другой.[12]

Reflected through and partaking of the presence of Christ, the world becomes an event of being. Perhaps it has become qualitatively a slightly different place once it has partaken of Sokolov's reflective art.

Notes to the Conclusion

1. David Remnick, 'Wellspring of the Russian Writer: Thirsting for his Native Language, Sasha Sokolov Returns' (hereafter 'Remnick'), *Washington Post* (28 September 1989).
2. Joseph Brodsky, 'A Poet and Prose' (hereafter 'A Poet and Prose'), in *Less Than One: Selected Essays* (New York: Farrar, Straus, Giroux, 1986), pp. 176–94 (p. 186).
3. Mikhail Bakhtin, 'K filosofii postupka' (hereafter 'K filosofii postupka'), in *Sobranie sochinenii*, 7 vols (Moscow: Russkie slovari, 1997–2003), I (2003), pp. 7–68 (p. 41).
4. This participatory and purifying quality of the novel's language has been noted by the theatre director Andrei Moguchii, who said that: 'я очищаюсь его языком'. Interview with Zhanna Zaretskaia in BIA, 20 February 2000 <http://bia-news.ru/news/36757.> [accessed January 2010].
5. Mark Lipovetsky, *Russian Postmodernist Fiction: Dialogue with Chaos* (Armonk, NY: M. E. Sharpe, 1998), pp. 236–37.
6. Joseph Brodsky, 'The Child of Civilization', in *Less Than One: Selected Essays* (New York: Farrar, Straus, Giroux, 1986), pp. 123–44 (p. 123).
7. See Alexander Boguslawski, 'Sokolov's *A School for Fools*: An Escape from Socialist Realism', *Slavic and East European Journal*, 27 (1983), 91–97; Richard C. Borden, 'Time, Backward! Sasha Sokolov and Valentin Kataev', *Canadian-American Slavic Studies*, 21 (1987), 247–63; Ludmilla L. Litus, 'Saša Sokolov's *Škola dlja durakov*: Aesopian Language and Intertextual Play', *Slavic and East European Journal*, 41 (1997), 114–34.

8. Olga Matich, 'Sasha Sokolov's *Palisandriia*: History and Myth', *The Russian Review*, 45 (1985), 415–26 (p. 426).
9. K filosofii postupka, p. 18.
10. 'Kommentarii', in Mikhail Bakhtin, *Sobranie sochinenii*, 7 vols (Moscow: Russkie slovari, 1997–2003), I (2003), pp. 343–867 (pp. 404–10).
11. Mikhail Bakhtin, 'Ritorika v meru svoei lzhivosti', in *Sobranie sochinenii*, 7 vols (Moscow: Russkie slovari, 1997–2003), V (1997), pp. 63–70 (p. 64).
12. K filosofii postupka, p. 19.

BIBLIOGRAPHY

Primary Sources

Works by Sasha Sokolov

Astrophobia, trans. by Michael H. Heim (New York: Grove Weidenfield, 1989)
'Florinit', *Zerkalo*, 35 (2010)
'Gazibo', *Zerkalo*, 33 (2009)
Mezhdu sobakoi i volkom (St Petersburg: Symposium, 2001)
Palisandriia (St Petersburg: Symposium, 2004)
'Palisandr Aleksandrovich, a, Palisandr Aleksandrovich? (Stranitsy iz romana *Palisandriia*)', *Dvadtsat' Dva*, 30 (1983), 29–57
'Rassuzhdenie', *Zerkalo*, 29 (2007)
School for Fools, trans. by Carl Proffer (Ann Arbor, MI: Ardis, 1977)
Shkola dlia durakov (St Petersburg: Symposium, 2001)
Shkola dlia durakov. Mezhdu sobakoi i volkom. Palisandriia. Esse (St Petersburg: Azbuka-klassika, 2009)
Trevozhnaia kukolka. Esse (St Petersburg: Azbuka-klassika, 2007)
Triptikh (Moscow: OGI, 2011)

Interviews

EROFEEV, VICTOR, 'Vremia dlia chastnykh besed ...', *Oktiabr'*, 8 (1989), 195–202
IVANOVA, NATALIA, 'Neestestvennyi otbor', *Moskovskii Komsomolets*, 215 (18 September 1988)
MKHEIDZE, MIKHAIL, 'Snezhnyi chelovek', *Playboy* (Russia) (2004), 48–53
PODSHIVALOV, IVAN, 'A Conversation with Sasha Sokolov: Moscow, 1989', trans. by Ludmilla Litus, *Canadian-American Slavic Studies*, 40 (2006), 352–66
POLOVETS, A., and RAKHLIN, S, 'Sasha Sokolov govorit', *Almanach Panorama*, 21 (1981), 8–12
REMNICK, DAVID, 'Wellspring of the Russian Writer: Thirsting for his Native Language, Sasha Sokolov Returns', *Washington Post* (28 September 1989)
SAPGIR, KIRA, 'V Russkoi Mysli — pisatel' Sasha Sokolov', *Russkaia mysl'*, 3386 (12 November 1981), 11
VAIMAN, NAUM, 'A Conversation with Sasha Sokolov (Over the Barrier: A Special Broadcast in Honor of Sasha Sokolov's 60th Birthday', *Canadian-American Slavic Studies*, 40 (2006), 367–78
VORONEL', A., and VORONEL', N., Ia khochu podniat' russkuiu prozu do urovnia poezii, *Dvadtsat' Dva*, 35 (1984), 179–86
VRUBEL'-GOLUBKINA, IRINA, 'Ia vsiu zhizn' vybiraiu luchshee. Chashche vsego bessoznatel'no ...', *Zerkalo*, 37 (2011)

Secondary Sources

ADAMS, H. C., 'The Dancing Mania', *Religious Manias* (London: Religious Tract Society), 16 August 1884, section 'Sunday at Home', pp. 513–15

ALTER, ROBERT, *Partial Magic: The Novel as a Self-Conscious Genre* (Berkeley, Los Angeles, and London: University of California Press, 1975)

ANTONOV-OVSEENKO, ANTON, 'Kar'era palacha', *Zvezda*, 9 (1988), 141–64

AUDEN, W. H., 'Musée des Beaux Arts', in *The English Auden: Poems, Essays and Dramatic Writings, 1927–1939*, ed. by Edward Mendelson (London and Boston: Faber and Faber, 1977), p. 237

AUERBACH, ERICH, *Mimesis: The Representation of Reality in Western Literature*, trans. by Willard R. Trask (Princeton: Princeton University Press, 1953)

BACHELARD, GASTON, *Water and Dreams: An Essay on the Imagination of Matter*, trans. by Edith R. Farrell (Dallas: Dallas Institute of Humanities and Culture, 1983)

BAKHTIN, MIKHAIL, 'Avtor i geroi v esteticheskoi deiatel'nosti', in *Sobranie sochinenii*, 7 vols (Moscow: Russkie slovari, 1997–2003), I (2003), pp. 69–263

—— 'Chelovek u zerkala', in *Sobranie sochinenii*, 7 vols (Moscow: Russkie slovari, 1997–2003), V (1997), p. 71

—— *The Dialogic Imagination: Four Essays by M. M. Bakhtin*, ed. by Michael Holquist, trans. by Caryl Emerson and Michael Holquist (Austin, TX: University of Texas Press, 2002)

—— 'Iazyk v khudozhestvennoi literature', in *Sobranie sochinenii*, 7 vols (Moscow: Russkie slovari, 1997–2003), V (1997), pp. 287–97

—— 'Iz arkhivnykh zapisei k rabote. Problemy rechevykh zhanrov', in *Sobranie sochinenii*, 7 vols (Moscow: Russkie slovari, 1997–2003), V (1997), pp. 207–86

—— 'K filosofii postupka', *in Sobranie sochinenii*, 7 vols (Moscow: Russkie slovari, 1997–2003), I (2003), pp. 7–68

—— 'K stilistike romana', in *Sobranie sochinenii*, 7 vols (Moscow: Russkie slovari, 1997–2003), V (1997), pp. 138–40

—— 'K voprosam metodologii estetiki slovesnogo tvorchestva. I. Problema formy, soderzhaniia i materiala v slovesnom khudozhestvennom tvorchestve', in *Sobranie sochinenii*, 7 vols (Moscow: Russkie slovari, 1997–2003), I (2003), pp. 265–325

—— 'Mnogoiazychie, kak predposylka razvitia romannogo slova', in *Sobranie sochinenii*, 7 vols (Moscow: Russkie slovari, 1997–2003), V (1997), pp. 157–58

—— 'Problema rechevykh zhanrov', in *Sobranie sochinenii*, 7 vols (Moscow: Russkie slovari, 1997–2003), V (1997), pp. 159–206

—— *Problemy poetiki Dostoevskogo* (Moscow: Sovetskaia Rossia, 1979)

—— 'Ritorika v meru svoei lzhivosti', in *Sobranie sochinenii*, 7 vols (Moscow: Russkie slovari, 1997–2003), V (1997), pp. 63–70

BAKSHTEIN, JOSEPH, 'On Conceptual Art in Russia', in *Between Spring and Summer: Soviet Conceptual Art in the Era of Late Communism*, ed. by David A. Ross (Boston: The Institute of the Contemporary Arts, 1990), pp. 73–82

BALINA, MARINA, NANCY CONDEE, and EVGENII DOBRENKO, eds, *Endquote: Sots-Art Literature and Soviet Grand Style* (Evanston, IL: Northwestern University Press, 2000)

BARTH, JOHN, *Lost in the Funhouse* (New York: Bantam Books, 1980)

BARTHES, ROLAND, *Empire of Signs*, trans. by Richard Howard (New York: Hill and Wang, 1994)
—— *The Neutral*, trans. by Rosalind E. Krauss and Denis Hollier (New York: Columbia University Press, 2007)
—— *The Responsibility of Forms: Critical Essays on Music, Art, and Representation*, trans. by Richard Howard (Berkeley and Los Angeles: University of California Press, 1985)
—— *The Rustle of Language*, trans. by Richard Howard (Berkeley and Los Angeles: University of California Press, 1989)
—— *S/Z*, trans. by Richard Miller (London: Jonathan Cape, 1975)
BAUDELAIRE, CHARLES, *The Painter of Modern Life and Other Essays*, trans. and ed. by Jonathan Mayne (London: Phaidon, 1995)
BEERS, WILLIAM, *Women and Sacrifice: Male Narcissism and the Psychology of Religion* (Detroit: Wayne State University Press, 1992)
BELL, MICHAEL, *Literature, Modernism and Myth: Belief and Responsibility in the Twentieth Century* (Cambridge: Cambridge University Press, 1997)
BENJAMIN, WALTER, *Illuminations*, trans. by Harry Zohn (New York: Schocken Books, 2007)
BENTALL, RICHARD P., *Madness Explained: Psychosis and Human Nature* (London: Penguin Books, 2004)
BERAHA, LAURA, 'The Last Rogue of History: Picaresque Elements in Sasha Sokolov's *Palisandriia*', *Canadian Slavonic Papers*, 35 (1993), 201–20
BERBEROVA, NINA, *Bez zakata; Malen'kaia devochka; Rasskazy; Stikhi (1924–26)* (Moscow: Izdatel'stvo imeni Sabashnikovykh, 1999)
BERGSON, HENRI, *Matter and Memory*, trans. by Nancy Margaret Paul and W. Scott Palmer (New York: Zone Books, 1988)
BERMAN, JEFFREY, *Narcissism and the Novel* (New York and London: New York University Press, 1990)
BERRY, ELLEN E. and ANESA MILLER-POGACAR, EDS, *Re-Entering the Sign: Articulating New Russian Culture* (Ann Arbor, MI: University of Michigan Press, 1995)
BITOV, ANDREI, 'Grust' vsego cheloveka', *Oktiabr'*, 3 (1989), 157–58
BLOK, ALEKSANDR, *Stikhotvoreniia i poemy* (Leningrad: Sovetskii pisatel', 1961)
BOBRINSKAIA, EKATERINA, *Russkii avangard: granitsy iskusstva* (Moscow: Gosudarstvennyi Institut Iskusstvoznaniia, 2006)
BOGUSLAWSKI, ALEXANDER, 'Death in Works of Sasha Sokolov', *Canadian-American Slavic Studies*, 21 (1987), 231–46
—— 'How Sokolov's *Mezhdu sobakoi i volkom* is Made: Structure and Design', *Canadian-American Slavic Studies*, 40 (2006), 201–32
—— 'Sokolov's *A School for Fools*: An Escape from Socialist Realism', *Slavic and East European Journal*, 27 (1983), 91–97
—— 'Vremia Palisandra Dal'berga', *Russian Language Journal*, 42 (1988), 221–29
BOHEEMEN-SAAF, VAN, CHRISTINE, *Joyce, Derrida, Lacan, and Trauma of History: Reading, Narrative and Postcolonialism* (Cambridge: Cambridge University Press, 1999)
BORDEN, RICHARD C., 'Time, Backward! Sasha Sokolov and Valentin Kataev', *Canadian-American Slavic Studies*, 21 (1987), 247–63

BORGES, JORGE LUIS, 'The Garden of Forking Paths', in *Ficcion* (Paris, London, and New York: Calder Publications, 1998), pp. 81–92

—— 'John Wilkins' Analytical Language', in *The Total Library: Non Fiction, 1922–1986*, trans. by Esther Allen, Suzanne Jill Levine, and Eliot Weinberger (London: The Penguin Press, 2000), pp. 229–32

—— *Labyrinths*, ed. and trans. by James E. Irby (London: Penguin Books, 1970)

—— *A Universal History of Iniquity*, trans. by Andrew Hurley (London: Penguin Books, 2001)

BOWKER, JOHN, *The Oxford Dictionary of World Religions* (New York and Oxford: Oxford University Press, 1997)

BOYD, MICHAEL, *The Reflexive Novel: Fiction as Critique* (London and Toronto: Associated university Presses, 1983)

BRODSKII, IOSIF, *Chast' rechi: Izbrannye stikhotvoreniia* (St Petersburg: Azbuka-klassika, 2009)

—— *Less Than One: Selected Essays* (New York: Farrar, Straus, Giroux, 1986)

BRODSKY, ANNA, 'The Death of Genius in the Works of Sasha Sokolov and Liudmila Petrushevskaia', *Canadian-American Slavic Studies*, 40 (2006), 279–304

—— *Poetic Autobiography in Russian Literature: Turgenev, Bunin, Nabokov, Sokolov* (Ann Arbor, MI: UMI Dissertation Services, 2007)

BRUHM, STEVEN, *Reflecting Narcissus: A Queer Aesthetic* (Minneapolis and London: University of Minnesota Press, 2001)

BRUHN, SIGLIND, 'A Concept of Paintings: "Musical Ekphrasis" in the Twentieth-Century' <http://www-personal.umich.edu> [accessed 30 November 2008]

BUNIN, IVAN, 'Zhizn' Arsen'eva. Iunost'', *Polnoe sobranie sochinenii*, 8 vols (Moscow: Voskresenie, 2006), V, 7–249

BURGIN, VICTOR, *The End of Art Theory: Criticism and Postmodernity* (London: Macmillan, 1986)

BURIKHIN, IGOR, 'S. Sokolov. Mezhdu sobakoi i volkom. Ardis, Ann Arbor, 1980', *Grani*, 118 (1980), 273–74

Butler's Lives of the Saints (hereafter 'Lives of the Saints'), ed. by Herbert Thurston S. J. and Donals Attwater, 3 vols (London: Burns and Oates, 1956), II, 545

CANARY, ROBERT H., and HENRY KOZICKI, eds, *The Writing of History: Literary Form and Historical Understanding* (Madison, WI: The University of Wisconsin Press, 1978)

CARAMITTI, MARIO, ' "Ia" kak igrovoe nachalo iskusstva (po materialam "Palisandrii")', *Canadian-American Slavic Studies*, 40 (2006), 305–16

CHAIANOV, ALEKSANDR, 'Puteshestvie moego brata Alekseia v stranu krest'ianskoi utopii', in *Venetsianskoe zerkalo* (Moscow: Sovremennik, 1989), pp. 161–208

CLARK, KATERINA, *The Soviet Novel: History as Ritual* (Bloomington and Indianapolis: Indiana University Press, 2000)

CONDEE, NANCY and PADUNOV, VLADIMIR, 'Makulakultura: Reprocessing Culture', *Stanford Slavic Studies*, 7 (1993), 53–80

CORE, PHILIP, *Camp: The Lie That Tells the Truth* (London: Plexus, 1984)

DÄLLENBACH, LUCIEN, *The Mirror in the Text*, trans. by Jeremy Whiteley and Emma Hughes (Cambridge: Polity Press, 1989)

DAVIS, DIANA K., *Through Other Creatures: Modes of Identification in 'A School for Fools' and 'Singing From the Well'* (Ann Arbor, MI: UMI Dissertation Services, 2007)

DELEUZE, GILLES and GUATTARI, FÉLIX, *Anti-Oedipus: Capitalism and Schizophrenia*, trans. by Robert Hurley, Mark Seem, and Helen R. Lane (London: Continuum, 2004)
DERRIDA, JACQUES, *Dissemination*, trans. by Barbara Johnson (London: Athlone Press, 1981)
—— *Of Grammatology*, trans. by Gayatri Chakravorty Spivak (Baltimore and London: Johns Hopkins University Press, 1976)
—— *Writing and Difference*, trans. by Alan Bass (London and New York: Routledge Classics, 2009)
DOBRENKO, EVGENY, 'Preodolenie ideologii: zametki o sots-arte', *Volga*, 11 (1990), 164-84
DOSTOEVSKII, FEDOR, *Besy* (Moscow: Sovremennik, 1993)
—— 'Brat'ia Karamazovy', in *Sobranie sochinenii*, 15 vols (Leningrad: Nauka, 1991), IX
—— 'Chto znachit slovo: "Striutskie"?', in 'Dnevnik pisatelia', 1877, sentiabr'-dekabr', 1880 avgust', in *Polnoe sobranie sochinenii*, 30 vols (Leningrad: Nauka, 1984), XXVI, 63-65
DUGANOV, RUDOL'F V., *Velimir Khlebnikov: Priroda tvorchestva* (Moscow: Sovetskii pisatel', 1990)
ECO, UMBERTO, *The Infinity of Lists: From Homer to Joyce*, trans. by Alastair McEwan (London: MacLehose Press, 2009)
—— 'Postmodernism, Irony, the Enjoyable', in *Postscript to 'The Name of the Rose'*, trans. by William Weaver (San Diego, New York, and London: Harcourt Brace Jovanovich Publishers, 1984), pp. 65-72
—— *On Ugliness*, trans. by Alastair McEwen (London: Harvill Secker, 2007)
EFIMOVA, ALLA, and LEV MANOVICH, eds, *Tekstura: Russian Essays on Visual Culture*, (Chicago and London: University of Chicago Press, 1993)
EGOROV, MIKHAIL I., 'Ustanovka na indeterminirovannoe produtsirovanie teksta v romane Sashi Sokolova "Shkola dlia durakov"', *Canadian-American Slavic Studies*, 40 (2006), 179-200
EIKHENBAUM, BORIS, 'Leskov i sovremennaia proza', in *Literatura: Teoriia, kritika, polemika* (Chicago, IL: Russian Study Series, 66, 1969), pp. 210-25
ELIADE, MIRCEA, *The Myth of the Eternal Return*, trans. by Willard R. Trask (London: Routledge and Kegan Paul, 1955)
—— *The Sacred and the Profane: The Nature of Religion*, trans. by Willard R. Trask (San Diego, New York, and London: Harcourt Brace Jovanovich Publishers, 1987)
—— *The Two and the One*, trans. by J. M. Cohen (London: Harvill Press, 1965)
EMERSON, CARYL, 'The Next Hundred Years of Mikhail Bakhtin (The View from the Classroom)', *Rhetoric Review*, 19 (2000), 12-27
EPSHTEIN, MIKHAIL, *After the Future: The Paradoxes of Postmodernism and Contemporary Russian Culture*, trans. by Anesa Miller-Pogacar (Amherst, MA: University of Massachusetts Press, 1995)
—— *Postmodern v russkoi literature* (Moscow: Vysshaia shkola, 2005)
—— 'Postmodernism, Communism and Sots-Art', in *Endquote: Sots-Art Literature and Soviet Grand Style*, ed. by Marina Balina, Nancy Condee, and Evgenii Dobrenko (Evanston, IL: Northwestern University Press, 2000), pp. 3-31
—— *Slovo i molchanie: Metafizika russkoi literatury* (Moscow: Vysshaia shkola, 2006)

—— *V Rossii: vse esse 1977–1990* (Ekaterinburg: U-Faktoria, 2005)
——, ALEXANDER GENIS and SLOBODANKA VLADIV-GLOVER, eds, *Russian Postmodernism*, trans. by Slobodanka Vladiv-Glover (New York, Oxford: Berghahn Books, 1999)
EREMIN, I., *Lektsii i stat'i po istorii drevnei russkoi literatury* (Leningrad: Izdatel'stvo Leningradskogo Universiteta, 1987)
ERLICH, VICTOR, *Russian Formalism: History — Doctrine* (New Haven and London: Yale University Press, 1981)
ERMOLINA, G. G., 'Vremia ot vetra. Nekotoryie problemy prostranstva i vremeni v "Shkole dlia durakov" Sashi Sokolova', in *Literatura 'tret'ei volny': sbornik nauchnykh statei*, ed. by V. P. Skobelev (Samara: 'Samarskii universitet', 1997), pp. 195–201
FEDOROV, NIKOLAI, 'Filosofiia obshchego dela', in *Sochineniia*, 3 vols (Moscow: Akademiia Nauk, Institut filosofii, 1982), I, 53–503
FLETCHER, ANGUS, ed., *The Literature of Fact: Selected Papers from the English Institute* (New York: Columbia University Press, 1976)
FOLEY, BARBARA, *Telling the Truth: Theory and Practice of Documentary Fiction* (Ithaca and London: Cornell University Press, 1986)
FOUCAULT, MICHEL, *The History of Sexuality: The Will to Knowledge*, 2 vols, trans. by Robert Hurley (London: Penguin Books, 1990), I
—— *Language, Counter-Memory, Practice: Selected Essays and Interviews*, trans. by Donald F. Bouchard and Sherry Simon, ed. by Donald F. Bouchard (Ithaca, NY: Cornell University Press, 1988)
—— *Madness and Civilization: A History of Insanity in the Age of Reason*, trans. by Richard Howard (New York: Vintage Books, 1973)
—— *The Order of Things: An Archeology of the Human Sciences*, trans. of *Les Mots et le chose* (New York: Vintage Books, 1973)
—— 'Aesthetics, Method and Epistemology', in *Essential Works of Foucault, 1954–1984*, 2 vols, ed. by James D. Faubion, trans. by Robert Hurley and others, (London: Penguin Books, 2000), II
FRANK, JOSEPH, *The Idea of Spatial Form* (New Brunswick and London: Rutgers University Press, 1991)
FREEDMAN, JOHN, 'Memory, Imagination and the Liberating Force of Literature in Sasha Sokolov's *A School for Fools*', *Canadian-American Slavic Studies*, 21 (1987), 265–78
FREUD, SIGMUND, 'Beyond the Pleasure Principle', in *The Standard Edition of Complete Psychological Works of Sigmund Freud*, 24 vols, trans. by James Strachey (London: Vintage, 2001), XVIII, pp. 7–64
—— *The Interpretation of Dreams*, trans. by James Strachey (London, Harmondsworth: Penguin, 1991)
—— *Leonardo da Vinci: A Memory of his Childhood*, trans. by Alan Tyson (London and New York: Routledge Classics, 2006)
—— 'On Narcissism: An Introduction', *The Standard Edition of the Compete Psychological Works of Sigmund Freud: On the History of the Psycho-Analytic Movement, Papers on Metapsychology and Other Works*, 24 vols, trans. by James Strachey (London: The Hogarth Press and the Institute of Psycho-Analysis, 1957), XIV, 73–102

—— 'The Uncanny', in *The Uncanny*, trans. by David McLintock (London: Penguin Books, 2003), pp. 121–62

GACHEV, GEORGY, 'National Images of the World', in *Re-Entering the Sign: Articulating New Russian Culture*, ed. by Ellen E. Berry and Anesa Miller-Pogacar (Ann Arbor, MI: University of Michigan Press, 1995), pp. 106–28

GELLER, LEONID, 'Na podstupakh k zhanru ekfrasisa. Russkii fon dlia nerusskikh kartin (i naoborot)', *Wiener Slawistischer Almanach, Sonderband*, 44 (1997), 151–71

——, ed., *Ekfrasis v russkoi literature: trudy Losannskogo simpoziuma* (Moscow: MIK, 2002)

GENETTE, GÉRARD, 'Complexe de Narcisse', in *Figures I–II: essays* (Paris: Seuil, 1966), pp. 21–28

—— *Palimpsests: Literature in the Second Degree*, trans. by Channa Newman and Claude Doubinsky (Lincoln, NB and London: University of Nebraska Press, 1997)

GENIS, ALEKSANDR, 'Lessons of *Shkola dlia dirakov* (Over the Barrier: A Special Broadcast in Honor of Sasha Sokolov's 60th Birthday)', *Canadian-American Slavic Studies*, 40 (2006), 341–49

GIBSON, WALTER S., *Bruegel* (London: Thames and Hudson, 2002)

—— *Pieter Bruegel and the Art of Laughter* (Berkeley, Los Angeles, and London: University of California Press, 2006)

GIRARD, RENÉ, 'Narcissism: The Freudian Myth Demythified by Proust', in *Psychoanalysis, Creativity, and Literature: A French-American Inquiry*, ed. by Alan Rolan (New York: Columbia University Press, 1978), pp. 292–311

—— *Oedipus Unbound: Selected Writings on Rivalry and Desire*, trans. and ed. by Mark. R. Anspach (Stanford, CA: Stanford University Press, 2004)

GLÜCK, GUSTAV, *Pieter Brueghel the Elder* (London: A. Zwemmer, 1951)

GOETHE, J. W., *Faust*, 2 vols, trans. by David Luke (Oxford and New York: Oxford University Press, 1994)

GOGOL', NIKOLAI, 'Mertvye dushi', in *Povesti. Mertvye dushi* (Moscow: AST Olimp, 1996), pp. 269–530

—— 'Portret', in *Sobraniie sochinenii*, 8 vols (Moscow: Terra-knizhnyi klub, 2001), III, pp. 61–110

—— 'Revizor', in Gogol', N. V., *Komedii*, (Leningrad: Iskusstvo, 1988), pp. 46–129

—— 'Shinel'', in *Sobraniie sochinenii*, 8 vols (Moscow: Terra-knizhnyi klub, 2001), III, pp. 111–39

GOR'KII, MAKSIM, *Detstvo, V liudiakh, Moi universitety* (Leningrad, 1971)

GOULD, ERIC, *Mythical Intentions in Modern Literature* (Princeton: Princeton University Press, 1981)

Govorit Dmitrii Aleksandrovich Prigov, ed. by Irina Balabanova (Moscow: OGI, 2001)

GRANT, MICHAEL, *Roman Myths* (London: Wiedenfeld and Nicholson, 1971)

GRAVES, ROBERT, *The Greek Myths* (London: Penguin Books, 1992)

GREEN, ANDRÉ, 'The Double and the Absent', in *Psychoanalysis, Creativity, and Literature: A French-American Inquiry*, ed. by Alan Rolan (New York: Columbia University Press, 1978), pp. 271–91

GRIGOR'EV, APOLLON, 'Vzgliad na russkuiu literaturu so smerti Pushkina: Stat'ia pervaia', in *Literaturnaia kritika* (Moscow: Khudozhestvennaia literatura, 1967), pp. 157–203

GROYS, BORIS, *Ilya Kabakov: The Man Who Flew into Space from his Apartment* (London: Afterall Books, 2006)
—— 'Stalinism as Aesthetic Phenomenon', in *Tekstura: Russian Essays on Visual Culture*, ed. by Alla Efimova and Lev Manovich (Chicago and London: University of Chicago Press, 1993), pp. 115–26
—— *The Total Art of Stalinism: Avant-garde, Aesthetic Dictatorship, and Beyond*, trans. by Charles Rougle (Princeton: Princeton University Press, 1992)
—— 'Zhizn' kak utopiia i utopiia kak zhizn': iskusstvo sots-arta', *Sintaksis*, 18 (1987), 171–81
GRUNBERGER, BELA, *New Essays on Narcissism*, trans. and ed. by David Macey (London: Free Association Books, 1989)
GUREEV, MAKSIM, 'Snimaetsia dokumental'noe kino', *Voprosy Literatury*, 2 (2011)
HACKING, IAN, *Rewriting Soul: Multiple Personality and the Sciences of Memory* (Princeton: Princeton University Press, 1995)
HAMILTON, VICTORIA, *Narcissus and Oedipus: The Children of Psychoanalysis* (London: Karnac Books, 1993)
HAVELOCK, ELLIS, *The Psychology of Sex* (New York: Random House, 1936)
HAWTHORN, JEREMY, *Multiple Personality and the Disintegration of Literary Character From Oliver Goldsmith to Sylvia Plath* (London: Edward Arnold, 1983)
HEFFERMAN, JAMES A. W., *Museum of Words: The Poetics of Ekphrasis from Homer to Ashbery* (Chicago and London: University of Chicago Press, 1993)
HELDT, BARBARA, 'Female Skaz in Sasha Sokolov's *Between Dog and Wolf*', *Canadian-American Slavic Studies*, 21 (1987), 279–85
HEUSSER, MARTIN, MICHÈLE HANNOOSH, ERIC HASKELL, LEO HOEK, DAVID SCOTT, and PETER DE VOOGD, eds, *On Verbal/Visual Representation: Word and Image Interactions* (Amsterdam, New York: Rodopi, 2005)
HICKS, JEREMY, *Mikhail Zoshchenko and the Poetics of Skaz* (Nottingham: Astra Press, 2000)
HODGKINSON, DEBORAH, 'The Significance and Insignificance of Time in Sasha Sokolov's *A School for Fools*', *Slovo*, 17 (2005), 65–74
HOLQUIST, MICHAEL, *Dialogism: Bakhtin and his World* (London and New York: Routledge, 2002)
The Holy Bible, New King James Version (Nashville, Dallas, Mexico City, Rio de Janeiro, and Beijing: Thomas Nelson, 1982)
HUBBS, JOANNA, *Mother Russia: The Feminine Myth in Russian Culture* (Bloomington and Indianapolis: Indiana University Press, 1993)
HUEVEL, VAN DEN, PIERRE, *Parole Mot Silence: Pour une poétique de l'enonciation* (Paris: Librairie José Corti, 1985)
HUTCHEON, LINDA, *Narcissistic Narrative: The Metafictional Paradox* (New York: Methuen, 1984)
—— *A Poetics of Postmodernism: History, Theory, Fiction* (New York and London: Routledge, 2005)
—— *A Theory of Parody: The Teachings of Twentieth-Century art Forms* (New York and London: Methuen, 1985)
IABLOKOV, E. A., ' "Nashel ia nachalo dorogi otsiuda — tuda" (o motivnoi structure romana Sashi Sokolova "Mezhdu sobakoi i volkom")', in *Literatura 'tret'ei volny': sbornik nauchnykh statei*, ed. by V. P. Skobelev (Samara: Samarskii universitet, 1997), pp. 202–14

Iazyk kak tvorchestvo, ed. by Z. Petrova and N. Fateeva (Moscow: Institut russkogo iazyka RAN, 1996)

Interart Poetics. Essays on the Interrelations of the Arts and Media, ed. by Ulla-Britta Lagerroth, Hans Lund, and Erik Hedling (Amsterdam and Atlanta, GA: Rodopi, 1997)

JACOBUS, MARY, *First Things: The Maternal Imagery in Literature, Art, and Psychoanalysis* (New York and London: Routledge, 1995)

JAKOBSON, ROMAN, 'Noveishaia russkaia poeziia: Podstupy k Khlebnikovu', in *Selected Writings: On Verse, Its Masters and Explorers*, (The Hague, Paris, and New York: Mouton Publishers, 1979), pp. 299-354

JAMESON, FREDRIC, 'Postmodernism, or The Cultural Logic of Late Capitalism', *New Left Review*, 146 (1948), 53-92

—— *The Prison-House of Language: A Critical Account of Structuralism and Russian Formalism* (Princeton: Princeton University Press, 1972)

JOHNSON, D. BARTON, 'Background Notes on Sokolov's *School for Fools* and *Between Dog and Wolf*: Conversations with the Author', *Canadian-American Slavic Studies*, 40 (2006), 331-39

—— 'The Galoshes Manifesto: A Motif in the Novels of Sasha Sokolov', *Oxford Slavonic Papers*, 22 (1989), 155-79

—— 'Literary Biography', *Canadian-American Slavic Studies*, 21 (1987), 203-30

—— '*Mezhdu sobakoi i volkom*: O fantasticheskom iskusstve Sashi Sokolova', *Vremia i my*, 64 (1982), 165-75

—— 'Sasha Sokolov's *Between Dog and Wolf* and the Modernist Tradition', in *The Third Wave: Russian Literature in Emigration*, ed. by Olga Matich and Michael Heim (Ann Arbor, MI: Ardis, 1984), pp. 208-17

—— 'Sasha Sokolov's Major Essays', *Canadian-American Slavic Studies*, 40 (2006), 233-50

—— 'Sasha Sokolov: The New Russian Avant-garde', *Critique: Studies in Contemporary Fiction*, 30 (1989), 163-78

—— 'Saša Sokolov's Palisandrija', *Slavic and East European Journal*, 30 (1986), 389-403

—— 'Sasha Sokolov's Twilight Cosmos: Themes and Motifs', *Slavic Review*, 45 (1986), 639-49

—— 'Saša Sokolov and Vladimir Nabokov', *Russian Language Journal*, 41 (1987), 153-62

—— 'A Structural Analysis of Sasha Sokolov's *School for Fools*: A Paradigmatic Novel', *Fiction and Drama in Eastern and Southeastern Europe: Evolution and Experiment in the Postwar Period*, ed. by Henrik Birnbaum and Thomas Eekman (Bloomington, IN: Slavica Publishers, Inc., 1980), pp. 207-237

JUNG, CARL, 'The Archetypes and the Collective Unconscious', in *The Collected Works*, 9 vols, trans. by R. F. G. Hull (London: Routledge and Kegan Paul, 1959), I

JUNG, CARL, and CARL KERENYI, *The Science of Mythology: Essays on the Myth of the Divine Child and the Mysteries of Eleusis*, trans. by R. F. C. Hull (London and New York: Routledge Classics, 2006)

KARRIKER, ALEXANDRA H., 'Double Vision: Sasha Sokolov's *School for Fools*', *World Literature Today*, 53 (1979), 610-14

—— 'Narrative Shifts and Cyclic Patterns in *A School for Fools*', *Canadian-American Slavic Studies*, 21 (1987), 287–99

KAZARINA, T. V., 'Estetism Sashi Sokolova kak nravstvennaia pozitsiia', in *Literatura 'tret'ei volny': Sbornik nauchnykh statei*, ed. by V. P. Skobelev (Samara: 'Samarskii universitet', 1997), pp. 189–94

KELLMAN, G. STEVEN, *The Self-Begetting Novel* (London: Macmillan, 1980)

KHLEBNIKOV, OLEG, 'The Orderly on Duty by the Time Switch', *Canadian-American Slavic Studies*, 40 (2006), 389–90

KHLEBNIKOV, VELIMIR, *Sobraniie sochinenii*, 3 vols (St Petersburg, 2001)

—— *Tvoreniia* (Moscow: Sovetskii pisatel', 1986)

—— *Stikhotvoreniia. Poemy. Dramy. Proza*, ed. by R.V. Duganov (Moscow: Sovetskaia Rossiia, 1986)

KHOLMOGOROVA, OLGA, *Sots-art* (Moscow: Galart, 1994)

KOCHHAR-LINDGREN, GRAY, *Narcissus Transformed: The Textual Subject in Psychoanalysis and Literature* (University Park, PA: The Pennsylvania State University Press, 1993)

KOHUT, HEINZ, 'Thoughts on Narcissism and Narcissistic Rage', in *Selected Writings of Heinz Kohut: 1950–1978: The Search for the Self*, ed. by Paul H. Ornstein (New York: International Universities Press, 1978), pp. 615–58

KOLB, HANNA, 'The Dissolution of Reality in Sasha Sokolov's Mezhdu Sobakoi i Volkom', in *Reconstructing the Canon: Russian Writing in the 1980s*, ed. by Arnold McMillin (London: Harwood Academic Publishers, 2000), pp. 193–223

'Kommentarii', in MIKHAIL BAKHTIN, *Sobranie sochinenii*, 7 vols (Moscow: Russkie slovari, 1997-2003), i (2003), pp. 343–867

KREID, VADIM, 'Zaitil'shchina', *Dvadtsat'dva*, 19 (1981), 213–18

KRIEGER, MURRAY, *Ekphrasis: The Illusion of the Natural Sign* (Baltimore: Johns Hopkins University Press, 1992)

KRISTEVA, JULIA, *Powers of Horror: An Essay on Abjection*, trans. by Leon S. Roudiez (New York: Columbia University Press, 1982)

—— *Tales of Love*, trans. by Leon S. Roudiez (New York: Columbia University Press, 1987)

LACAN, JACQUES, 'The Mirror Stage as the Formative of the Function of the I', in *Écrits: A Selection*, trans. by Alan Sheridan (London: Routledge, 1993), pp. 1–7

—— *Écrits: A Selection*, trans. by Alan Sheridan (London: Routledge, 1993)

—— *The Language of the Self: The Function of Language in Psychoanalysis*, trans. by Antony Wilden (Baltimore and London: John Hopkins University Press, 1981)

—— 'The Psychoses, 1955–1956', in *The Seminar of Jacques Lacan*, Book III, ed. by Jacques-Alain Miller, trans. by Russell Grigg (New York: Norton, 1993)

LAMBERT, GREGG, *The Return of the Baroque in Modern Culture* (New York and London: Continuum, 2004)

LANNE, JEAN-CLAUDE, 'O raznykh aspektakh ekfrasisa u Velimira Khlebnikova' in *Ekfrasis v russkoi literature: trudy Losannskogo simpoziuma*, ed. Leonid Geller (Moscow: MIK, 2002), pp. 71–86

LASCH, CHRISTOPHER, *The Culture of Narcissism: American Life in an Age of Diminishing Expectations* (New York: Norton, 1978)

LAVELLE, LOUIS, *The Dilemma of Narcissus*, trans. by W. T. Gairner (London and New York: George Allen and Unwin, 1973)

LEEMING, DAVID, *The Oxford Companion to World Mythology* (Oxford: Oxford University Press, 2005)
LEIDERMAN, NAUM, and MARK LIPOVETSKII, 'Romany Sashi Sokolova', in *Sovremennaia russkaia literatura: Kniga 2: Semidesiatye gody (1968–1986)*, ed. by N. Leiderman and M. Lipovetskii (Moscow: URSS, 2001), pp. 274–80
—— —— 'Zhizn' posle smerti, ili Novye svedeniia o realizme', *Novyi Mir*, 7 (1993), 233–52
—— ——, eds, *Sovremennaia russkaia literatura: Kniga 1: Literatura 'Ottepeli' (1953–1968)* (Moscow: URSS, 2001)
—— ——, eds, *Sovremennaia russkaia literatura: Kniga 2: Semidesiatye gody (1968–1986)* (Moscow: URSS, 2001)
LERMONTOV, MIKHAIL, *Geroi nashego vremeni* (Moscow: Goslitizdat, 1941)
—— 'Stikhotvorieniia', *Izbrannye sochineniia*, 3 vols (Moscow: Russkaia kniga, 1996)
LESKOV, NIKOLAI, 'Levsha (Skaz o tul'skom kosom Levshe i o stal'noi blokhe)', *Povesti i rasskazy* (Leningrad: Lenizdat, 1966), pp. 358–89
LINDSAY, KENNETH C. and HUPPÉ, BERNARD, 'Meaning and Method in Brueghel's Painting', *The Journal of Aesthetics and Art Criticism*, 14.3 (1956), 376–86
LIPOVETSKII, MARK, *Paralogii: Transformatsiia (post)modernistskogo diskursa v kul'ture 1920–2000-h godov* (Moscow: Novoe literaturnoe obozrenie, 2008)
—— *Russkii postmodernism: ocherki istoricheskoi poetiki* (Ekaterinburg: Ural'skii gosudarstvenny pedogogicheskii universitet, 1997)
—— *Russian Postmodernist Fiction: Dialogue with Chaos* (Armonk, NY: M. E. Sharpe, 1998)
LITUS, LUDMILLA L., *Saša Sokolov's "Skola dlja durakov": Form, Language, Intertext, and Allusion* (Ann Arbor, MI: UMI Dissertation Services, 2007)
—— 'Intertextuality in *Škola dlja durakov* Revisited: Sokolov, Gogol, and the Others', *Russian Language Journal*, 52 (1998), 99–137
—— 'Sasha Sokolov's Journey from "Samizdat" to Russia's Favorite "Classic": 1976–2006', *Canadian-American Slavic Studies*, 40 (2006), 393–424
—— 'Saša Sokolov's *Škola dlja durakov*: Aesopian Language and Intertextual Play', *Slavic and East European Journal*, 41 (1997), 114–34
LITUS, LUDMILLA L., and JOHNSON, D. BARTON, 'Sasha Sokolov: A Selected Annotated Bibliography (1967–2006)', *Canadian-American Slavic Studies*, 40 (2006), 425–94
LOSSKII, VLADIMIR, *Ocherk misticheskogo bogosloviia Vostochnoi Tserkvi. Dogmaticheskoe bogosloviie* (Moscow: SEI, 1991)
LOTMAN, IURII, 'Lektsii po struktural'noi poetike, in *Iu. M. Lotman i tartusskomoskovskaia semioticheskaia shkola*, ed. by A. D. Koshelev (Moscow: Gnosis, 1994), pp. 17–263
—— *Ob iskusstve. Struktura khudozhestvennogo teksta. Semiotika kino i problemy kinoestetiki. Stat'i. Zametki. Vystupleniia* (St Petersburg: Iskusstvo-SPB, 1998)
—— 'Stat'i po istorii russkoi literatury. Teoriia i semiotika drugikh iskusstv. Mekhanizmy kul'tury. Melkie zametki', in *Izbrannye stat'i*, 3 vols (Tallin: Aleksandra, 1993), III
—— 'Stat'i po semiotike i tipologii kultury', in *Izbrannye stat'i*, 3 vols (Tallin: Aleksandra, 1993), I

LYOTARD, JEAN-FRANÇOIS, *The Postmodern Condition: A Report on Knowledge*, trans. by Geoff Bennington and Brian Massumi (Minneapolis: University of Minnesota Press, 1984)
MALER, I., 'Imeiushchii v rukakh tsvety', *Dvadtsat' Dva*, 16 (1980), 219–20
MAN, PAUL DE, 'The Rhetoric of Blindness: Jacque Derrida's Reading of Rousseau', in *Blindness and Insight: Essays in the Rhetoric of Contemporary Criticism* (New York and Oxford: Oxford University Press, 1971), pp. 102–41
MANDEL'SHTAM, Osip, 'Komissarzhevskaia', in 'Egipetskaia marka', in *Sobranie sochinenii*, 2 vols, ed. by G. P. Struve and B. A. Fillipov (New York: Inter-Library Association, 1966), II, 137–39
MARKOV, VLADIMIR, *Russian Futurism: A History* (London: Macgibbon and Kee, 1968)
MATICH, OLGA, '*Palisandriia*: Dissidentskii mif i ego razvenchanie', *Sintaksis*, 15 (1986), 86–102
—— 'Sasha Sokolov and his Literary Context', *Canadian-American Slavic Studies*, 21 (1987), 301–19
—— 'Sasha Sokolov's *Palisandriia*: History and Myth', *The Russian Review*, 45 (1985), 415–26
McDOWELL, KAREN RICE, *The Reemergence of Medieval Word-Weaving in Sasha Sokolov's 'Shkola dlia durakov': Invoking the Word* (Ann Arbor, MI: UMI Dissertation Services, 2007)
McMILLIN, ARNOLD, 'Aberration or the Future: The Avant-Garde Novels of Sasha Sokolov', in *From Pushkin to Palisandriia: Essays on the Russian Novel in Honour of Richard Freeborn*, ed. by A. McMillin (London: Macmillan, 1990), pp. 229–43
MELETINSKY, ELEAZAR, *Literaturnyie arkhetipy i universalii* (Moscow, 2001)
—— *The Poetics of Myth*, trans. by Guy Lanoue and Alexandre Sadetsky (New York and London: Routledge, 2000)
MITCHELL, W. J. T., *Picture Theory: Essays on Verbal and Visual Representation* (Chicago and London: University of Chicago Press, 1994)
MOODY, FRED, 'Madness and the Pattern of Freedom in Sasha Sokolov's *A School for Fools*', *Russian Literature Triquarterly*, 16–17 (1979), 7–32
MUSORGSKII, MODEST, *Izbrannye pis'ma* (Moscow: Gosudarstvennoe muzykal'noe izdatel'stvo, 1953)
NAIMAN, ERIC, 'Historectomies: On the Metaphysics of Reproduction in a Utopian Age' in *Sexuality and the Body in Russian Culture*, ed. by Jane T. Costlow, Stephanie Sandler, and Judith Vowles (Stanford, CA: Stanford University Press, 1993), pp. 255–76
Narcissism and the Text: Studies in Literature and the Psychology of Self, ed. by Lynne Layton and Barbara Ann Schapiro (New York and London: New York University Press, 1986)
NEKRASOV, NIKOLAI, 'Stikhotovorenia i poemy: 1861–1874', in *Sobranie sochinenii*, 4 vols (Moscow: Pravda, 1979)
NEUMANN, ERICH, *The Origins and History of Consciousness* (London: Karnac Book, 1989)
New Catholic Encyclopedia, 17 vols (New York: McGraw-Hill Book Company, 1967)
NIETZSCHE, FRIEDRICH, *The Will to Power*, trans. by Walter Kaufmann and R. J. Hollingdale (New York: Vintage Books, 1968)

ONG, WALTER, *Interfaces of the World: Studies in the Evolution of Consciousness and Culture* (Ithaca and London: Cornell University Press, 1977)
—— *Orality and Literacy: The Technologizing of the Word* (London and New York: Methuen, 1982)
OVID, *Metamorphoses*, trans. by Frank Justus Miller, 2 vols (London and Cambridge, MA: Loeb Classical Library, 1960), I
PALENCIA-ROTH, MICHAEL, *Myth and the Modern Novel: Garcia Marquez, Mann and Joyce* (New York and London: Garland Publishing, 1987)
PASTERNAK, BORIS, *Doktor Zhivago* (Moscow: Knizhnaia palata, 1989)
PATER, WALTER, 'Leonardo da Vinci', in *Studies in the History of Renaissance* (Oxford: Oxford University Press, 2010), pp. 56–72
PAYNE, MICHAEL, *Reading Theory: An Introduction to Lacan, Derrida, and Kristeva* (Oxford and Cambridge, MA: Blackwell, 1993)
PETERSON, NADYA L., *Subversive Imaginations: Fantastic Prose and the End of Soviet Literature, 1970s–1990s* (Boulder, CO and Oxford: Westview Press, 1997)
PRIGOV, DMITRII, *Evgenii Onegin Pushkina* (St Petersburg: MitkiLibris & Krasnyi matros, 1998)
PROUST, MARCEL, 'Within a Budding Grove', in *Remembrance of Things Past*, 12 vols, trans. by C. K. Scott Moncrieff (London: Chatto & Windus, 1961), III–IV
PUSHKIN, ALEKSANDR, *Izbrannye proizvedeniia*, 2 vols (Moscow: Khudozhestvennaia literatura, 1970)
—— *Evgenii Onegin* (Moscow: Gosudarstvennoe izdatel'stvo detskoi literatury Ministerstva prosveshcheniia RSFSR, 1960)
—— 'Kapitanskaia dochka', in *Izbrannye proizvedeniia. Povesti* (L'vov: Kameniar, 1988), pp. 162–246
—— 'Stikhotvorieniia. Skazki', in *Sochineniia*, 3 vols (Moscow: Goslitizdat, 1962), I
ROBERTS, GRAHAM, *The Last Soviet Avant-garde: OBERIU — Fact, Fiction, Metafiction* (Cambridge: Cambridge University Press, 1997)
ROBIN, REGINE, *Socialist Realism: An Impossible Aesthetic* (Stanford, CA: Stanford University Press, 1992)
ROGERS, THOMAS F., *Myth and Symbolism in Soviet Fiction: Images of the Savior Hero, Great Mother, Anima, and Child in Selected Novels and Films* (San Francisco: Mellen Research University Press, 1992)
RORTY, RICHARD, 'Texts and Lumps', *New Literary History*, 17.1 (1985), 1–16
ROSE, MARGARET A., *Parody/Meta-Fiction: An Analysis of Parody as a Critical Mirror of the Writing and Reception of Fiction* (London: Croom Helm, 1979)
—— *Parody: Ancient, Modern, and Post-Modern* (Cambridge: Cambridge University Press, 1993)
ROSENFRANZ, KAREN LINK, *Hunter of Themes: The Interplay of Word and Thing in the Works of Sigizmund Krizizanovskij* (New York: Peter Lang, 2005)
ROSS, DAVID A., ed., *Between Spring and Summer: Soviet Conceptual Art in the Era of Late Communism*, (Boston: The Institute of the Contemporary Arts, 1990)
ROSSI, WILLIAM, *The Sex Life of the Foot and Shoe* (Ware: Wordsworth Editions, 1989)
RUBINS, MARIA, *Plasticheskaia radost' krasoty: Akmeizm i Parnas* (St Petersburg: Akademicheskii proekt, 2003)
RUDNEV, VADIM, *Morfologiia real'nosti: Issledovanie po 'filosofii teksta'* (Moscow: Gnozis, 1996)

RUDOVA, LARISSA, 'The Dystopian Vision in Sasha Sokolov's *Palisandriia*', *Canadian-American Slavic Studies*, 40 (2006), 163–77

—— 'Reading *Palisandria*: Of Menippean Satire and Sots-Art', in *Endquote: Sots-Art Literature and Soviet Grand Style*, ed. by Marina Balina, Nancy Condee, and Evgenii Dobrenko (Evanston, IL: Northwestern University Press, 2000), pp. 211–24

RUSS, MICHAEL, *Mussorgsky: Pictures at an Exhibition* (Cambridge: Cambridge University Press, 1992)

RYAN, KAREN, 'Sokolov's *Palisandriya*: The Art of History', in *Twentieth-Century Russian Literature: Selected Papers from the Fifth World Congress of Central and East European Studies, Warsaw 1995*, ed. by Karen L. Ryan, Barry P. Scherr, and Ronald J. Hill (London: Macmillan, 2000), pp. 215–27

SAPGIR, KIRA, 'Dal'nii bereg Palisandra', *Kontinent*, 46 (1985), 385–89

SASS, LOUIS A., *Madness and Modernism: Insanity in the Light of Modern Art, Literature, and Thought* (Cambridge, MA: Harvard University Press, 1996)

SCHILLER, FRIEDRICH, *On the Aesthetic Education of Man: In a Series of Letters*, ed. and trans by E. M. Wilkinson and L.A. Willoughby (Oxford: The Clarendon Press, 1967)

SCHOLES, ROBERT, *Fabulation and Metafiction* (Chicago and London: University of Illinois Press, 1979)

SCHOPENHAUER, ARTHUR, 'The Representation Independent of the Principle of Sufficient Reason: The Platonic Idea: The Object of Art', in *The World as Will and Representation*, 2 vols, trans. by E. F. Payne (New York: Dover Publications, 1969), I, Book 3, pp. 167–267

SHAPIRO, GAVRIEL, *Nikolai Gogol and the Baroque cultural Heritage* (University Park, PA: The Pennsylvania State University Press, 1993)

SHKLOVSKY, VIKTOR, *O teorii prozy* (Moscow: Sovetskii pisatel', 1983)

SIMMONS, CYNTHIA, 'Incarnation of the Hero Archetype in Sokolov's *School for Fools*', in *The Supernatural in Slavic and Baltic Literature: Essays in Honour of Victor Terras*, ed. by Amy Mandelker and Roberta Reeder (Columbus, OH: Slavica Publishers, 1988), pp. 275–89

—— '*School for Fools*: The Spirit of an "Abnormal" Condition', *Their Father's Voice: Vassily Aksyonov, Venedict Erofeev, Eduard Limonov, and Sasha Sokolov*, ed. by Cynthia Simmons (New York: Peter Lang, 1993), pp. 125–58

SINIAVSKII, ANDREI, *Ivan-durak: Ocherk russkoi narodnoi very* (Moscow: Agraf, 2001)

—— 'Stalin — geroi i khudozhnik ispalinskoi epokhi', *Sintaksis*, 19 (1987), 106–25

SKOROPANOVA, IRINA, *Postmodernistskaia russkaia literatura: novaia filosofia, novy iazyk* (St Petersburg: Nevskii Prostor, 2001)

SKRINE, PETER N., *The Baroque: Literature and Culture in Seventeenth-Century Europe* (London: Methuen, 1978)

SMIRNOV, IGOR' P., 'Barokko i opyt poeticheskoi kul'tury nachala XX v.', in *Slavianskoe barokko: Istoriko-kul'turnye problemy epokhi*, ed. by A. I. Rogov's (Moscow: Nauka, 1979), pp. 335–61

—— 'Nepoznavaemyi sub'ekt': bessub'ektnost', polisub'ektnost', inosub'ektnost'", *Beseda*, 6 (1987), 127–43

SMIRNOV, IGOR', 'O nartsisticheskom tekste (diakhronia i psikhoanaliz)', *Wiener Slawistischer Almanach*, 12 (1983), 21–45

SMITH, GERALD S., 'The Verse in Sasha Sokolov's *Between Dog and Wolf*', *Canadian-American Slavic Studies*, 21 (1987), 321-45

SMITH, WILLIAM, *Smith's Bible Dictionary* (1901)

SONTAG, SUSAN, *Against Interpretation and Other Essays* (London: Penguin Classics, 2009)

SPAAS, LIEVE, ed., *Echoes of Narcissus*, (New York and Oxford: Berghahn Books, 2000)

SUGERMAN, SHIRLEY, *Sin and Madness: Studies in Narcissism* (Philadelphia: The Westminster Press, 1976)

SUKHOTIN, MIKHAIL, *Tsentony i marginalia* (Moscow: Novoe Literaturnoe Obozrenie, 2001)

SUSLOV, ALEKSANDER, *The 'New Art' Tradition in Modern Russian Prose* (Unpublished PhD Dissertation, Georgetown University, Washington DC, 1984)

TERTZ, ABRAM, 'Chto takoe sotsialisticheskii realizm?', *Fantasticheskii mir Abrama Tertza* (Paris: Mezhdunarodnoe literaturnoe sodruzhestvo, 1967), pp. 401-46

—— 'On Socialist Realism', in *The Trial Begins and On Socialist Realism*, trans. by George Dennis (Berkeley and Los Angeles: University of California Press, 1982), pp. 127-219

—— *Progulki s Pushkinym* (London: Overseas Publications Interchange in Association with Collins, 1975)

TOKER, LEONA, 'Gamesman's Sketches (Found in a Bottle): A Reading of Sasha Sokolov's *Between Dog and Wolf*', *Canadian-American Slavic Studies*, 21 (1987), 347-67

TOSTAIA, TATIANA, 'O Sashe Sokolve', *Ogonek*, 33 (1988), 20-23

TSVETKOV, ALEKSEI, 'Uroki Merkatora', in Sasha Sokolov, *Trevozhnaia kukolka. Esse* (St Petersburg: Azbuka-klassika, 2007), pp. 167-90

TSVETKOV, ALEKSEI, *Edem* (Ann Arbor, MI: Ardis Publishers, 1985)

TUMANOV, VLADIMIR, 'A Tale Told by Two Idiots: Krik idiota v "Shkole dlia durakov" S. Sokolova i v "Shume i iarosti" U. Folknera', *Russian Language Journal*, 48 (1994), 137-55

TUPITSYN, MARGARITA, *Margins of Soviet Art: Socialist Realism to the Present* (Milan: Giancarlo Politi, 1989)

TURGENEV, IVAN, *Sobranie sochinenii*, 12 vols (Moscow: Khudozhestvennaia literatura, 1979)

—— *Zapiski okhotnika* (Leningrad: Gosudarstvennoe izdatel'stvo khudozhestvennoi literatury, 1945)

—— 'Russkii iazyk', in *Polnoe sobranie sochinenii i pisem*, 28 vols (Moscow and Leningrad: Nauka, 1967), xiii, p. 198

TYNIANOV, IURII, *Poetika, Istoriia literatury, Kino* (Moscow: Nauka, 1977)

UŽAREVIĆ, JOSIP, 'Simul'tanizm vremen?', *Russian, Croatian and Serbian, Czech and Slovak, Polish Literature*, 51 (2002), 344-53

VAIL', PETR, and Genis, Aleksandr, 'Soslagatel'noe naklonenie istorii: tsvetnik rossiiskogo anakhronizma', *Grani*, 139 (1986), 137-64

VARI, ERZSEBET, '"Literatura [...] — iskusstvo obrashcheniia so slovom": Zametki o povesti "Shkola dlia durakov" Sashi Sokolova', *Studia Slavica Academiae Scientiarum Hungaricae*, 47 (2002), 427-50

VASARI, GIORGIO, *Le vite dei più eccellenti pittori, scultori e architetti*, 2 vols, ed. by Licia e Carlo L. Ragghianti (Milan: Rizzoli, 1971-1973)

VAVULINA, ANASTASIIA, 'Sasha Sokolov: Osobennosti khronotopa v "Shkole dlia durakov"', *Canadian-American Slavic Studies*, 40 (2006), 251–78

VEL'BERG, BORIS, 'Mezhdu sobakoi i volkom', *Novyi amerikanets*, 206 (1984), 14–15

VERNON, JOHN, *The Garden and the Map: Schizophrenia in Twentieth-Century Literature and Culture* (Chicago: University of Illinois Press, 1973)

VINGE, LOUISE, *The Narcissus Theme in Western European Literature up to the Early 19th Century*, trans. by Robert Dewsnap and Nigel Reeves (Lund: Skånska Centraltryckeriet, 1967)

VOJDOVIĆ, JASMINA, 'Otkliki simultanizma v postmodernistskoi proze (*Shkola dlia durakov* S. Sokolova)', *Russian, Croatian and Serbian, Czech and Slovak, Polish Literature*, 51 (2002), 355–70

VROON, ROLAND, 'From Liturgy to Literature: Prayer and Play in the Early Russian Baroque', in *Culture and Authority in the Baroque*, ed. by Massimo Ciavolella and Patrick Coleman (Toronto, Buffalo, and London: University of Toronto Press, 2005), pp. 122–37

WAKAMIYA, LISA RYOKO, 'Transformation, Forgetting and Fate: Self-Representation in the Essays of Sasha Sokolov', *Canadian-American Slavic Studies*, 40 (2006), 305–16

WEIDLE, WLADIMIR, *Russia: Absent and Present*, trans. by A. Gordon Smith (London: Hollis and Carter, 1952)

WILDE, OSCAR, 'The Nightingale and the Rose', in *The Complete Oscar Wilde* (New York, Avenel: Crescent Books, 1995), pp. 286-90

WILLIAMS, CARLOS WILLIAM, 'Pictures from Brughel', in *Selected Poems*, ed. by Charles Tomlinson (London: Penguin Books, 2000), pp. 209-26

WINDLE, KEVIN, 'From Orge to "Uncle Lawrence": The Evolution of the Myth of Beria in Russian Fiction from 1953 to the Present', *Australian Slavonic and East European Studies*, 3.1 (1989), 1–16

WOOLF, VIRGINIA, *Orlando: A Biography* (Ware: Wordsworth Classics, 2003)

ZAMIATIN, EVGENII, 'Novaia russkaia proza', in *Izbrannye prozivedeniia*, 2 vols (Moscow: Khudozhestvennaia literatura, 1990), II, 352–66

—— 'O sintetizme', in *Izbrannye prozivedeniia*, 2 vols (Moscow: Khudozhestvennaia literatura, 1990), II, 378–86

ZETLIN, MIKHAIL, *The Five: The Evolution of the Russian School of Music*, trans. by George Panin (New York: International Universities Press, 1959)

ZHOLKOVSKII, ALEXANDER, 'Vliublenno-blednye nartsissy o vremeni i o sebe', *Beseda*, 6 (1987), 144–77

ZHOLKOVSKII, ALEXANDR, 'Perechityvaia izbrannye opiski Gogolia', in *Bluzhdaiushchie sny* (Moscow: Sovetskii Pisatel', 1992), pp. 86–110

—— 'Posviashchaetsia S.', *Sintaksis*, 18 (1987), 203–12

—— 'The Stylistic Roots of Palisandriia', *Canadian-American Slavic Studies*, 21 (1987), 369–400

—— *Text Counter Text: Readings in Russian Literary History* (Stanford, CA: Stanford University Press, 1994)

ZINIK, ZINOVY, 'Sots-Art, in *Tekstura: Russian Essays on Visual Culture*, ed. by Alla Efimova and Lev Manovich (Chicago and London: University of Chicago Press, 1993), pp. 70–88

ZIOLKOWSKI, MARGARET, 'In the Land of the Lonely Goatsucker: Ornithic Imagery in *A School for Fools* and *Between Dog and Wolf*', *Canadian-American Slavic Studies*, 21 (1987), 401–16

ŽIŽEK, SLAVOJ, 'The Fetish of the Party', in *Lacan, Politics, Aesthetics*, ed. by Willy Apollon and Richard Feldstein (Albany, NY: The State University of New York Press, 1996), pp. 3–29

—— *Looking Awry: An Introduction to Jacques Lacan through Popular Culture* (Cambridge, MA and London: The MIT Press, 1991)

—— *The Sublime Object of Ideology* (London, New York: Verso, 2008)

ZORIN, ANDREI, 'Nasylaiushchii Veter', *Novyi Mir*, 12 (1989), 250–53

INDEX

Aksakov, Sergei 57, 59, 91 n. 28
Aleksandr Nevsky 74
Allilueva, Nadezhda 108
Allilueva, Svetlana 110
Andrei Belyi Prize 9, 15 n. 33
androgyne 114, 117
Andropov, Iurii 100, 116
Antonov-Ovseenko, Anton, *Executioner's Carrier* (*Kariera palacha*) 117
Auden, W. H. 63, 90
  'Musée des Beaux Arts' 63, 93 n. 68
Avtorkhanov, Abdurakhman, *The Mystery of Stalin's Death: Beriia's Plot* (*Zagadka smerti Stalina: zagovor Beria*) 110

Bachelard, Gaston 45 n. 2
Bakhtin, Mikhail 3, 4, 12, 14 nn. 21 & 29, 22, 36, 41, 44, 45 n. 18, 52, 78, 89, 98 n. 220, 112, 121, 130, 131, 132, 132 n. 3
  answerability 130
  chronotope 78, 130
  the event of being (*sobytie bytiia*) 131, 132
  outsidedness 4, 89, 130
  surplus of vision 4, 89,
Balzac, Honoré de, *The Human Comedy* (*La Comédie Humaine*) 107
Barth, John, 49 n. 128
Barthes, Roland 13 n. 1
Baudelaire, Charles 113, 126 n. 81
Belyi, Andrei 11
Bentall, Richard 46 n. 37
Berberova, Nina 6, 110, 126 n. 75
Bergson, Henri 45 n. 1
Beriia, Lavrentii 99, 100, 104, 105, 112, 114, 116, 117
Bitov, Andrei 16 n. 49, 18 n. 91,
Bleuler, Eugen 25
Blok, Aleksandr, 'The Twelve' ('Dvenadtsat'') 120
Bobrinskaia, Ekaterina 93 n. 82
Boguslawski, Aleksandr 16 n. 58, 46 n. 34, 132 n. 7
Borges, Jorge Luis 30, 31, 84
  John Wilkins' Analytical Language 30, 67 n. 32
Breton, André 6, 46 n. 36
  Surrealist Manifestoes 6

Brezhnev, Leonid 100, 102, 108, 116
Broch, Herman 114, 127 n. 95
Brodskii, Iosif 5, 6, 15 n. 31, 132 n. 2
Brueghel, Pieter (the Elder) 60–64, 90, 92 n. 51, 92–93 n. 63, 93 nn. 64 & 67, 97 n. 193
  The Census at Bethlehem 63
  Christ Carrying the Cross 63
  Gibson, Walter 92 nn. 48 & 50
  Gloomy Day 60
  Glück, Gustav 63, 92 n. 49, 93 n. 67
  Hunters in the Snow 60, 61–63, 92 n. 51
  Landscape with the Fall of Icarus 63
  Lindsay, Kenneth and Huppé, Bernard 93 n. 67
  The Parable of the Blind 97 n. 193
  Return of the Herd 60
  The Slaughter of the Innocents 63
Bruhm, Steven 40, 48 n. 108
Bruhn, Siglind 92 n. 55
Bulgakov, Mikhail, *Master and Margarita* 32

Camp 13, 99, 113–15, 126 nn. 85 & 92
Catherine the Great 108, 114, 117
Cervantes, Miguel 42, 91 n. 36
  Don Quixote 42, 58
Christ 37, 63, 73, 120, 132
Chukovskii, Kornei, *Mukha-Tsokotukha* 83, 96 n. 178
Cocteau, Jean 126 n. 92
Conceptualism 11, 71, 101
Core, Philip 99, 114, 123 n. 1, 126 n. 92
Cronos 103, 105, 109

Dali, Salvador, *Secret Life of Salvador Dali* 6
Dällenbach, Lucien 12, 18 n. 96, 32, 42, 47 n. 68, 49 n. 121
  mise en abyme 12, 32, 35, 47, 68, 107
Danaë 103, 108
Dandy 13, 113
Daniil Zatochnik 75
Davis, Diana 45 n. 17
Debussy, Claude 113
Deleuze, Gilles and Guattari, Felix 97 n. 216, 124 n. 22
  deterritorialization 89, 97 n. 216, 130

Derrida, Jacques 4, 14 nn. 26 & 27, 58, 75, 82, 85, 87–89, 92 n. 40, 96 nn. 174 & 181, 97 nn. 197, 203, 206, 207 & 209, 98 nn. 218 & 219
  deconstruction 12, 75, 109, 115, 123
  differance 4, 75
  dissemination 87–89
  supplement 4, 13, 14 n. 27, 36, 72, 89, 103
dissident 10, 110, 112, 122, 128 n. 129
Dogen 26
Don Juan 117, 129
Dostoevskii, Fedor 36, 43, 46 n. 36, 70, 88, 91 n. 38, 97 n. 214, 111, 131
  The Brothers Karamazov 88, 97 n. 214
  Crime and Punishment 43, 49 n. 125
  The Double 36, 46 n. 36
  The Notes from the Underground 46 n. 36
Duchamp, Marcel 70
  A Fountain 70
  ready-made 70, 82
Duganov, Rudol'f 58, 91 n. 38
Duncan, Peter 127 n. 123

Echo 2–5, 19, 21, 37, 44, 45, 129
Eco, Umberto 28, 30, 47 nn. 53, 61 & 63, 126 n. 93
ekphrasis 61–64, 86, 112, 129
  Hefferman, James 93 nn. 65 & 72
  Krieger, Murray 92 n. 61
  Mitchell, Thomas 62, 92 n. 62
  Philostratus the Elder, *Imagines* 62
Eliade, Mircea 118, 127 n. 116
Elijah 73
Epshtein, Mikhail 10, 17 nn. 88, 89 & 90, 97 n. 213, 102, 121, 122, 124 nn. 22 & 23
  arrière-garde 10, 11, 121, 122
  phenomenalism 11
Erofeev, Viktor 18 n. 91
Esenin, Sergei, *The Persian Themes* (*Persidkie motivy*) 117
Eucharist, 12, 86
  see also Holy Communion

Faulkner, William 6, 9, 46 n. 36
Fedorov, Nikolai 104
Flaubert, Gustave 91 n. 36
  Madame Bovary 58
Freud, Sigmund 14 n. 19, 17 n. 82, 40, 48 nn. 106 & 107, 70, 74, 94 n. 106, 96 n. 181, 106, 112, 115, 117, 128 n. 129
  Gschnas 70, 94 n. 106
  narcissism 3, 10, 11, 12, 14 n. 19, 21, 40, 41, 48 n. 90, 121
  return of the repressed 102
sublimation 40, 41, 89, 112, 115
uncanny (Unheimlich) 43, 66, 72, 73, 74, 112, 115, 120

Garshin, Vsevolod 105
Genis, Aleksandr 6, 20, 120, 127 n. 122
Goethe, Johann Wolfgang von, *Faust* 104, 124 nn. 35 & 36
Gogol', Nikolai 7, 36, 46 n. 36, 66, 67, 70, 81, 93 nn. 81 & 85, 105, 111, 124 n. 38
  Dead Souls (*Mertvye dushi*) 67, 93 n. 85
  Nose (*Nos*) 105, 124 n. 38
  The Portrait (*Portret*) 66, 93 n. 81
Gor'kii, Maksim, *In the World* (*V liudiakh*) 43, 49 n. 123
Grois, Boris 17 nn. 85 & 87, 114, 120, 123 n. 12, 125 n. 62, 126 n. 94, 128 nn. 125 & 126
Grossman, Vasilii, *Everything Flows* (*Vse techet*) 111
Gureev, Maksim, *But Landscape is Impeccable* (*A peizazh bezuprechen*) 13 n. 12

Hacking, Ian 45 n. 19
Hamilton, Victoria 41, 44, 49 n. 115
Havelock, Ellis 95 n. 125
Heim, Michael 106, 124 n. 20
Heldt, Barbara 89, 95 n. 136, 98 n. 217
Heuvel, Pierre van den 70
  objet trouvé 70
  objet volé 70
Holy Communion, 84, 129
  see also Eucharist
Holy Fool 117, 132
Homer 28, 30, 62, 100, 105,
  Iliad 28, 62, 100,
  Odyssey 100
Hutcheon, Linda 10, 12, 17 n. 84, 35, 47 nn. 82 & 83
  historiographic metafiction 10
  narrative narcissism 12, 35

Il'ia Muromets 75
Ivanov, Viacheslav 131
Ivanova, Natalia 7, 16 n. 53

Jameson, Fredric 11, 18 n. 95
Johnson, Barbara 87, 97 n. 207
Johnson, Don Barton 7, 8, 10, 14 n. 15, 15 nn. 43 & 46, 16 nn. 59, 61 & 63, 17 n. 81, 25, 29, 45 nn. 5 & 8, 46 nn. 35 & 49, 47 n. 57, 51, 54, 71, 80, 90 n. 3, 92 n. 51, 94 n. 109, 95 nn. 124 & 126, 96 nn. 154, 159 & 160, 120, 125 n. 41, 54 & 62, 127 nn. 113 & 121

Joyce, James 6, 7, 8, 30, 100
  Finergans Wake 8
  The Ulysses 100
Jung, Carl 17 n. 82, 117, 128 n. 129

Kabakov, Il'ia 97 n. 198
Kant, Immanuel 65, 111
Kaplan, Fanny 108
Karriker, Alexandra 36, 47 n. 71, 48 nn. 84 & 89
Kawabata, Yasunari 26
Khlebnikov, Velemir 8, 9, 57, 58, 90, 91 nn. 37 & 38, 98 n. 221
Kholmogorova, Olga 127 nn. 99 & 102
Khrushchev, Nikita 100, 120
Kitsch 112, 114, 115, 126 n. 93
Kolb, Hanna 69, 70, 76, 78, 90 n. 5, 91 n. 35, 95 nn. 134, 135 & 150, 97 n. 187
Komar, Vitalii and Melamid, Aleksandr 101, 116, 123 nn. 10 & 11
  Comrade Stalin and the Muses 101
Kristeva, Julia 12, 18 n. 97, 41, 42, 44, 48 n. 109
  abject 12, 122
Krupskaia, Nadezhda 127 n. 123
Kuprin, Aleksandr 7

Lacan, Jacques 3, 14 nn. 20 & 30, 44, 87
  the mirror stage 3
  point de capiton 87
Lenin, Vladimir 24, 108, 120, 127 n. 123
Lermontov, Mikhail 43, 49 n. 124, 57, 67, 68, 74, 94 nn. 90, 93 & 94
  Hero of Our Time (Geroi nashego vremeni) 43, 49 n. 124, 67, 68, 94 nn. 90, 91, 93 & 94
  'A Leaf' 57
  The Novice (Mtsyri) 74
Limonov, Eduard 10, 110
  It's me, Edie (Eto ia — Edichka) 10
Lipovetskii, Mark 11, 18 nn. 91, 92 & 93, 75, 77, 97 n. 216, 130
Liriope 2, 40
Litus, Ludmilla 27, 46 nn. 34, 43, 46 & 48, 132 n. 7
Lotman, Iurii 32, 58

Mandel'shtam, Osip 5, 49 n. 126, 122
Maramzin, Vladimir 6, 15 n. 37
Matich, Olga 10, 17 n. 82, 109, 120, 124 nn. 21 & 28, 125 n. 68, 126 n. 70, 128 nn. 124 & 129, 133 n. 8
McDowell, Karen Rice 37, 48 n. 88
McMillin, Arnold 15 n. 44, 18 n. 94, 94 n. 105, 96 n. 159

memory 12, 19–21, 27, 36, 43, 44, 45 n. 1, 79, 87, 89, 97 n. 203
Mighty Handful (Moguchaia Kuchka) 61
  Balakirev, Mily 61
  Borodin, Aleksandr 61
  Cui, Cesar 61
  Rimskii-Korsakov, Nikolai 61
  Stasov, Vladimir 61
  Zetlin, Mikhail 92 n. 56
möbius strip 65, 69, 72, 79
modernism 6, 10, 11, 46 n. 36, 51, 71, 121
Moguchii, Andrei 9, 17 n. 70, 132 n. 4
multiple personality disorder 20, 22, 45 n. 19
Musorgskii, Modest 61–63, 90, 92 n. 57
  Hartman, Victor 61, 62
  see also Mighty Handful
  Pictures at an Exhibition 61, 92 n. 52
  Russ, Michael 92 nn. 53 & 54
Musset, Alfred de 113

Nabokov, Vladimir 5, 6–8, 10, 11, 19, 20, 36, 54, 66, 92 n. 46, 113
  Gift (Dar) 7, 92 n. 46
  Lolita 7, 10, 36, 113
Narcissus 2–4, 12, 14 n. 18, 19, 21, 22, 37, 40–44, 48 n. 90, 105
Nekrasov, Nikolai 59, 60, 77, 92 n. 44
  'Orina, the Mother of a Soldier' 59, 77, 92 n. 43
neo-Baroque 11, 18 n. 91
Neumann, Erich 106, 125 nn. 52 & 53
Nietzsche, Friedrich 115

Oedipus 80, 83, 102, 115, 121, 124 n. 22
Ong, Walter 83, 96 nn. 172, 182 & 183

Pasternak, Boris 5, 60, 80, 96 n. 166
  Doctor Zhivago 60, 80, 92 n. 45, 96 nn. 164, 165 & 166
Pavlova, Karolina, *Double Life (Dvoinaia zhizn')* 92 n. 46
Perrault, Charles, *Cinderella* 74, 75
Perseus 103
Pharisees 85
Pil'niak, Boris, *Mother Moist Earth (Mat' syra zemlia)* 77
Plato 120
Platonov, Andrei 8, 15 n. 37, 16 n. 60
Poe, Edgar Allan 7, 36, 37
  William Wilson 36
  Doppelganger 36, 37
pop art 101

postmodernism 11, 71, 109
Proffer, Ellendea and Carl 5–8, 10, 15 nn. 39 & 42, 16 n. 62, 17 n. 72, 19, 45 n. 4, 54
Proust, Marcel, *In Search of Lost Time* 111, 113, 125 n. 42, 126 n. 82
Pushkin, Aleksandr 54–57, 59, 60, 77, 84, 90, 91 n. 38, 92 n. 44, 103
  'Approaching Izhory' ('Pod'ezzhaia pod Izhory') 55, 56, 91 n. 23
  The Captain's Daughter (Kapitanskaia dochka) 56, 103
  Count Nulin (Graf Nulin) 55
  Evgenii Onegin 54, 55, 57, 71
  The Gypsies (Tsygany) 55
  'Winter. What are we to do at this time?...' (Zima. Chto delat' nam v derevne?') 55
Putin, Vladimir 127 n. 123

Rabelais, François 30
Rank, Otto 48 n. 90
Rasputin, Grigorii 99, 108, 114
recycling 67–70, 84
reflection 2–4, 12, 20, 21, 37–41, 44, 45, 48 n. 94, 64, 78, 89, 90, 101, 105, 118, 123, 129, 130
Robbe-Grillet, Alan 46 n. 36
Romanova, Princess, Anastasiia 111, 122
Romulus and Remus 75, 103
Rossi, William 95 n. 125
Rousseau, Jean-Jacques, *Essay on the Origin of Languages* 89
Rudova, Larissa 17 nn. 76 & 83, 121, 127 n. 120, 128 n. 128
Ryan, Karen 109, 124 nn. 14 & 28, 125 n. 68

Sass, Louis 12, 22, 25, 29, 46 nn. 21, 39 & 40, 47 n. 57
  glossomania 25
  schizophrenia 12, 20, 22, 25, 29, 36, 45 n. 19, 129, 131
Saul 23
Saussure, Ferdinand de 87
Schnittke, Alfred 11
  polystylistic technique 11
Schopenhauer, Arthur 114
sexuality 27, 28, 33, 35, 40–41, 74, 76, 83, 95 n. 125, 96 n. 181, 101–02, 105–06, 108, 114–18, 122, 127 n. 104, 129
  incest 102, 107–09, 119, 124 n. 20
  gerontophilia 102, 115,
  necrophilia 104, 121
  nymphomania 35
Silver Age 6

Siniavskii, Andrei 100, 101, 123 n. 13, 127 n. 109
  see also Tertz, Abram
skaz 33, 52, 53, 68–71, 74, 76, 77, 80, 82, 83, 85, 87, 89 , 129, 131
  Eikhenbaum, Boris 80, 90 n. 8, 96 n. 167
  Hicks, Jeremy 90 nn. 7 & 8, 96 n. 167
  Smith, Gerald 16 n. 61, 55, 59, 91 nn. 15, 16 & 21, 92 nn. 41, 44, 46 & 47
SMOG 5, 15 nn. 32 & 33
socialist realism 100, 101, 114, 116, 123 nn. 8, 9 & 13
Sokolov, Sasha:
  All the Colours of the Rainbow (Vse tsveta radugi) 2
  Astrophobia 9, 10
    see also *Palisandriia*
  Between Dog and Wolf (Mezhdu sobakoi i volkom) 7–9, 10, 12, 18 n. 94, 27, 51–98, 107, 110, 129, 130
  Gazebo (Gazibo) 1
  Meditation (Rassuzhdenie) 1
  Palisandriia 9–11, 12, 27, 99–128, 129, 130
    see also *Astrophobia*
  Philornite (Filortnit) 1
  proetry (proeziia) 1
  School for Fools (Shkola dlia durakov) 5–8, 10–12, 16 n. 55, 17 n.70, 19–49, 106, 79, 83, 107, 129, 130
  The Old Helmsman (Staryi shturman) 2
  Triptych (Triptikh) 1
Soloukhin, Vladimir 110
Solzhenitsyn, Aleksandr 110
Sontag, Susan 113, 114, 126 nn. 86, 87, 89 & 91
sots-art 10, 101, 110, 115, 123 nn. 10 & 11, 127 nn. 99 & 102
space 5, 12, 21, 44, 65, 71, 76–82, 89, 97 n. 216, 104, 108, 123, 130
St Alphaeus 73
St Cyril 80
St George 73
St Jeremy 73
St John, Gospel of 88
St Matthew, Gospel of 85, 88
St Nicholas 69, 73
St Paul 23, 73
St Thomas 73
St Vitus 22–24
Stalin, Iosif 24, 99–103, 108, 110, 112, 114, 117, 120, 122, 123 n. 8, 126 n. 96, 127 nn. 109 & 123, 128 n. 129
Sterne, Laurence 10, 105
Stevenson, Robert Louis *Dr Jekyll and Mr Hyde* 36

symbolism 5, 6

Tertz, Abram, 123 nn. 2 & 9
    see also Siniavskii, Andrei
time 5, 9, 10, 12, 35, 44, 71, 76, 78–80, 90,
    97 n. 216, 100, 104, 105, 108, 118, 121, 123,
    124 n. 29, 125 nn. 42 & 54, 130
Tiresias 2, 21
Tiutchev, Fedor 91 n. 38
Tolstaia, Tatiana 7, 18 n. 91
Tolstoi, Lev 117
    Anna Karenina 43
    Yardstick (*Kholstomer*) 117
Tsiolkovskii, Konstantin 104
Tsvetaeva, Marina 5
Tsvetkov, Aleksei 8, 90 n. 3
Turgenev, Ivan 57–60, 74, 90, 91 n. 28, 96 n. 166
    Russian Language (*Russkii iazyk*) 91 n. 34
    Sportsman Sketches (*Zapiski okhotnika*) 59

Vail', Petr 120, 127 n. 122
Vega, Lope de 117, 127 n. 104, 129
Vernon, John 46 n. 38
Vinci, Leonardo da 39–41, 48 nn. 106 & 107
    La Gioconda 39–41

Pater, Walter 48 nn. 105 & 112
Vasari, Giorgio 40
Vishnevskii, Vsevolod, *The Optimistic Tragedy*
    (*Optimisticheskaia tragediia*) 107
Vladimov Georgii, 110, 128 n. 129
Vysotskii, Vladimir 8

Wanderers (Peredvizhniki) 57, 61
    Polenov, Vasilii 57
    Repin, Il'ia 92 n. 57
    Savrasov, Aleksei 57
Weidle, Vladimir 6
Wilde, Oscar, *The Picture of Dorian Gray* 36,
    37, 66, 105
Williams, William Carlos, *Pictures from
    Brueghel* 64
Woolf, Virginia 6, 46 n. 36
word-weaving 8

Zadonshchina 8
Zholkovskii, Aleksandr 10, 17 nn. 79 & 80, 124
    nn. 14, 15 & 16, 126 n. 74
Zorin, Andrei 9, 17 nn. 67 & 68, 19, 20, 45 n. 6,
    92 n. 51, 93 n. 64

www.ingramcontent.com/pod-product-compliance
Lightning Source LLC
Chambersburg PA
CBHW071505150426
43191CB00009B/1426